Words Aptly Spoken®
AMERICAN DOCUMENTS
SECOND EDITION

a study of the documents that shaped the United States

compiled and edited by Jen Greenholt

Jen Greenholt, *Words Aptly Spoken*® Series
American Documents, second edition
First edition printed 2006. Second edition printed 2011.

©2011 Classical Conversations® MultiMedia. All rights reserved.

Published by Classical Conversations, Inc.
255 Air Tool Drive
Southern Pines, NC 28387
www.ClassicalConversations.com | www.ClassicalConversationsBooks.com

Cover design by Classical Conversations. Cover image courtesy Library of Congress, *Washington's entry into New York: on the evacuation of the city by the British, Nov. 25th. 1783*, Currier & Ives, Reproduction Number LC-USZC2-3310.

Printed in the United States of America.
All rights reserved. No part of this publication may be reproduced, stored in a retrieval system, or transmitted in any form by any means, electronic, mechanical, photocopy, recording, or otherwise, without prior permission of the author, except as provided by USA copyright law.

ISBN: 978-0-9829845-4-3

Acknowledgments

Many thanks to the editors and readers at Classical Conversations, especially Pam Greenholt and Denise Moore, for taking the time to make the details right. Special thanks to Judy Palmer for her close editing to match the original documents.

To God be the glory.

Foreword

What do you think of when you hear the word "history"? Does it have a positive connotation or a negative one? For many, the idea of history brings to mind elderly teachers droning on and on about this date when that obscurely named figure went before this unimportant council to deliver that news about the rebellion of this farmer and—you get the picture.

While it is possible to make history a dull subject that has little or no contemporary relevance, in its pure form, history is alive with insights into our world. Did you know, for example, that women's rights leaders once crafted an updated version of the Declaration of Independence that stressed the injustice done to women? Or that Osama Bin Laden was once considered an ally of the United States during the Cold War?

The interest history holds for you is connected to the interest you put into learning about history. If you can think of history in terms of a great story in which you are still taking part, then you will be able to find connections between your life and the events of the past.

You cannot understand the modern system of American government without looking at its historical roots. But instead of the usual route of a textbook-style discussion on the history of government, this book follows the theme of a great story, looking at the narratives that shaped this history. If you allow the voices of great Americans to speak for themselves, you will gain insight into the logic behind the system of government that may seem natural and "American."

If you have ever watched or read about a trial in one of the higher courts, especially the Supreme Court, you will know that "past precedent" (how the issue has been handled in the past) is extremely important. The same is often true for the laws and policies of a government. In reading about the history of American government, you gain insight into the rationale for decisions that are made today. Many of these decisions, drawn from the legal precedent of *Brown v. Board of Education* or from the Constitution, for example, are largely based on the documents you will read.

As with the other collections in the *Words Aptly Spoken*® series, *American Documents* contains a series of questions about each work. Review Questions ensure that you understand the basic plot, characters, setting, and message of each historical document. Thought Questions take the themes and ideas raised by each author and help you apply them to other, more familiar situations.

All new to this edition, general comprehension questions at the beginning of the book and at the start of each new section will help you navigate the genres in this collection (speeches, poetry, essays, and legal documents) as you compare and contrast their content on the level of ideas. In addition, writing practices at the end of each section will give you practical insight into the use of different genres. Finally, new expanded introductions to each piece provide background information about not only the authors and content of the documents, but also the historical context in which they were written.

Best wishes and happy reading!

Table of Contents

Foreword 5
A Note for Parents: Tools for the Journey 9
List of the United States Presidents..13
Outline of the U.S. Constitution 19
Comprehension Questions..20

STUDY GUIDES

What's That You Say? **Speeches**..21
    "Liberty or Death," by Patrick Henry..23
    "First Inaugural Address," by George Washington 27
    "In Favor of the Federal Constitution" (excerpts),
        by James Madison 31
    "The Monroe Doctrine," by James Monroe.....................................35
    "Seneca Falls Declaration of Sentiments,"
        by Elizabeth Cady Stanton...39
    "On the Slavery Question," by John C. Calhoun 43
    "A House Divided," by Abraham Lincoln.......................................51
    "Inaugural Address," by Jefferson Davis...57
    "Gettysburg Address," by Abraham Lincoln 61
    "Atlanta Exposition Address," by Booker T. Washington..................63
    "The Man with the Muck-Rake," by Theodore Roosevelt...............67
    "War Message," by Woodrow Wilson 75
    "League of Nations Speech" (excerpt), by Henry Cabot Lodge 83
    "Pearl Harbor Address," by Franklin D. Roosevelt.........................87
    "The Marshall Plan," by George C. Marshall..................................91
    "Inaugural Address," by John F. Kennedy 95
    "First Inaugural Address," by Ronald Reagan 99

Is it Time to Rhyme? **Poetry** 105
    "Pocahontas," William M. Thackeray...107
    "Five Kernels of Corn," by Hezekiah Butterworth 109
    "Nathan Hale," by Francis M. Finch...111
    "Valley Forge" (excerpt), by Thomas B. Read 115
    "Defence of Fort McHenry," by Francis Scott Key...........................119
    "Defense of the Alamo," by Joaquin Miller.....................................123
    "Liberty for All," by William L. Garrison..125
    "The New Colossus," by Emma Lazarus..127
    "The Men of the *Maine*," by Clinton Scollard 129
    "Panama," by James Roche...133

Can You Write That Down? **Articles and Essays** 137
   "Apologia" (excerpt), by Christopher Columbus 139
   "The Federalist: Number 30," by Alexander Hamilton 141
   "The Federalist: Number 47," by James Madison 145
   "Farewell Address," by George Washington 151
   "The American Language" (excerpt), by H.L. Mencken 163

Where's the Evidence? **Legal Documents** 169
   The Mayflower Compact 171
   The Declaration of Independence 173
   The Articles of the Confederation 177
   The U.S. Constitution 185
   The Amendments to the U.S. Constitution 195
   The Northwest Ordinance 203
   The Missouri Compromise, by Henry Clay 209
   The Emancipation Proclamation, by Abraham Lincoln 215
   The Pledge of Allegiance, by Francis Bellamy 219
   Dred Scott v. Sandford, by Roger B. Taney 221
   Brown v. Board of Education of Topeka, by Earl Warren 231

Looking Back, Looking Forward 237
Endnotes 239
Photo Credits 241

A Note for Parents: Tools for the Journey

If you have ever heard Shakespeare performed before a live audience and marveled at the ease with which the words flowed from the actors' lips; if you have ever envied people who can call on Milton, Dickens, Joyce, and Lewis to lend eloquence to their argument; if you have skimmed a list of the hundred greatest novels of all time and winced as you remembered struggling to finish *The Grapes of Wrath* in high school—you may think that the great conversations of literature are forever closed to you.

The good news is, they're not! Whether you are a student, an adult, a parent, a child, or all of the above, you have the capability to train yourself not only to read great literature, but also to share its beauty, truth, and joy with others.

Although most people learn to read as children, the art of deliberately engaging with the content and ideas of a novel or short story requires ongoing practice.

The *Words Aptly Spoken* series is based on the classical model of education,[1] which breaks learning into three natural stages: grammar, dialectic, and rhetoric. In the grammar stage, you learn the vocabulary of a subject. In the dialectic stage, you learn to develop logical arguments and analyze others' ideas. In the rhetoric stage, you explore the consequences of ideas as you form and express your own. This guide will help you as you begin to apply the classical model to the study of literature.

Why American Documents?

If you think the word "literature" refers only to fiction, you may be surprised to see the documents that formed the U.S. government included in a series of literature guides. Are these documents even literature? Although there is no easy answer to that question, several important features of the documents in this collection explain their presence in "An Introduction to Classical Literature."

Scrooge and Frankenstein are familiar figures, but popular manifestations may differ widely from their literary sources. In the same way, "separate but equal," "cruel and unusual punishment," and "liberty or death" are powerful phrases, but they can be misinterpreted outside their original contexts.

When you study literature, you learn to interpret what you read by paying close attention to the clues in the text. You will need the same skills to read these documents. Each document tells a story about what America could or should be, and many of them have influenced the United States profoundly. By studying the arguments, persuasive techniques, and ideas that made American government what it is today, you will be equipped to imagine how it might be different tomorrow.

How to Use This Book

Despite popular belief, reading is not wholly instinctive. Because comprehension, analysis, and critical thinking require practice, each story in this collection comes with a set of questions designed to give structure and guidance to your reading. Treat these questions

---

[1] See Dorothy Sayers' essay, "The Lost Tools of Learning."

as tools not only for reading, but also for writing, leading discussion, and sharing your ideas with others.

Review Questions pull out the **grammar** for each selection: Who is it about? (Characters) What happens? (Plot) Where does it take place? (Setting) What is the message? (Theme) What is the scope or time frame? (Focus), and so on. For readers of all ages, repeatedly asking these questions will generate good reading habits; eventually, as you read, your brain will automatically take note of this information and store it for future use.

Thought Questions are an exercise in **dialectic**, taking the basic elements from the review questions and encouraging you to analyze that information in light of other knowledge. As you become more familiar with the building blocks of a story, you should begin to ask questions of your own. What does this mean for me? How should I respond to this argument? You can use the thought questions as a jump-start for your own thinking process, as training tools for leading discussion, or as topics for essays and book reports.

You may not be able to answer the questions after just one reading, and because these stories are short, you should take time to read each story at least twice. The first time should be for general enjoyment and to get a feel for the author's writing style. The next reading should look a little deeper at the underlying issues the author confronts.

If you cannot answer some of the questions by the time you have finished the selection, consider going back and re-reading sections you may only have skimmed the first time. A word of caution: don't merely "look up" the answers to the questions and skim the rest. Once established, this habit will make it harder for you to read and understand more difficult books. After all, self-respecting Olympic runners know that they would be at a severe disadvantage in the actual games if they secretly completed only half of their daily training regimen. In the same way, the results you achieve as a reader will reflect the quality and consistency of your training.

Because most of these documents were written a long time ago, some of the language and sentence structures may be difficult to understand. The following tips will make your task easier:

- First, read each piece multiple times. None (with the possible exception of the Constitution) are long, and re-reading them will allow you to notice details you missed.
- Second, read with a dictionary. When you come to an unfamiliar word, look it up and jot down a definition. The next time you read the piece, substitute familiar terminology.
- Third, if a piece is especially complicated, rewrite it paragraph by paragraph in your own words. This exercise will allow you to modernize the language and ideas.

Finally, writing practice exercises at the end of each section will guide you to a better understanding of the different genres represented by these historical documents as you practice rewriting the documents in your own words.

The Journey in Perspective

One of the most important things to remember as you start—or resume—this journey is that it doesn't happen overnight. The art of leading and sharing in conversations about classical literature takes a lifetime to refine. You must begin with the fundamentals: learning to read closely, taking notes, and developing the vocabulary to structure your ideas and explain them to others (grammar). You must practice: adding new techniques, revising old ones, and comparing the results (dialectic). And then you will be ready to start all over again as you share the joy of the journey with others around you (rhetoric). Let's get started!

List of the U.S. Presidents

These basic facts about the presidents are an important part of the grammar of American government. As you read, use these names and dates to organize your knowledge about U.S. government.

Take time to assign each text you read to its proper place in the timeline, and pay attention to the themes that emerge. Remember, comparing a historical document to other events and texts from that same period of history can tell you something about prominent attitudes and concerns at that time.

1 George Washington
2 terms, 1789–1797
None (1st term)
Federalist (2nd)

Vice President:
John Adams

2 John Adams
1 term, 1797–1801
Federalist

Vice President:
Thomas Jefferson

3 Thomas Jefferson
2 terms, 1801–1809
Democratic-Republican

Vice Presidents:
Aaron Burr
George Clinton

4 James Madison
2 terms, 1809–1817
Democratic-Republican
Vice Presidents:
George Clinton
Elbridge Gerry

5 James Monroe
2 terms, 1817–1825
Democratic-Republican

Vice President:
Daniel D. Tompkins

6 John Quincy Adams
1 term, 1825–1829
Democratic-Republican

Vice President:
John C. Calhoun

7 Andrew Jackson
2 terms, 1829–1837
Democratic

Vice Presidents:
John C. Calhoun
Martin Van Buren

8 Martin Van Buren
1 term, 1837–1841
Democratic

Vice President:
Richard M. Johnson

9 William H. Harrison
1 term, 1841
Whig

Vice President:
John Tyler

14 Franklin Pierce
1 term, 1853–1857
Democratic

Vice President:
William R. King

10 John Tyler
1 term, 1841–1845
Whig
Vice President: None

15 James Buchanan
1 term, 1857–1861
Democratic

Vice President:
John C. Breckinridge

11 James K. Polk
1 term, 1845–1849
Democratic

Vice President:
George M. Dallas

16 Abraham Lincoln
1 term, 1861–1865
Republican

Vice Presidents:
Hannibal Hamlin
Andrew Johnson

12 Zachary Taylor
1 term, 1849–1850
Whig

Vice President:
Millard Fillmore

17 Andrew Johnson
1 term, 1865–1869
Democratic
Vice President: None

13 Millard Fillmore
1 term, 1850–1853
Whig
Vice President: None

18 Ulysses S. Grant
2 terms, 1869–1877
Republican

Vice Presidents:
Schuyler Colfax
Henry Wilson

List of the U.S. Presidents

19 Rutherford B. Hayes
1 term, 1877–1881
Republican

Vice President:
William A. Wheeler

24 Grover Cleveland
1 term, 1893–1897
Democratic

Vice President:
Adlai E. Stevenson

20 James A. Garfield
1 term, 1881
Republican

Vice President:
Chester A. Arthur

25 William McKinley
1 term, 1897–1901
Republican

Vice Presidents:
Garret A. Hobart
Theodore Roosevelt

21 Chester A. Arthur
1 term, 1881–1885
Republican
Vice President: None

26 Theodore Roosevelt
2 terms, 1901–1909
Republican

Vice President:
Charles W. Fairbanks

22 Grover Cleveland
1 term, 1885–1889
Democratic

Vice President:
Thomas A. Hendricks

27 William H. Taft
1 term, 1909–1913
Republican

Vice President:
James S. Sherman

23 Benjamin Harrison
1 term, 1889–1893
Republican

Vice President:
Levi P. Morton

28 Woodrow Wilson
2 terms, 1913–1921
Democratic

Vice President:
Thomas R. Marshall

29 Warren G. Harding

1 term, 1921–1923
Republican

Vice President:
Calvin Coolidge

30 Calvin Coolidge

2 terms, 1923–1929
Republican

Vice President:
Charles G. Dawes

31 Herbert C. Hoover

1 term, 1929–1933
Republican

Vice President:
Charles Curtis

32 Franklin D. Roosevelt

3 terms, 1933–1945
Democratic
Vice Presidents:
John N. Garner
Henry A. Wallace
Harry S. Truman

33 Harry S. Truman

2 terms, 1945–1953
Democratic

Vice President:
Alben W. Barkley

34 Dwight D. Eisenhower

2 terms, 1953–1961
Republican

Vice President:
Richard M. Nixon

35 John F. Kennedy

1 term, 1961–1963
Democratic

Vice President:
Lyndon B. Johnson

36 Lyndon B. Johnson

2 terms, 1963–1969
Democratic

Vice President:
Hubert H. Humphrey

37 Richard M. Nixon

2 terms, 1969–1974
Republican

Vice President:
Spiro T. Agnew
Gerald R. Ford

38 Gerald R. Ford

1 term, 1974–1977
Republican

Vice President:
Nelson A. Rockefeller

List of the U.S. Presidents

39 James E. Carter
1 term, 1977–1981
Democratic

Vice President:
Walter F. Mondale

40 Ronald W. Reagan
2 terms, 1981–1989
Republican

Vice President:
George H. W. Bush

41 George H. W. Bush
1 term, 1989–1993
Republican

Vice President:
J. Danforth Quayle

42 William J. Clinton
2 terms, 1993–2001
Democratic

Vice President:
Albert Gore, Jr.

43 George W. Bush
2 terms, 2001–2009
Republican

Vice President:
Richard Cheney

44 Barack H. Obama
2 terms, 2009–2017
Democratic

Vice President:
Joseph Biden

45 Donald J. Trump
1 term, 2017–
Republican

Vice President:
Michael R. Pence

Outline of the U.S. Constitution

As the foundational document of U.S. government, the Constitution is one very important piece of grammar you need to know as you study the history of American government.

Articles

I. Legislative branch
II. Executive branch
III. Judicial branch
IV. The states and the federal government
V. Method of amendment
VI. General provisions (supremacy clause)
VII. Ratification of the Constitution

Amendments

The Bill of Rights
1. Five freedoms: speech, press, religion, petition, and assembly
2. Right to bear and keep arms
3. Quartering of troops
4. Limiting right of search and seizure
5. Trial by jury guaranteed; private property respected; no self-incrimination
6. Rights of accused persons
7. Rules of common law
8. Excessive bail, fines, and punishment prohibited
9. Rights retained by the people
10. Powers reserved to states and people

11. Limiting powers of federal courts
12. Election of President and Vice President separated
13. Abolition of slavery
14. Citizenship defined
15. Right to vote not denied by race, color, or slavery
16. Income tax
17. Direct election of senators
18. National prohibition
19. Women's suffrage
20. Beginning of presidential/congressional terms (lame duck)
21. Repealed prohibition
22. Two-term limit for presidency
23. Electoral College
24. No poll tax
25. Succession to the presidency
26. Voting age becomes 18
27. Salaries of senators and representatives take effect after election

Comprehension Questions

Every document is different, and the documents in this collection represent a wide variety of genres, both fiction and nonfiction, each with its own grammar. Learning to ask questions and analyze ideas across genres is an important part of progressing to the dialectic stage of learning. Certain questions are useful to make sure you are reading closely on the idea level and pay attention to the differences between genres.

Audience

Who seems to be the audience for this piece? How do you know?
How much prior knowledge about the subject does the author assume the audience has?
Does the author address the audience directly? If so, what is his or her tone?

Content

What opening information does the author use to catch the audience's attention?
Does the author give background information? If so, how is that information presented?
Is the document primarily fact or opinion?
What final idea does the author impress on his or her audience?

Style

How would you describe the author's writing style? Flowery? Matter-of-fact?
Does the purpose seem to be to inform, to entertain, to persuade, or something else?
What images or comparisons does the author use to make his or her points?

Worldview

Does the author associate him- or herself with a particular cause or movement?
What larger statements does the document make about the world?
What does the author imply about human nature?
What kind of story does this document tell about America or the U.S. government?

Your Perspective

Did you agree with the author's ideas? Why or why not?
Is this document still relevant today?
What influence do you think this document has had on American identity?

What's That You Say? SPEECHES

The power of oratory plays a large role in the history of nations around the world. The ability to speak persuasively is invaluable to politicians, activists, and ordinary citizens who want to make a difference.

Because speeches are written to be delivered orally, they use a different set of conventions than documents that are meant to be read. The best way to get a feel for a speech is to read it aloud or have someone else read it to you. Either way, pay particular attention to the following questions:

- How long is the speech?
- Who seems to be the intended audience?
- What is the tone of the speech?
- How formal is the speaker's language?
- What parts of the speech would you emphasize if you were the speaker?
- What effect do you think the speaker was trying to achieve? How do you know?

These speeches are a sample of those that have triggered, contributed to, or responded to important events in American history. As you read, look for the tools that each speaker uses to accomplish his or her objectives.

Remember, most speeches are presented once, but they don't cease to have influence immediately afterward. Instead, subsequent audiences listen to recordings of the speech or see it in written form. Think carefully about how the speech impacted you, and ask yourself how the effects might differ for audiences hearing the speech live, hearing a recording, and reading a transcript.

"Liberty or Death"
Patrick Henry

Patrick Henry (1736–1799) grew up in Virginia and was educated to become a lawyer. He was elected to the Virginia House of Burgesses in 1765, where he proposed the Stamp Act Resolutions in response to British taxation of public documents. Similar radicalism and defiance became a feature of Henry's politics, and in 1774, he represented Virginia at the First Continental Congress. Henry delivered the following speech on March 23, 1775, before the Virginia Congressional delegates in an attempt to persuade Virginia to prepare for revolution. The famous line, "Give me liberty or give me death!" became a slogan for the Revolutionary War. Henry's persuasion was successful, and the delegates passed his resolutions. During the war, Henry went on to serve three consecutive terms and one additional term as governor of Virginia.

No man thinks more highly than I do of the patriotism, as well as abilities, of the very worthy gentlemen who have just addressed the House. But different men often see the same subject in different lights; and, therefore, I hope that it will not be thought disrespectful to those gentlemen, if, entertaining as I do opinions of a character very opposite to theirs, I shall speak forth my sentiments freely and without reserve.

This is no time for ceremony. The question before the House is one of awful moment to this country. For my own part I consider it as nothing less than a question of freedom or slavery; and in proportion to the magnitude of the subject ought to be the freedom of the debate. It is only in this way that we can hope to arrive at truth, and fulfill the great responsibility which we hold to God and our country. Should I keep back my opinions at such a time, through fear of giving offense, I should consider myself as guilty of treason towards my country, and of an act of disloyalty towards the majesty of Heaven, which I revere above all earthly kings.

Mr. President, it is natural to man to indulge in the illusions of hope. We are apt to shut our eyes against a painful truth, and listen to the song of that siren, till she transforms us into beasts. Is this the part of wise men, engaged in a great and arduous struggle for liberty? Are we disposed to be of the number of those who, having eyes, see not, and having ears, hear not, the things which so nearly concern their temporal salvation?

For my part, whatever anguish of spirit it may cost, I am willing to know the whole truth—to know the worst and to provide for it. I have but one lamp by which my feet are guided; and that is the lamp of experience. I know of no way of judging of the future but by the past. And judging by the past, I wish to know what there has been in the conduct of the British ministry for the last ten years, to justify those hopes with which gentlemen have been pleased to solace themselves and the House?

Is it that insidious smile with which our petition has been lately received? Trust it not, sir; it will prove a snare to your feet. Suffer not yourselves to be betrayed with a kiss. Ask yourselves how this gracious reception of our petition comports with these warlike preparations which cover our waters and darken our land. Are fleets and armies necessary to a work of love and reconciliation? Have we shown ourselves so unwilling to be reconciled that force must be called in to win back our love? Let us not deceive ourselves, sir. These are the implements of war and subjugation—the last arguments to which kings resort. I ask gentlemen, sir, what means this martial array, if its purpose be not to force us to submission? Can gentlemen assign any other possible motives for it? Has Great Britain any enemy, in this quarter of the world, to call for all this accumulation of navies and armies?

No, sir, she has none. They are meant for us; they can be meant for no other. They are sent over to bind and rivet upon us those chains which the British ministry have been so long forging. And what have we to oppose to them? Shall we try argument? Sir, we have been trying that for the last ten years. Have we anything new to offer on the subject? Nothing.

We have held the subject up in every light of which it is capable; but it has been all in vain. Shall we resort to entreaty and humble supplication? What terms shall we find which have not been already exhausted? Let us not, I beseech you, sir, deceive ourselves longer.

Sir, we have done everything that could be done to avert the storm which is now coming on. We have petitioned; we have remonstrated; we have supplicated; we have prostrated ourselves before the throne, and have implored its interposition to arrest the tyrannical hands of the ministry and Parliament.

Our petitions have been slighted; our remonstrances have produced additional violence and insult; our supplications have been disregarded; and we have been spurned, with contempt, from the foot of the throne. In vain, after these things, may we indulge the fond hope of peace and reconciliation. There is no longer any room for hope.

If we wish to be free—if we mean to preserve inviolate those inestimable privileges for which we have been so long contending—if we mean not basely to abandon the noble struggle in which we have been so long engaged, and which we have pledged ourselves never to abandon until the glorious object of our contest shall be obtained, we must fight! I repeat it, sir, we must fight! An appeal to arms and to the God of Hosts is all that is left us!

They tell us, sir, that we are weak—unable to cope with

so formidable an adversary. But when shall we be stronger? Will it be the next week, or the next year? Will it be when we are totally disarmed, and when a British guard shall be stationed in every house? Shall we gather strength by irresolution and inaction? Shall we acquire the means of effectual resistance, by lying supinely on our backs, and hugging the delusive phantom of hope, until our enemies shall have bound us hand and foot?

Sir, we are not weak, if we make a proper use of the means which the God of nature hath placed in our power. Three millions of people, armed in the holy cause of liberty, and in such a country as that which we possess, are invincible by any force which our enemy can send against us. Besides, sir, we shall not fight our battles alone. There is a just God who presides over the destinies of nations, and who will raise up friends to fight our battles for us.

The battle, sir, is not to the strong alone; it is to the vigilant, the active, the brave. Besides, sir, we have no election. If we were base enough to desire it, it is now too late to retire from the contest. There is no retreat but in submission and slavery! Our chains are forged! Their clanking may be heard on the plains of Boston! The war is inevitable—and let it come! I repeat it, sir, let it come!

It is in vain, sir, to extenuate the matter. Gentlemen may cry, "Peace! Peace!"—but there is no peace. The war is actually begun! The next gale that sweeps from the north will bring to our ears the clash of resounding arms! Our brethren are already in the field! Why stand we here idle? What is it that gentlemen wish? What would they have? Is life so dear, or peace so sweet, as to be purchased at the price of chains and slavery? Forbid it, Almighty God! I know not what course others may take; but as for me, give me liberty, or give me death!

Review Questions

1. "Different men often see the same subjects in different lights" is a tactful way of saying what?
2. Why did Henry not keep back his opinions? To which authority was he submitting himself?
3. By what one lamp were Henry's feet guided? *experience*
4. Why did Henry claim the British were not sincere in their reception of the colonists' petitions?
5. According to Henry, what was the only choice that was left?

Thought Questions

1. What does it mean to be free? What is the opposite of freedom?
2. Were you aware that, at the time of this speech, the leaders of the Revolutionary movement owned slaves? Does this seem hypocritical to you?
3. Is it hard to negotiate peacefully when an army is standing nearby? Why or why not?
4. Are life and peace dearer to you than liberty? Be honest, and defend your answer.
5. Several revolutions have had slogans relating to the idea of liberty/equality or death. Is that slogan appropriate? What expectations does it place on revolutionaries? What does it assume?

"First Inaugural Address"
George Washington

George Washington (1732–1799) was born into a plantation family in Virginia. In his early life, he worked as a surveyor before he was commissioned in the military and went on to serve under General Braddock in the French and Indian War. Back in Virginia, he was a member of the House of Burgesses. In 1775, as a delegate to the Second Continental Congress, Washington was elected Commander in Chief of the Continental Army. After the Revolutionary War ended, however, Washington voluntarily stepped down from the position. When the U.S. Constitution was ratified, the Electoral College unanimously elected Washington the first president of the new United States. He delivered his inaugural address in New York City on April 30, 1789.

Fellow Citizens of the Senate and the House of Representatives.

Among the vicissitudes incident to life, no event could have filled me with greater anxieties than that of which the notification was transmitted by your order, and received on the fourteenth day of the present month. On the one hand, I was summoned by my Country, whose voice I can never hear but with veneration and love, from a retreat which I had chosen with the fondest predilection, and, in my flattering hopes, with an immutable decision, as the asylum of my declining years: a retreat which was rendered every day more necessary as well as more dear to me, by the addition of habit to inclination, and of frequent interruptions in my health to the gradual waste committed on it by time. On the other hand, the magnitude and difficulty of the trust to which the voice of my Country called me, being sufficient to awaken in the wisest and most experienced of her citizens, a distrustful scrutiny into his qualifications, could not but overwhelm with despondence, one, who, inheriting inferior endowments from nature and unpracticed in the duties of civil administration, ought to be peculiarly conscious of his own deficiencies. In this conflict of emotions, all I dare aver, is, that it has been my faithful study to collect my duty from a just appreciation of every circumstance, by which it might be affected. All I dare hope, is, that, if in executing this task I have been too much swayed by a grateful remembrance of former instances, or by an affectionate sensibility to this transcendent proof, of the confidence of my fellow-citizens; and have thence too little consulted my incapacity as well as disinclination for the weighty and untried cares before me; my error will be palliated by the motives which misled me, and its consequences be judged by my Country, with some share of the partiality in which they originated.

Such being the impressions under which I have, in obedience to the public summons, repaired to the present station; it would be peculiarly improper to omit in this first official Act, my fervent supplications to that Almighty Being who rules over the Universe, who presides in the Councils of Nations, and whose providential aids can supply every human defect, that his benediction may consecrate to the liberties and happiness of the People of the United States, a Government instituted by themselves for these essential purposes: and may enable every instrument employed in its administration to execute with success, the functions allotted to his charge. In tendering this homage to the Great Author of every public and private good I assure myself that it expresses your sentiments not less than my own; nor those of my fellow-citizens at large, less than either. No People can be bound to acknowledge and adore the invisible hand, which conducts the Affairs of men more than the People of the United States. Every step, by which they have advanced to the character of an independent nation, seems to have been distinguished by some token of providential agency. And in the important revolution just accomplished in the system of their United Government, the tranquil deliberations and voluntary consent of so many distinct communities, from which the event has resulted, cannot be compared with the means by which most Governments have been established, without some return of pious gratitude along with an humble anticipation of the future blessings which the past seem to presage. These reflections, arising out of the present crisis, have forced themselves too strongly on my mind to be suppressed. You will join with me I trust in thinking, that there are none under the influence of which, the proceedings of a new and free Government can more auspiciously commence.

By the article establishing the Executive Department, it is made the duty of the President "to recommend to your consideration, such measures as he shall judge necessary and expedient." The circumstances under which I now meet you, will acquit me from entering into that subject, farther than to refer to the Great Constitutional Charter under which you are assembled; and which, in defining your powers, designates the objects to which your attention is to be given. It will be more consistent with those circumstances, and far more congenial with the feelings which actuate me, to substitute, in place of a recommendation of particular measures, the tribute that is due to the talents, the rectitude, and the patriotism which adorn the characters selected to devise and adopt them. In these honorable qualifications, I behold the surest pledges, that as on one side, no local prejudices, or attachments; no separate views, nor party animosities, will misdirect the comprehensive and equal eye which ought to watch over this great assemblage of communities and interests: so, on another, that the foundations of our National policy will be laid in the pure and immutable principles of private morality; and the pre-eminence of a free Government, be exemplified by all the attributes which can win the affections of its Citizens, and command the respect of the world.

I dwell on this prospect with every satisfaction which an ardent love for my Country can inspire: since there is no truth more thoroughly established, than that there exists in the economy and course of nature, an indissoluble union between virtue and happiness, between duty and advantage, between the genuine maxims of an honest and magnanimous policy, and the solid rewards of public prosperity and felicity: Since we ought to be no less persuaded that the propitious smiles of Heaven, can never be expected on a nation that disregards the eternal rules of order and right, which Heaven itself has ordained: And since the preservation of the sacred fire of liberty, and the destiny of the Republican model of Government, are justly considered as deeply, perhaps as finally staked, on the experiment entrusted to the hands of the American people.

Besides the ordinary objects submitted to your care, it will remain with your judgment to decide, how far an exercise of the occasional power delegated by the Fifth article of the Constitution is rendered expedient at the present juncture by the nature of objections which have been urged against the System, or by the degree of inquietude which has given birth to them. Instead of undertaking particular recommendations on this subject, in which I could be guided by no lights derived from official opportunities, I shall again give way to my entire confidence in your discernment and pursuit of the public good: For I assure myself that whilst you carefully avoid every alteration which might endanger the benefits of an United and effective Government, or which ought to await the future lessons of experience; a reverence for the characteristic rights of freemen, and a regard for the public harmony, will sufficiently influence your deliberations on the question how far the former can be more impregnably fortified, or the latter be safely and advantageously promoted.

To the preceding observations I have one to add, which will be most properly addressed to the House of Representatives. It concerns myself, and will therefore be as brief as possible. When I was first honored with a call into the Service of my Country, then on the eve of an arduous struggle for its liberties, the light in which I contemplated my duty required that I should renounce every pecuniary compensation. From this resolution I have in no instance departed. And being still under the impressions which produced it, I must decline as inapplicable to myself, any share in the personal emoluments, which may be indispensably included in a permanent provision for the Executive Department; and must accordingly pray that the pecuniary estimates for the Station in which I am placed, may, during my continuance in it, be limited to such actual expenditures as the public good may be thought to require.

Having thus imported to you my sentiments, as they have been awakened by the occasion which brings us together, I shall take my present leave; but not without resorting once more to the benign parent of the human race, in humble supplication that since he has been pleased to favor the American people, with opportunities for deliberating in perfect tranquility, and dispositions for deciding with unparalleled unanimity on a form of Government, for the security of their Union, and the advancement of their happiness; so his divine blessing may be equally conspicuous in the enlarged views, the temperate consultations, and the wise measures on which the success of this Government must depend.

Review Questions

1. Did Washington want the presidency? What reasons did he give?
2. Why did Washington think he was unqualified? (Name two reasons.)
3. What did Washington carefully avoid omitting from this "first official Act"?
4. What role did Washington say God played in the United States' early history?
5. To what was Washington referring when he said (para. 4), "There is no truth more thoroughly established"?

Thought Questions

1. What is the role of humility in leadership? Do we still value humility in the business world? Which is ranked more highly, humility or self-confidence?
2. What would you consider to be the role of God in America's development?
3. Do you think the government is granted a certain amount of power by the people, or does the government grant a certain amount of power to the people? Explain your answer.
4. Washington concluded with praise to God for the unanimity of America's choice of government. How important is unanimity in nationwide decisions? Is majority rule always best?
5. Should the presidency be a paid position? Why or why not?

"In Favor of the Federal Constitution" (excerpts)
James Madison

James Madison (1751–1836) was a Virginian who was deeply involved in the early writing of American government. He contributed to the Virginia Constitution and was an active participant in the Constitutional Convention. On June 6, 1788, Madison gave a speech refuting Patrick Henry's argument against giving additional powers to the federal government. Henry supported the revision of the Articles of the Confederation; Madison supported a federal constitution. Madison's speech answered many of the fears of the anti-federalists and helped to secure favorable opinion for the federal constitution. Madison went on to contribute to the Bill of Rights as well, and he became known as the "Father of the Constitution." In 1808, Madison was elected president, from which position he led the United States into the War of 1812.

We ought, sir, to examine the Constitution on its own merits solely. We are to inquire whether it will promote the public happiness; its aptitude to produce this desirable object ought to be the exclusive subject of our present researches. In this pursuit, we ought not to address our arguments to the feelings and passions but to those understandings and judgments which were selected by the people of this country, to decide this great question by a calm and rational investigation.

I hope that gentlemen, in displaying their abilities on this occasion, instead of giving opinions and making assertions, will condescend to prove and demonstrate by a fair and regular discussion. It gives me pain to hear gentlemen continually distorting the natural construction of language; for it is sufficient if any human production can stand a fair discussion. Before I proceed to make some additions to the reasons which have been adduced by my honorable friend over the way, I must take the liberty to make some observations on what was said by another gentleman.

He told us that this Constitution ought to be rejected because it endangered the public liberty, in his opinion, in many instances. Give me leave to make answer to that observation. Let the dangers which this system is supposed to be replete with be clearly pointed out. If any dangerous and unnecessary powers be given to the general legislature, let them be plainly demonstrated; and let us not rest satisfied with general assertions of danger, without examination. If powers be necessary, apparent danger is not a sufficient reason against conceding them. He has suggested that licentiousness has seldom produced the loss of liberty, but that the tyranny of rulers has almost always effected it. Since the general civilization of mankind I believe there are more instances of the abridgment of the freedom of the people by gradual and silent encroachments of those in power than by violent and sudden usurpations; but, on a candid examination of history, we shall find that turbulence, violence, and abuse of power, by the majority trampling on the rights of the minority, have produced factions and commotions which, in republics, have more frequently than any other cause, produced despotism. If we go over the whole history of ancient and modern republics we shall find their destruction to have generally resulted from those causes. If we consider the peculiar situation of the United States, and what are the sources of that diversity of sentiment which pervades its inhabitants, we shall find great danger to fear that the same causes may terminate here in the same fatal effects which they produced in those republics. This danger ought to be wisely guarded against.

I must confess I have not been able to find his usual consistency in the gentleman's argument on this occasion. He informs us that the people of the country are at perfect repose; that is, every man enjoys the fruits of his labor peaceably and securely, and that everything is in perfect tranquility and safety. I wish sincerely that this were true. If this be their happy situation, why has every state acknowledged the contrary? Why were deputies from all the states sent to the general convention? Why have complaints of national and individual distresses been echoed and reechoed throughout the continent? Why has our general government been so shamefully disgraced and our Constitution violated? Wherefore have laws been made to authorize a change, and wherefore are we now assembled here? A federal government is formed for the protection of its individual members. Ours has attacked itself with impunity. Its authority has been disobeyed and despised.

I think I perceive a glaring inconsistency in another of his arguments. He complains of this Constitution because it requires the consent of at least three-fourths of the states to introduce amendments which shall be necessary for the happiness of the people...In the first case, he asserts that a majority ought to have the power of altering the government when found to be inadequate to the security of public happiness. In the last case, he affirms that even three-fourths of the community have not a right to alter a government which experience has proved to be subversive of national felicity! nay, that the most necessary and urgent alterations cannot be made without the absolute unanimity of all the states! Does not the thirteenth article of the Confederation expressly require that no alteration shall be made without the unanimous consent of all the states? Could anything in theory be more perniciously improvident and injudicious than this submission of the will of the majority to the most trifling minority? Have not experience and practice actually manifested this theoretical inconvenience to be extremely impolitic?

The power of raising and supporting armies is exclaimed against as dangerous and unnecessary. I wish there were no necessity of vesting this power in the general government. But suppose a foreign nation were to declare war against the United States; must not the general legislature have the power of defending the United States? Ought it to be known to foreign nations that the general government of the United States of America has no power to raise and support an army, even in the utmost danger, when attacked by external enemies? Would not their knowledge of such a circumstance stimulate them to fall upon us?

If, sir, Congress be not invested with this power, any powerful nation, prompted by ambition or avarice, will be invited by our weakness to attack us; and such an attack by disciplined veterans would certainly be attended with success, when only opposed by irregular, undisciplined militia.

Give me leave to say something of the nature of the government and to show that it is safe and just to vest it with the power of taxation. There are a number of opinions, but the principal question is whether it be a federal or a consolidated government. In order to judge properly of the question before us, we must consider it minutely in its principal parts. I conceive myself that it is of a mixed nature; it is in a manner unprecedented; we cannot find one express example in the experience of the world. It stands by itself. In some respects it is a government of a federal nature; in others, it is of a consolidated nature. Even if we attend to the manner in which the Constitution is investigated, ratified, and made the act of the people of America, I can say, notwithstanding what the honorable gentleman has alleged, that this government is not completely consolidated, nor is it entirely federal. Who are parties to it? The people — but not the people as composing one great body, but the people as composing thirteen sovereignties. Were it, as the gentleman asserts, a consolidated government, the assent of a majority of the people would be sufficient for its establishment; and, as a majority have adopted it already, the remaining states would be bound by the act of the majority, even if they unanimously rejected it. Were it such a government as is suggested it would be now binding on the people of this state without their having had the privilege of deliberating on it. But, sir, no state is bound by it, as it is, without its own consent. Should all the states adopt it, it will be then a government established by the thirteen states of America, not through the intervention of the legislatures, but by the people at large. In this particular respect the distinction between the existing and the proposed governments is very material. The existing system has been derived from the dependent derivative authority of the legislatures of the states; whereas, this is derived from the superior power of the people.

If we look at the manner in which alterations are to be made in it, the same idea is, in some degree, attended to. By the new system a majority of the states cannot introduce amendments, nor are all the states required for that purpose; three-fourths of them must concur in alterations. In this there is a departure from the federal idea. The members of the national House of Representatives are to be chosen by the people at large, in proportion to the numbers in the respective districts. When we come to the Senate, its members are elected by the states in their equal and political capacity. But had the government been completely consolidated, the Senate would have been chosen by the people in their individual capacity, in the same manner as the members of the other house. Thus it is of a complicated nature; and this complication, I trust, will be found to exclude the evils of absolute consolidation, as well as of a mere confederacy…

Those who wish to become federal representatives must depend on their credit with that class of men who will be the most popular in their counties, who generally represent the people in the state governments; they can, therefore, never succeed in any measure contrary to the wishes of those on whom they depend. It is almost certain, therefore, that the deliberations of the members of the federal House of Representatives will be directed to the interests of the people of America. As to the other branch, the senators will be appointed by the legislatures; and, though elected for six years, I do not conceive they will so soon forget the source from whence they derive their political existence. This election of one branch of the federal by the state legislatures secures an absolute dependence of the former on the latter. The biennial exclusion of one-third will lessen the facility of a combination and may put a stop to intrigues. I appeal to our past experience whether they will attend to the interests of their constituent states. Have not those gentlemen who have been honored with seats in Congress, often signalized themselves by their attachment to their seats?

I wish this government may answer the expectation of its friends and foil the apprehension of its enemies. I hope the patriotism of the people will continue and be a sufficient guard to their liberties. I believe its tendency will be that the state governments will counteract the general interest and ultimately prevail. The number of the representatives is yet sufficient for our safety and will gradually increase; and, if we consider their different sources of information, the number will not appear too small.

Review Questions

1. What basis for evaluating the Constitution did Madison advocate?
2. What did it mean to distort "the natural construction of language"?
3. What did Madison list as Henry's main arguments? Summarize Madison's responses.
4. To what factors did Madison attribute the destruction of ancient and modern republics?
5. What inconsistencies did Madison point out in Henry's arguments?

Thought Questions

1. How, in your opinion, would Madison respond to the assertion that change is dangerous and should be avoided?
2. Madison cited threat of foreign invasion as a reason for the government to raise an army. Is this also a good reason for the government to be able to institute a draft? Why or why not?
3. Madison claimed that: "no state is bound by [the federal government] as it is, without its own consent." Do you think this is true? On the basis of this statement, were the southern states justified in seceding from the union?
4. Why did Madison think that representatives would do what was in the interest of their constituents? Do you agree? Defend your answer.
5. Do you see any inconsistencies or weaknesses in Madison's arguments? Did he convince you?

"The Monroe Doctrine"
James Monroe

James Monroe (1758–1831) was born in Virginia, and after fighting in the Revolutionary War, he returned to Virginia to practice law. He went on to serve in the Senate and as Foreign Minister to France. Monroe was elected president in 1816 and served two terms. In his seventh annual message to Congress, presented on December 2, 1823, he outlined the foreign policy that would become known as the Monroe Doctrine. He claimed that the United States had the right to protect Latin America and the land south of the Bering Strait from foreign aggression or further European colonization. The speech represents one of the first instances in which the United States stood up to world colonial powers. The doctrine began to be widely cited in defense of foreign policy decisions in the 1860s, and it was reaffirmed and amended by Theodore Roosevelt in 1904.

At the proposal of the Russian Imperial Government, made through the minister of the Emperor residing here, a full power and instructions have been transmitted to the Minister of the United States at St. Petersburg to arrange, by amicable negotiation, the respective rights and interests of the two nations on the northwest coast of this continent. A similar proposal has been made by His Imperial Majesty to the Government of Great Britain, which has likewise been acceded to. The Government of the United States has been desirous, by this friendly proceeding, of manifesting the great value which they have invariably attached to the friendship of the Emperor, and their solicitude to cultivate the best understanding with his Government. In the discussions to which this interest has given rise, and in the arrangements by which they may terminate the occasion has been judged proper for asserting, as a principle in which the rights and interests of the United States are involved, that the American continents, by the free and independent condition which they have assumed and maintain, are henceforth not to be considered as subjects for future colonization by any European powers…

It was stated at the commencement of the last session that a great effort was then making in Spain and Portugal, to improve the condition of the people of those countries, and that it appeared to be conducted with extraordinary moderation. It need scarcely be remarked, that the result has been, so far, very different from what was then anticipated. Of events in that quarter of the globe, with which we have so much intercourse, and from which we

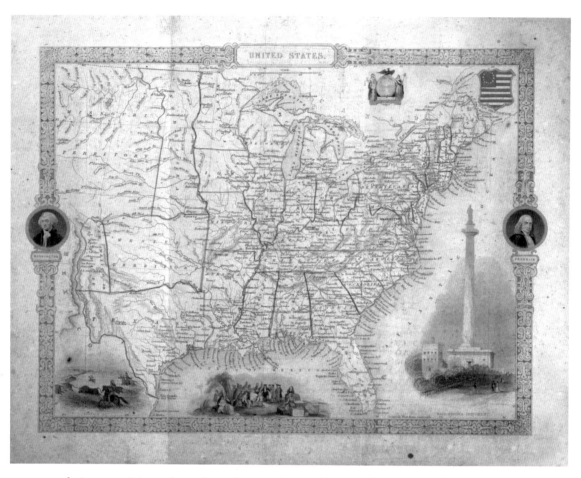

derive our origin, we have always been anxious and interested spectators. The citizens of the United States cherish sentiments the most friendly, in favor of the liberty and happiness of their fellow men on that side of the Atlantic. In the wars of the European powers, in matters relating to themselves, we have never taken any part, nor does it comport with our policy to do so. It is only when our rights are invaded, or seriously menaced, that we resent injuries, or make preparation for our defence. With the movements in this hemisphere, we are, of necessity, more immediately connected, and by causes which must be obvious to all enlightened and impartial observers. The political system of the allied powers is essentially different, in this respect, from that of America. This difference proceeds from that which exists in their respective governments. And to the defence of our own, which has been achieved by the loss of so much blood and treasure, and matured by the wisdom of their most enlightened citizens, and under which we have enjoyed unexampled felicity, this whole nation is devoted.

We owe it, therefore, to candor, and to the amicable relations existing between the United States and those powers, to declare, that we should consider any attempt on their part to extend their system to any portion of this hemisphere, as dangerous to our peace and safety. With the existing colonies or dependencies of any European power we have not interfered, and shall not interfere. But with the governments who have declared their independence, and maintained it, and whose independence we have, on great consideration, and on just principles, acknowledged, we could not view any interposition for the purpose of oppressing them, or controlling, in any other manner, their destiny, by any European power in any other light than as the manifestation of an unfriendly disposition towards the United States. In the war between those new governments and Spain we declared our neutrality at the time of their recognition, and to this we have adhered, and shall continue to adhere, provided no change shall occur, which, in the judgement of the competent authorities of this government, shall make a corresponding change, on the part of the United States, indispensable to their security.

The late events in Spain and Portugal, shew that Europe is still unsettled. Of this important fact, no stronger proof can be adduced than that the allied powers should have thought it proper, on any principle satisfactory to themselves, to have interposed, by force, in the internal concerns of Spain. To what extent such interposition may be carried, on the same principle, is a question, to which all independent powers, whose governments differ from theirs, are interested; even those most remote, and surely none more so than the United States. Our policy, in regard to Europe, which was adopted at an early stage of the wars which have so long agitated that quarter of the globe, nevertheless remains the same, which is, not to interfere in the internal concerns of any of its powers; to consider the government de facto as the legitimate government for us; to cultivate friendly relations with it, and to preserve those relations by a frank, firm, and manly policy; meeting, in all instances, the just claims of every power; submitting to injuries from none.

But, in regard to these continents, circumstances are eminently and conspicuously different. It is impossible that the allied powers should extend their political system to any portion of either continent, without endangering our peace and happiness: nor can any one believe that our Southern Brethren, if left to themselves, would adopt it of their own accord. It is equally impossible, therefore, that we should behold such interposition, in any form, with indifference. If we look to the comparative strength and resources of Spain and those new governments, and their distance from each other, it must be obvious that she can never subdue them. It is still the true policy of the United States to leave the parties to themselves, in the hope that other powers will pursue the same course.

Review Questions

1. What portion of the Americas did Russia want to claim?
2. What warning did Monroe issue to other imperial powers (see end of opening paragraph)?
3. Did Monroe recommend involvement in the affairs of other nations?
4. How were the allied powers' political systems different from the United States', according to Monroe?
5. What showed Monroe that Europe was still unsettled?

Thought Questions

1. What did the United States consider "as dangerous to our peace and safety"? Why?
2. How did this doctrine represent a change in the way America was viewed by the world?
3. Which countries did Monroe claim U.S. protection over? What is the relationship between the United States and those countries today?
4. What message was Monroe attempting to convey to the European powers? How do you think they received the message?
5. How long did the United States maintain its policy of non-interference in world affairs? What eventually caused the United States to change this policy?

"Seneca Falls Declaration of Sentiments"
Elizabeth Cady Stanton

Elizabeth Cady Stanton (1815–1902) was born in New York, where she received an informal legal education from her father to complement her formal schooling. Stanton was a talented writer and an advocate of women's rights. She was one of the organizers of the first national women's rights convention, which was held in 1848 in Seneca Falls, New York. On July 19, at the opening of the convention, Stanton read this "Declaration of Sentiments" to the assembly. After minor revisions, it was unanimously adopted. The statement was composed on the model of the Declaration of Independence; it proposed extending to women the rights Americans had fought for in the Revolutionary War. After the convention, Stanton remained active in the movement, working closely with Susan B. Anthony and serving as president of the National Woman Suffrage Association.

When, in the course of human events, it becomes necessary for one portion of the family of man to assume among the people of the earth a position different from that which they have hitherto occupied, but one to which the laws of nature and of nature's God entitle them, a decent respect to the opinions of mankind requires that they should declare the causes that impel them to such a course.

We hold these truths to be self-evident: that all men and women are created equal; that they are endowed by their Creator with certain inalienable rights; that among these are life, liberty, and the pursuit of happiness; that to secure these rights governments are instituted, deriving their just powers from the consent of the governed. Whenever any form of government becomes destructive of these ends, it is the right of those who suffer from it to refuse allegiance to it, and to insist upon the institution of a new government, laying its foundation on such principles, and organizing its powers in such form, as to them shall seem most likely to effect their safety and happiness. Prudence, indeed, will dictate that governments long established should not be changed for light and transient causes; and accordingly all experience hath shown that mankind are more disposed to suffer, while evils are sufferable, than to right themselves by abolishing the forms to which they were accustomed. But when a long train of abuses and usurpations, pursuing invariably the same object, evinces a design to reduce them under absolute despotism, it is their duty to throw off such government, and to provide new guards for their future security. Such has been the patient sufferance of the women under this government, and such is now the necessity which constrains them to demand the equal station to which they are entitled.

The history of mankind is a history of repeated injuries and usurpations on the part of man toward woman, having in direct object the establishment of an absolute tyranny over her. To prove this, let facts be submitted to a candid world.

He has never permitted her to exercise her inalienable right to the elective franchise.

He has compelled her to submit to laws, in the formation of which she had no voice.

He has withheld from her rights which are given to the most ignorant and degraded men—both natives and foreigners.

Stanton (seated) and Susan B. Anthony

Having deprived her of this first right of a citizen, the elective franchise, thereby leaving her without representation in the halls of legislation, he has oppressed her on all sides.

He has made her, if married, in the eye of the law, civilly dead.

He has taken from her all right in property, even to the wages she earns.

He has made her, morally, an irresponsible being, as she can commit many crimes with impunity, provided they be done in the presence of her husband. In the covenant of marriage, she is compelled to promise obedience to her husband, he becoming to all intents and purposes, her master—the law giving him power to deprive her of her liberty, and to administer chastisement.

He has so framed the laws of divorce, as to what shall be the proper causes, and in case of separation, to whom the guardianship of the children shall be given, as to be wholly regardless of the happiness of women—the law, in all cases, going upon a false supposition of the supremacy of man, and giving all power into his hands.

After depriving her of all rights as a married woman, if single, and the owner of property, he has taxed her to support a government which recognizes her only when her property can be made profitable to it.

He has monopolized nearly all the profitable employments, and from those she is permitted to follow, she receives but a scanty remuneration. He closes against her all the avenues to wealth and distinction which he considers most honorable to himself. As a teacher of theology, medicine, or law, she is not known.

He has denied her the facilities for obtaining a thorough education, all colleges being closed against her.

He allows her in Church, as well as State, but a subordinate position, claiming Apostolic authority for her exclusion from the ministry, and, with some exceptions, from any public participation in the affairs of the Church.

He has created a false public sentiment by giving to the world a different code of morals for men and women, by which moral delinquencies which exclude women from society, are not only tolerated, but deemed of little account in man.

He has usurped the prerogative of Jehovah himself, claiming it as his right to assign for her a sphere of action, when that belongs to her conscience and to her God.

He has endeavored, in every way that he could, to destroy her confidence in her own powers, to lessen her self-respect, and to make her willing to lead a dependent and abject life.

Now, in view of this entire disfranchisement of one-half the people of this country, their social and religious degradation—in view of the unjust laws above mentioned, and because women do feel themselves aggrieved, oppressed, and fraudulently deprived of their most sacred rights, we insist that they have immediate admission to all the rights and privileges which belong to them as citizens of the United States.

In entering upon the great work before us, we anticipate no small amount of misconception, misrepresentation, and ridicule; but we shall use every instrumentality within our power to effect our object. We shall employ agents, circulate tracts, petition the State and National legislatures, and endeavor to enlist the pulpit and the press in our behalf. We hope this Convention will be followed by a series of Conventions embracing every part of the country.

Review Questions

1. How was this similar to the Declaration of Independence? How was it different?
2. What did Stanton mean when she said men "usurped the prerogative of Jehovah himself"?
3. Define *disfranchisement* (disenfranchisement). Have you ever personally experienced disenfranchisement?
4. What did this speech attempt to accomplish?
5. What were the tools of the women's rights movement? Did they expect to have success?

Thought Questions

1. In the first section, was Stanton speaking of a literal government, or was she referring to social institutions like patriarchy?
2. What does it mean to say that a woman is "civilly dead" after she is married? Do you agree?
3. Should married couples maintain separate property rights? Explain your answer.
4. Why did Stanton complain about the fact that women can commit crimes with impunity (without punishment)? Isn't this a good thing? If not, why not?
5. Should men and women have different codes of morals? Would any situations justify this?

"On the Slavery Question"
John C. Calhoun

John Caldwell Calhoun (1782–1850) was born in South Carolina, where, after completing school, he returned to practice law. Calhoun then turned to politics and served in both the South Carolina and the U.S. House of Representatives, and as secretary of war. He was elected vice president twice: once alongside John Quincy Adams and once with Andrew Jackson. He went on to serve in the Senate and as secretary of state under President Tyler. Later in his career, Calhoun became an outspoken supporter of the South and slavery. On March 4, 1850, in response to Henry Clay's Missouri Compromise, Calhoun prepared a speech for the Senate, but because he was too ill to read it himself, Virginia Senator James M. Mason read it on his behalf. Calhoun died only a few weeks later.

I have, senators, believed from the first that the agitation of the subject of slavery would, if not prevented by some timely and effective measure, end in disunion. Entertaining this opinion, I have, on all proper occasions, endeavored to call the attention of both the two great parties which divided the country to adopt some measure to prevent so great a disaster, but without success. The agitation has been permitted to proceed with almost no attempt to resist it, until it has reached a point when it can no longer be disguised or denied that the Union is in danger. You have thus had forced upon you the greatest and gravest question that can ever come under your consideration: How can the Union be preserved?

To give a satisfactory answer to this mighty question, it is indispensable to have an accurate and thorough knowledge of the nature and the character of the cause by which the Union is endangered. Without such knowledge it is impossible to pronounce with any certainty, by what measure it can be saved; just as it would be impossible for a physician to pronounce in the case of some dangerous disease, with any certainty, by what remedy the patient could be saved, without similar knowledge of the nature and character of the cause which produce it. The first question, then, presented for consideration in the investigation I propose to make in order to obtain such knowledge is: What is it that has endangered the Union?

To this question there can be but one answer,—that the immediate cause is the almost universal discontent which pervades all the States composing the Southern section of the Union. This widely extended discontent is not of recent origin. It commenced with the agitation of the slavery question and has been increasing ever since. The next question, going one step further back, is: What has caused this widely diffused and almost universal discontent?

It is a great mistake to suppose, as is by some, that it originated with demagogs who excited the discontent with the intention of aiding their personal advancement, or with the disappointed ambition of certain politicians who resorted to it as the means of retrieving their fortunes. On the contrary, all the great political influences of the section were arrayed against excitement, and exerted to the utmost to keep the people quiet. The great mass of the people of the South were divided, as in the other section, into Whigs and Democrats. The leaders and the presses of both parties in the South were very solicitous to prevent excitement and to preserve quiet; because it was seen that the effects of the former would necessarily tend to weaken, if not destroy, the political ties which united them with their respective parties in the other section.

Those who know the strength of party ties will readily appreciate the immense force which this cause exerted against agitation and in favor of preserving quiet. But, great as it was, it was not sufficient to prevent the widespread discontent which now pervades the section.

No; some cause far deeper and more powerful than the one supposed must exist, to account for discontent so wide and deep. The question then recurs: What is the cause of this discontent? It will be found in the belief of the people of the Southern States, as prevalent as the discontent itself, that they can not remain, as things now are, consistently with honor and safety, in the Union. The next question to be considered is: What has caused this belief?

One of the causes is, undoubtedly, to be traced to the long-continued agitation of the slave question on the part of the North, and the many aggressions which they have made on the rights of the South during the time. I will not enumerate them at present, as it will be done hereafter in its proper place.

There is another lying back of it—with which this is intimately connected—that may be regarded as the great and primary cause. This is to be found in the fact that the equilibrium between the two sections in the government as it stood when the Constitution was ratified and the government put in action has been destroyed. At that time there was nearly a perfect equilibrium between the two, which afforded ample means to each to protect itself against the aggression of the other; but, as it now stands, one section has the exclusive power of controlling the government, which leaves the other without any adequate means of protecting itself against its encroachment and oppression.

The result of the whole is to give the Northern section a predominance in every department of the government, and thereby concentrate in it the two elements which constitute the federal government: a majority of States, and a majority of their population, estimated in federal numbers. Whatever section concentrates the two in itself possesses the control of the entire government.

But we are just at the close of the sixth decade and the commencement of the seventh. The census is to be taken this year, which must add greatly to the decided preponderance of the North in the House of Representatives and in the Electoral College. The prospect is, also, that a great increase will be added to its present preponderance in the Senate, during the period of the decade, by the addition of new States. Two Territories, Oregon and Minnesota, are already in progress, and strenuous efforts are making to bring in three additional States from the Territory recently conquered from Mexico; which, if successful, will add three other States in a short time to the Northern section, making five States, and increasing the present number of its States from fifteen to twenty, and of its senators from thirty to forty.

On the contrary, there is not a single Territory in progress in the Southern section, and no certainty that any additional State will be added to it during the decade. The prospect then is, that the two sections in the Senate, should the efforts now made to exclude the South from the newly acquired Territories succeed, will stand, before the end of the decade, twenty Northern States to fourteen Southern (considering Delaware as neutral), and forty Northern senators to twenty-eight Southern. This great increase of senators, added to the great increase of members of the House of Representatives and the Electoral College on the part of the North, which must take place under the next decade, will effectually and irretrievably destroy the equilibrium which existed when the government commenced.

Had this destruction been the operation of time without the interference of government, the South would have had no reason to complain; but such was not the fact. It was caused by the legislation of this government, which was appointed as the common agent of all and charged with the protection of the interests and security of all.

The legislation by which it has been effected may be classed under three heads: The first is that series of acts by which the South has been excluded from the common territory belonging to all the States as members of the federal Union—which have had the effect of extending vastly the portion allotted to the Northern section, and restricting within narrow limits the portion left the South. The next consists in adopting a system of revenue and disbursements by which an undue proportion of the burden of taxation has been imposed upon the South, and an undue proportion of its proceeds appropriated to the North. And the last is a system of political measures by which the original character of the government has been radically changed. I propose to bestow upon each of these, in the order they stand, a few remarks, with the view of showing that it is owing to the action of this government that the equilibrium between the two sections has been destroyed, and the whole powers of the system centered in a sectional majority.

I have not included the territory recently acquired by the treaty with Mexico. The North is making the most strenuous efforts to appropriate the whole to herself, by excluding the South from every foot of it. If she should succeed, it will add to that from which the South has already been excluded 526,078 square miles, and would increase the whole which the North has appropriated to herself to 1,764,023, not including the portion that she may succeed in excluding us from in Texas. To sum up the whole, the United States, since they declared their independence, have acquired 2,373,046 square miles of territory, from which the North will have excluded the South, if she should succeed in monopolizing the newly-acquired

Territories, about three-fourths of the whole, leaving to the South but about one-fourth. Such is the first and great cause that has destroyed the equilibrium between the two sections in the government.

The next is the system of revenue and disbursements which has been adopted by the government. It is well known that the government has derived its revenue mainly from duties on imports. I shall not undertake to show that such duties must necessarily fall mainly on the exporting States, and that the South, as the great exporting portion of the Union, has in reality paid vastly more than her due proportion of the revenue; because I deem it unnecessary, as the subject has on so many occasions been fully discussed. Nor shall I, for the same reason, undertake to show that a far greater portion of the revenue has been disbursed in the North, than its due share; and that the joint effect of these causes has been to transfer a vast amount from South to North, which, under an equal system of revenue and disbursements, would not have been lost to her. If to this be added that many of the duties were imposed, not for revenue but for protection—that is, intended to put money, not in the Treasury, but directly into the pocket of the manufacturers—some conception may be formed of the immense amount which in the long course of sixty years has been transferred from South to North. There are no data by which it can be estimated with any certainty; but it is safe to say that it amounts to hundreds of millions of dollars. Under the most moderate estimate it would be sufficient to add greatly to the wealthy of the North, and thus greatly increase her population by attracting immigration from all quarters to that section.

This, combined with the great primary cause, amply explains why the North has acquired a preponderance in every department of the government by its disproportionate increase of population and States. The former, as has been shown, has increased, in fifty years, 2,400,000 over that of the South. This increase of population during so long a period is satisfactorily accounted for by the number of immigrants, and the increase of their descendants, which have been attracted to the Northern section from Europe and the South, in consequence of the advantages derived from the causes assigned. If they had not existed—if the South had retained all the capital which has been extracted from her by the fiscal action of the government; and if it had not been excluded by the Ordinance of 1787 and the Missouri Compromise, from the region lying between the Ohio and the Mississippi Rivers, and between the Mississippi and the Rocky Mountains north of 36ø 30'—it scarcely admits of a doubt that it would have divided the immigration with the North, and by retaining her own people would have at least equaled the North in population under the census of 1840, and probably under that about to be taken. She would also, if she had retained her equal rights in those territories, have maintained an equality in the number of States with the North, and have preserved the equilibrium between the two sections that existed at the commencement of the government. The loss, then, of the equilibrium is to be attributed to the action of this government.

There is a question of vital importance to the Southern section, in reference to which the views and feelings of the two sections are as opposite and hostile as they can possibly be. I refer to the relation between the two races in the Southern section, which constitutes a vital portion of her social organization. Every portion of the North entertains views and feelings more or less hostile to it. Those most opposed and hostile regard it as a sin, and consider themselves under the most sacred obligation to use every effort to destroy it.

Indeed, to the extent that they conceive that they have power, they regard themselves as implicated in the sin, and responsible for not suppressing it by the use of all and every means. Those less opposed and hostile regard it as a crime—an offense against humanity, as they call it and, altho not so fanatical, feel themselves bound to use all efforts to effect the same object; while those who are least opposed and hostile regard it as a blot and a stain on the character of what they call the "nation," and feel themselves accordingly bound to give it no countenance or support. On the contrary, the Southern section regards the relation as one which can not be destroyed without subjecting the two races to the greatest calamity, and the section to poverty, desolation, and wretchedness; and accordingly they feel bound by every consideration of interest and safety to defend it.

Unless something decisive is done, I again ask, What is to stop this agitation before the great and final object at which it aims—the abolition of slavery in the States—is consummated? Is it, then, not certain that if something is not done to arrest it, the South will be forced to choose between abolition and secession? Indeed, as events are now moving, it will not require the South to secede in order to dissolve the Union. Agitation will of itself effect it, of which its past history furnishes abundant proof—as I shall next proceed to show.

It is a great mistake to suppose that disunion can be effected by a single blow. The cords which bind these States together in one common Union are far too numerous and powerful for that. Disunion must be the work of time. It is only through a long process, and successively, that the cords can be snapped until the whole fabric falls asunder. Already the agitation of the slavery question has snapped some of the most important, and has greatly weakened all the others.

If the agitation goes on, the same force, acting with increased intensity, as has been shown, will finally snap every cord, when nothing will be left to hold the States together except force. But surely that can with no propriety of language be called a Union when the only means by which the weaker is held connected with the stronger portion is force. It may, indeed, keep them connected; but the connection will partake much more of the character of subjugation on the part of the weaker to the stronger than the union of free, independent, and sovereign States in one confederation, as they stood in the early stages of the government, and which only is worthy of the sacred name of Union.

Having now, senators, explained what it is that endangers the Union, and traced it to its cause, and explained its nature and character, the question again recurs, How can the Union be saved? To this I answer, there is but one way by which it can be, and that is by adopting such measures as will satisfy the States belonging to the Southern section that they can remain in the Union consistently with their honor and their safety. There is, again, only one way by which this can be effected, and that is by removing the causes by which this belief has been produced. Do this, and discontent will cease, harmony and kind feelings between the sections be restored, and every apprehension of danger to the Union removed. The question, then, is, How can this be done? There is but one way by which it can with any certainty; and that is by a full and final settlement, on the principle of justice, of all the questions at issue between the two sections. The South asks for justice, simple justice, and less she ought not to take. She has no compromise to offer but the Constitution, and no concession or surrender to make. She has already surrendered so much that she has little left to surrender. Such a settlement would go to the root of the evil, and remove all cause of discontent, by satisfying the South that she could remain honorably and safely in the Union, and thereby restore the harmony and fraternal feelings between the sections which existed anterior to the Missouri agitation. Nothing else can, with any certainty, finally and for ever settle the question at issue, terminate agitation, and save the Union.

But can this be done? Yes, easily; not by the weaker party, for it can of itself do nothing—not even protect itself—but by the stronger. The North has only to will it to accomplish it—to do justice by conceding to the South an equal right in the acquired territory, and to do her duty by causing the stipulations relative to fugitive slaves to be faithfully fulfilled—to cease the agitation of the slave question, and to provide for the insertion of a provision in the Constitution, by an amendment, which will restore to the South, in substance, the power she possessed of protecting herself before the equilibrium between the sections was destroyed by the action of this government. There will be no difficulty in devising such a provision—one that will protect the South, and which at the same time will improve and strengthen the government instead of impairing and weakening it.

But will the North agree to this? It is for her to answer the question. But, I will say, she can not refuse if she has half the love of the Union which she professes to have, or without justly exposing herself to the charge that her love of power and aggrandizement is far greater than her love of the Union. At all events, the responsibility of saving the Union rests on the North, and not on the South. The South can not save it by any act of hers, and the North may save it without any sacrifice whatever, unless to do justice and to perform her duties under the Constitution should be regarded by her as a sacrifice.

It is time, senators, that there should be an open and manly avowal on all sides as to what is intended to be done. If the question is not now settled, it is uncertain whether it ever can hereafter be; and we, as the representatives of the States of this Union regarded as governments, should come to a distinct understanding as to our respective views, in order to ascertain whether the great questions at issue can be settled or not. If you who represent the stronger portion, can not agree to settle them on the broad principle of justice and duty, say so; and let the States we both represent agree to separate and part in peace.

If you are unwilling we should part in peace, tell us so; and we shall know what to do when you reduce the question to submission or resistance. If you remain silent, you will compel us to infer by your acts what you intend. In that case California will become the test question. If you admit her under all the difficulties that oppose her admission, you compel us to infer that you intend to exclude us from the whole of the acquired Territories, with the intention of destroying irretrievably the equilibrium between the two sections. We should be blind not to perceive in that case that your real objects are power and aggrandizement, and infatuated, not to act accordingly.

I have now, senators, done my duty in expressing my opinions fully, freely, and candidly on this solemn occasion. In doing so I have been governed by the motives which have governed me in all the stages of the agitation of the slavery question since its commencement. I have exerted myself during the whole period to arrest it, with the intention of saving the Union if it could be done; and if it could not, to save the section where it has pleased providence to cast my lot, and which I sincerely believe has justice and the Constitution on its side. Having faithfully done my duty to the best of my ability, both to the Union and my section, throughout this agitation, I shall have the consolation, let what will come, that I am free from all responsibility.

Review Questions

1. What did Calhoun believe would be the end result of the issue of slavery?
2. What did Calhoun say endangered the Union? How did he think the Union could be saved?
3. What was the "question of vital importance to the Southern section" according to Calhoun?
4. According to Calhoun, on what basis did Southerners defend slavery?
5. What "cords" did Calhoun say still bound the Union together?

Thought Questions

1. Which side, North or South, had predominance in the House? The Senate? Why did it matter?
2. It is now a common principle that checks and balances (separation of power) are central to a successful government. Does this make sense in light of the facts Calhoun mentioned?
3. Do you believe the primary cause of the Civil War was slavery? Why or why not?
4. What sequence of events led to the state of civil unrest? Whom did Calhoun blame?
5. Would compromise have prevented the Civil War? Would it have been worth the cost?

"A House Divided"
Abraham Lincoln

Abraham Lincoln (1809–1865) was born in Kentucky and then moved with his family to the backwoods of Illinois, where he had little access to formal schooling; however, he made education a personal priority. As an adult, he served in the militia during the Black Hawk War of 1832, and after one failed political campaign was elected to the Illinois state legislature at the age of twenty-five. During this time, Lincoln also earned a license to practice law. Returning to politics, he ran for the Senate in 1858. He accepted his party's nomination with the following speech, given June 16, 1858 at the Illinois Republican Convention. Although he lost the race, his debates with Stephen Douglas earned him a reputation as a powerful orator, and, two years later, the Republican nomination for president.

Mr. President and Gentlemen of the Convention:

If we could first know where we are, and whither we are tending, we could better judge what to do, and how to do it. We are now far into the fifth year since a policy was initiated with the avowed object, and confident promise, of putting an end to slavery agitation. Under the operation of that policy, that agitation has not only not ceased, but has constantly augmented. In my opinion, it will not cease, until a crisis shall have been reached and passed. "A house divided against itself cannot stand." I believe this government cannot endure permanently half slave and half free. I do not expect the Union to be dissolved — I do not expect the house to fall — but I do expect it will cease to be divided. It will become all one thing, or all the other. Either the opponents of slavery will arrest the further spread of it, and place it where the public mind shall rest in the belief that it is in the course of ultimate extinction; or its advocates will push it forward, till it shall become alike lawful in all the States, old as well as new — North as well as South.

Have we no tendency to the latter condition?

Let any one who doubts, carefully contemplate that now almost complete legal combination — piece of machinery, so to speak — compounded of the Nebraska doctrine, and the *Dred Scott* decision. Let him consider not only what work the machinery is adapted to do, and how well adapted; but also, let him study the history of its construction, and trace, if he can, or rather fail, if he can, to trace the evidences of design, and concert of action, among its chief architects, from the beginning.

The new year of 1854 found slavery excluded from more than half the States by State Constitutions, and from most of the national territory by Congressional prohibition. Four days later, commenced the struggle which ended in repealing that Congressional prohibition. This opened all the national territory to slavery, and was the first point gained.

But, so far, Congress only had acted; and an endorsement by the people, real or apparent, was indispensable, to save the point already gained, and give chance for more.

This necessity had not been overlooked; but had been provided for, as well as might be, in the notable argument of "squatter sovereignty," otherwise called "sacred right of self-government," which latter phrase, though expressive of the only rightful basis of any government, was so perverted in this attempted use of it as to amount to just this: That if any one man choose to enslave another, no third man shall be allowed to object. That argument was incorporated into the Nebraska Bill itself, in the language which follows: "It being the true intent and meaning of this act not to legislate slavery into any Territory or State, nor to exclude it therefrom; but to leave the people thereof perfectly free to form and regulate their domestic institutions in their own way, subject only to the Constitution of the United States." Then opened the roar of loose declamation in favor of "Squatter Sovereignty," and "sacred right of self-government." "But," said opposition members, "let us amend the bill so as to expressly declare that the people of the Territory may exclude slavery." "Not we," said the friends of the measure; and down they voted the amendment.

While the Nebraska Bill was passing through Congress, a law case involving the question of a Negro's freedom, by reason of his owner having voluntarily taken him first into a free State and then into a Territory covered by the Congressional prohibition, and held him as a slave for a long time in each, was passing through the U.S. Circuit Court for the District of Missouri; and both Nebraska Bill and law suit were brought to a decision in the same month of May, 1854. The Negro's name was "Dred Scott," which name now designates the decision finally made in the case. Before the then next Presidential election, the law case came to, and was argued in, the Supreme Court of the United States; but the decision of it was deferred until after the election. Still, before the election, Senator Trumbull, on the floor of the Senate, requested the leading advocate of the Nebraska Bill to state his opinion whether the people of a Territory can constitutionally exclude slavery from their limits; and the latter answers: "That is a question for the Supreme Court."

The election came. Mr. Buchanan was elected, and the indorsement [sic], such as it was, secured. That was the second point gained. The indorsement, however, fell short of a clear popular majority by nearly four hundred thousand votes, and so, perhaps, was not overwhelmingly reliable and satisfactory. The outgoing President, in his last annual message, as impressively as possible, echoed back upon the people the weight and authority of the indorsement. The Supreme Court met again; did not announce their decision, but ordered a re-argument. The Presidential inauguration came, and still no decision of the court; but the incoming President in his inaugural address, fervently exhorted the people to abide by the forthcoming decision, whatever it might be. Then, in a few days, came the decision.

The reputed author of the Nebraska Bill finds an early occasion to make a speech at this capital indorsing the *Dred Scott* decision, and vehemently denouncing all opposition to it. The new President, too, seizes the early occasion of the Silliman letter to indorse and strongly construe that decision, and to express his astonishment that any different view had ever been entertained!

At length a squabble springs up between the President and the author of the Nebraska Bill, on the mere question of fact, whether the Lecompton Constitution was or was not, in any just sense, made by the people of Kansas; and in that quarrel the latter declares that all he wants is a fair vote for the people, and that he cares not whether slavery be voted down or voted up. I do not understand his declaration that he cares not whether slavery be voted down or voted up, to be intended by him other than as an apt definition of the policy he would impress upon the public mind—the principle for which he declares he has suffered so much, and is ready to suffer to the end. And well may he cling to that principle. If he has any parental feeling, well may he cling to it. That principle is the only shred left of his original Nebraska doctrine. Under the *Dred Scott* decision "squatter sovereignty" squatted out of existence, tumbled down like temporary scaffolding—like the mould at the foundry served through one blast and fell back into loose sand—helped to carry an election, and then was kicked to the winds. His late joint struggle with the Republicans, against the Lecompton Constitution, involves nothing of the original Nebraska doctrine. That struggle was made on a point—the right of a people to make their own constitution—upon which he and the Republicans have never differed.

The several points of the *Dred Scott* decision, in connection, with Senator Douglas's "care not" policy, constitute the piece of machinery, in its present state of advancement. This was the third point gained. The working points of that machinery are:

First, that no Negro slave, imported as such from Africa, and no descendant of such slave, can ever be a citizen of any State, in the sense of that term as used in the Constitution of the United States. This point is made in order to deprive the Negro, in every possible event, of the benefit of that provision of the United States Constitution, which declares that "The citizens of each State, shall be entitled to all privileges and immunities of citizens in the several States."

Secondly, that "subject to the Constitution of the United States," neither Congress nor a Territorial Legislature can exclude slavery from any United States territory. This point is made in order that individual men may fill up the Territories with slaves, without danger of losing them as property, and thus to enhance the chances of permanency to the institution through all the future.

Thirdly, that whether the holding a Negro in actual slavery in a free State, makes him free, as against the holder, the United States courts will not decide, but will leave to be decided by the courts of any slave State the Negro may be forced into by the master. This point is made, not to be pressed immediately; but, if acquiesced in for awhile, and apparently indorsed by the people at an election, then to sustain the logical conclusion that what Dred Scott's master might lawfully do with Dred Scott, in the free State of Illinois, every other master may lawfully do with any other one, or one thousand slaves, in Illinois, or in any other free State.

Auxiliary to all this, and working hand in hand with it, the Nebraska doctrine, or what is left of it, is to educate and mould public opinion, at least Northern public opinion, not to care whether slavery is voted down or voted up. This shows exactly where we now are; and partially, also, whither we are tending.

It will throw additional light on the latter, to go back, and run the mind over the string of historical facts already stated. Several things will now appear less dark and mysterious than they did when they were transpiring. The people were to be left "perfectly free," "subject only to the Constitution." What the Constitution had to do with it, outsiders could not then see. Plainly enough now, it was an exactly fitted niche, for the *Dred Scott* decision to afterward come in, and declare the perfect freedom of the people to be just no freedom at all. Why was the amendment, expressly declaring the right of the people, voted down? Plainly enough now: the adoption of it would have spoiled the niche for the *Dred Scott* decision. Why was the court decision held up? Why even a Senator's individual opinion withheld, till after the Presidential election? Plainly enough now: the speaking out then would have damaged the perfectly free argument upon which the election was to be carried. Why the outgoing President's felicitation on the endorsement? Why the delay of a reargument? Why the incoming President's advance exhortation in favor of the decision? These things look like the cautious patting and petting of a spirited horse preparatory to mounting him, when it is dreaded that he may give the rider a fall. And why the hasty after-endorsement of the decision by the President and others?

We cannot absolutely know that all these exact adaptations are the result of preconcert. But when we see a lot of framed timbers, different portions of which we know have been gotten out at different times and places and by different workmen—Stephen, Franklin, Roger and James, for instance—and when we see these timbers joined together, and see they exactly make the frame of a house or a mill, all the tenons and mortices exactly fitting, and all the lengths and proportions of the different pieces exactly adapted to their respective places, and not a piece too many or too few—not omitting even scaffolding—or, if a single piece be lacking, we see the place in the frame exactly fitted and prepared yet to bring such a piece in – in such a case, we find it impossible not to believe that Stephen and Franklin and Roger and James all understood one another from the beginning, and all worked upon a common plan or draft drawn up before the first blow was struck.

It should not be overlooked that, by the Nebraska Bill, the people of a State as well as Territory, were to be left "perfectly free," "subject only to the Constitution." Why mention a State? They were legislating for Territories, and not for or about States. Certainly the people of a State are and ought to be subject to the Constitution of the United States; but why is mention of this lugged into this merely Territorial law? Why are the people of a Territory and the people of a State therein lumped together, and their relation to the Constitution therein treated as being precisely the same? While the opinion of the court, by Chief Justice Taney, in the *Dred Scott* case, and the separate opinions of all the concurring Judges, expressly declare that the Constitution of the United States neither permits Congress nor a Territorial Legislature to exclude slavery from any United States Territory, they all omit to declare whether or not the same Constitution permits a State, or the people of a State, to exclude it.

Possibly, this is a mere omission; but who can be quite sure, if McLean or Curtis had sought to get into the opinion a declaration of unlimited power in the people of a State to exclude slavery from their limits, just as Chase and Mace sought to get such declaration, in behalf of the people of a Territory, into the Nebraska Bill; —I ask, who can be quite sure that it would not have been voted down in the one case as it had been in the other? The nearest approach to the point of declaring the power of a State over slavery, is made by Judge Nelson. He approaches it more than once, using the precise idea, and almost the language, too, of the Nebraska act. On one occasion, his exact language is, "except in cases where the power is restrained by the Constitution of the United States, the law of the State is supreme over the subject of slavery within its jurisdiction." In what cases the power of the States is so restrained by the United States Constitution, is left an open question, precisely as the same question, as to the restraint on the power of the Territories, was left open in the Nebraska act.

Put this and that together, and we have another nice little niche, which we may, ere long, see filled with another Supreme Court decision, declaring that the Constitution of the United States does not permit a State to exclude slavery from its limits. And this may especially be expected if the doctrine of "care not whether slavery be voted down or voted up," shall gain upon the public mind sufficiently to give promise that such a decision can be maintained when made.

Such a decision is all that slavery now lacks of being alike lawful in all the States. Welcome, or unwelcome, such decision is probably coming, and will soon be upon us, unless the power of the present political dynasty shall be met and overthrown. We shall lie down pleasantly dreaming that the people of Missouri are on the verge of making their State free, and we shall awake to the reality instead, that the Supreme Court has made Illinois a slave State. To meet and overthrow the power of that dynasty, is the work now before all those who would prevent that consummation. That is what we have to do. How can we best do it?

There are those who denounce us openly to their own friends, and yet whisper us softly, that Senator Douglas is the aptest instrument there is with which to effect that object. They wish us to infer all, from the fact that he now has a little quarrel with the present head of the dynasty; and that he has regularly voted with us on a single point, upon which he and we have never differed. They remind us that he is a great man, and that the largest of us are very small ones. Let this be granted. But "a living dog is better than a dead lion." Judge Douglas, if not a dead lion, for this work, is at least a caged and toothless one. How can he oppose the advances of slavery? He don't care anything about it. His avowed mission is impressing the "public heart" to care nothing about it. A leading Douglas democratic newspaper thinks Douglas's superior talent will be needed to resist the revival of the African slave trade. Does Douglas believe an effort to revive that trade is approaching? He has not said so. Does he really think so? But if it is, how can he resist it? For years he has labored to prove it a sacred right of white men to take Negro slaves into the new Territories. Can he possibly show that it is less a sacred right to buy them where they can be bought cheapest? And unquestionably they can be bought cheaper in Africa than in Virginia. He has done all in his power to reduce the whole question of slavery to one of a mere right of property; and as such, how can he oppose the foreign slave trade—how can he refuse that trade in that "property" shall be "perfectly free"—unless he does it as a protection to the home production? And as the home producers will probably not ask the protection, he will be wholly without a ground of opposition.

Senator Douglas holds, we know, that a man may rightfully be wiser to-day than he was yesterday – that he may rightfully change when he finds himself wrong. But can we, for that reason, run ahead, and infer that he will make any particular change, of which he, himself, has given no intimation? Can we safely base our action upon any such vague inference? Now, as ever, I wish not to misrepresent Judge Douglas's position, question his motives, or do aught that can be personally offensive to him. Whenever, if ever, he and we can come together on principle so that our cause may have assistance from his great ability, I hope to have interposed no adventitious obstacle. But clearly, he is not now with us—he does not pretend to be—he does not promise ever to be.

Our cause, then, must be entrusted to, and conducted by, its own undoubted friends

—those whose hands are free, whose hearts are in the work – who do care for the result. Two years ago the Republicans of the nation mustered over thirteen hundred thousand strong. We did this under the single impulse of resistance to a common danger, with every external circumstance against us. Of strange, discordant, and even hostile elements, we gathered from the four winds, and formed and fought the battle through, under the constant hot fire of a disciplined, proud and pampered enemy. Did we brave all then, to falter now?—now, when that same enemy is wavering, dissevered and belligerent? The result is not doubtful. We shall not fail—if we stand firm, we shall not fail. Wise counsels may accelerate, or mistakes delay it, but, sooner or later, the victory is sure to come.

Review Questions

1. What two possibilities did Lincoln see for the future for the Union?
2. What was the Nebraska Bill? The *Dred Scott* case? How did Lincoln relate the two?
3. Explain, in your own words, the three parts of the "machinery" enabled by the two events from the previous question. (Hint: Lincoln refers to them as "points.")
4. What niche in the Constitution justified the *Dred Scott* decision?
5. To what did Lincoln compare the mechanism of slavery? To whom did he credit this product?

Thought Questions

1. Can you think of any other example of a house divided? Does Lincoln's statement apply?
2. Do you agree with Lincoln that the Constitution was phrased to allow slavery to continue?
3. The Supreme Court has always emphasized past precedent, i.e., previous court decisions. What kind of precedent did the *Dred Scott* decision create?
4. Lincoln said their cause must be given to "those whose hands are free." Reflect on this statement. Who were "those whose hands are free"? Why were they more worthy to be responsible for the success of Lincoln's cause?
5. How do you think Lincoln's speech would have affected you? Can you understand why he offended some and inspired others? Which emotion would you have felt?

"Inaugural Address"
Jefferson Davis

Jefferson Davis (1807/1808–1889) was born in Kentucky. Davis attended the U.S. Military Academy at West Point and served in the territories before moving to Mississippi, where he became involved in local and state politics. In 1845, he was elected to the House of Representatives. Davis returned to military service during the Mexican War, but after the war ended, he took up politics again. When Lincoln was elected president, Davis resigned from the Senate, and in 1861 he was elected President of the Confederate States. His inaugural address, delivered February 18, 1861, reflects the uncertainty under which he entered office. After the Civil War ended in 1865, Davis was imprisoned for two years under steadily deteriorating health. In 1867 he stood trial for treason, but after many delays, he was finally granted amnesty in 1869.

Gentlemen of the Congress of the Confederate States of America, Friends and Fellow-Citizens:

Called to the difficult and responsible station of Chief Executive of the Provisional Government which you have instituted, I approach the discharge of the duties assigned to me with an humble distrust of my abilities, but with a sustaining confidence in the wisdom of those who are to guide and aid me in the administration of public affairs, and an abiding faith in the virtue and patriotism of the people.

Looking forward to the speedy establishment of a permanent government to take the place of this, and which, by its greater moral and physical power, will be better able to combat with the many difficulties which arise from the conflicting interests of separate nations, I enter upon the duties of the office, to which I have been chosen, with the hope that the beginning of our career, as a Confederacy, may not be obstructed by hostile opposition to our enjoyment of the separate existence and independence which we have asserted, and, with the blessing of Providence, intend to maintain. Our present condition, achieved in a manner unprecedented in the history of nations, illustrates the American idea that governments rest upon the consent of the governed, and that it is the right of the people to alter or abolish governments whenever they become destructive of the ends for which they were established.

The declared purpose of the compact of union from which we have withdrawn, was "to establish justice, insure domestic tranquility, provide for the common defense, promote the general welfare;" and when in the judgment of the sovereign States now composing this Confederacy, it had been perverted from the purposes for which it was ordained, and had ceased to answer the ends for which it was established, a peaceful appeal to the ballot-box, declared that so far as they were concerned, the government created by that compact should cease to exist. In this they merely asserted a right which the Declaration of Independence of 1776 had defined to be inalienable. Of the time and occasion for its exercise, they as sovereigns, were the final judges, each for itself. The impartial and enlightened verdict of mankind will vindicate the rectitude of our conduct, and He, who knows the hearts of men, will judge of the sincerity with which we labored to preserve the government of our fathers in its spirit. The right solemnly proclaimed at the birth of the States and which has been affirmed and re-affirmed in the bills of rights of States subsequently admitted into the Union of 1789, undeniably recognizes in the people the power to resume the authority delegated for the purposes of government. Thus the sovereign States, here represented, proceeded to form this Confederacy, and it is by abuse of language that their act has been denominated a revolution. They formed a new alliance, but within each State its government has remained, and the rights of person and property have not been disturbed. The agent, through whom they communicated with foreign nations, is changed; but this does not necessarily interrupt their international relations.

Sustained by the consciousness that the transition from the former Union to the present Confederacy has not proceeded from a disregard on our part of just obligations, or any failure to perform any constitutional duty; moved by no interest or passion to invade the rights of others; anxious to cultivate peace and commerce with all nations, if we may not hope to avoid war, we may at least expect that posterity will acquit us of having needlessly engaged in it. Doubly justified by the absence of wrong on our part, and by wanton aggression on the part of others, there can be no cause to doubt that the courage and patriotism of the people of the Confederate States will be found equal to any measures of defense which honor and security may require.

An agricultural people, whose chief interest is the export of a commodity required in every manufacturing country, our true policy is peace and the freest trade which our necessities will permit. It is alike our interest, and that of all those to whom we would sell and from whom we would buy, that there should be fewest practicable restrictions upon the interchange of commodities. There can be but little rivalry between ours and any manufacturing or navigating community, such as the northeastern States of the American Union. It must follow, therefore, that a mutual interest would invite good will and kind offices. If, however, passion or the lust of dominion should cloud the judgment or inflame the ambition of those States, we must prepare to meet the emergency, and to maintain, by the final arbitrament of the sword, the position which we have assumed among the nations of the earth. We have entered upon the career of independence, and it must be inflexibly pursued. Through many years of controversy with our late associates, the Northern States, we have vainly endeavored to secure tranquility, and to obtain respect for the rights to which we are entitled.

As a necessity, not a choice, we have resorted to the remedy of separation; and henceforth our energies must be directed to the conduct of our own affairs, and the perpetuity of the Confederacy which we have formed. If a just perception of mutual interest shall permit us peaceably to pursue our separate political career, my most earnest desire will have been fulfilled; but if this be denied to us, and the integrity of our territory and jurisdiction be assailed it, it will but remain for us, with firm resolve, to appeal to arms and invoke the blessings of Providence on a just cause.

As a consequence of our new condition, and with a view to meet anticipated wants, it will be necessary to provide for the speedy and efficient organization of branches of the Executive Department, having special charge of foreign intercourse, finance, military affairs, and the postal service.

For purposes of defense, the Confederate States may, under ordinary circumstances, rely mainly upon the militia; but it is deemed advisable, in the present condition of affairs, that there should be a well-instructed and disciplined army, more numerous than would usually be required on a peace establishment. I also suggest that, for the protection of our harbors and commerce on the high seas, a navy adapted to those objects will be required. These necessities have doubtless engaged the attention of Congress.

With a Constitution differing only from that of our fathers, in so far as it is explanatory of their well-known intent, freed from the sectional conflicts which have interfered with the pursuit of the general welfare, it is not unreasonable to expect that States from which we have recently parted, may seek to unite their fortunes with ours under the government which we have instituted. For this your Constitution makes adequate provision; but beyond this,

if I mistake not, the judgment and will of the people, a re-union with the States from which we have separated is neither practicable nor desirable.

To increase the power, develop the resources, and promote the happiness of the Confederacy, it is requisite that there should be so much homogeneity that the welfare of every portion shall be the aim of the whole. Where this does not exist, antagonisms are engendered which must and should result in separation.

Actuated solely by the desire to preserve our own rights and promote our own welfare, the separation of the Confederate States has been marked by no aggression upon others, and followed by no domestic convulsion. Our industrial pursuits have received no check; the cultivation of our fields has progressed as heretofore; and even should we be involved in war, there would be no considerable diminution in the production of the staples which have constituted our exports, and in which the commercial world has an interest scarcely less than our own. This common interest of the producer and consumer can only be interrupted by an exterior force, which should obstruct its transmission to foreign markets – a course of conduct which would be as unjust towards us as it would be detrimental to manufacturing and commercial interests abroad. Should reason guide the action of the government from which we have separated, a policy so detrimental to the civilized world, the Northern States included, could not be dictated by even the strongest desire to inflict injury upon us; but if otherwise, a terrible responsibility will rest upon it, and the suffering of millions will bear testimony to the folly and wickedness of our aggressors. In the meantime, there will remain to us, besides the ordinary means before suggested, the well-known resources for retaliation upon the commerce of the enemy.

Experience in public stations, of subordinate grades to this which your kindness has conferred, has taught me that care, and toil, and disappointment, are the price of official elevation. You will see many errors to forgive, many deficiencies to tolerate, but you shall not find in me either a want of zeal or fidelity to the cause that is to me highest in hope and of most enduring affection. Your generosity has bestowed upon me an undeserved distinction — one which I never sought nor desired. Upon the continuance of that sentiment, and upon your wisdom and patriotism, I rely to direct and support me in the performance of the duty required at my hands.

We have changed the constituent parts but not the system of our government. The constitution formed by our fathers is that of these Confederates States, in their exposition of it; and, in the judicial construction it has received, we have a light that reveals its true meaning.

Thus instructed as to the just interpretation of the instrument, and ever remembering that all offices are but trusts held for the people, and that delegated powers are to be strictly construed, I will hope by due diligence in the performance of my duties, though I may disappoint your expectations, yet to retain, when retiring, something of the good will and confidence which welcomed my entrance into office.

It is joyous, in the midst of perilous times, to look around upon a people united in heart, where one purpose of high resolve animates and actuates the whole—where the sacrifices to be made are not weighed in the balance against honor, and right, and liberty, and equality. Obstacles may retard—they cannot long prevent—the progress of a movement sanctified by its justice, and sustained by a virtuous people. Reverently let us invoke the God of our fathers to guide and protect us in our efforts to perpetuate the principles which, by his blessing, they were able to vindicate, establish, and transmit to their posterity, and with a continuance of His favor, ever gratefully acknowledged, we may hopefully look forward to success, to peace, and to prosperity.

Review Questions

1. Did Davis view his position as a permanent one? Did he want it to be permanent?
2. To which right from the Declaration of Independence had the Confederacy appealed?
3. Did Davis advocate free or regulated trade?
4. What form of military was Davis proposing? What reasons did he give?
5. Had the Confederacy radically changed its form of government?

Thought Questions

1. Did the secession result in any major upheaval on a social or economic level?
2. What did Davis say "will vindicate the rectitude of [our] conduct"? Was he right?
3. Based on what Davis said, what were the primary arguments against the secession?
4. Was it conceivable, in your opinion, for the Northern states to allow the Southern states to form their own nation? Why do you think they chose not to allow this to happen?
5. Assuming that the Confederacy had been allowed to exist, how different would your life be?

"Gettysburg Address"
Abraham Lincoln

In the midst of growing concerns about slavery and the fate of the Union, Lincoln was elected president in 1860. Because Lincoln was known to be opposed to slavery, his election tipped the balance for many Southern states. South Carolina seceded from the Union in January 1861, followed by six other states. They were later joined by four more states to form the Confederate States of America. Tensions escalated until April 12, when firing on Fort Sumter in South Carolina initiated the Civil War. Lincoln delivered the following speech two years later, on November 19, 1863, at the Soldiers' National Cemetery at Gettysburg, Pennsylvania. The war would continue throughout his presidency. Lincoln was assassinated by John Wilkes Booth on April 14, 1865, less than a week after General Lee surrendered at Appomattox.

Four score and seven years ago our fathers brought forth on this continent, a new nation, conceived in Liberty, and dedicated to the proposition that all men are created equal.

Now we are engaged in a great civil war, testing whether that nation, or any nation so conceived and so dedicated, can long endure. We are met on a great battle-field of that war. We have come to dedicate a portion of that field, as a final resting place for those who here gave their lives that that nation might live. It is altogether fitting and proper that we should do this.

But, in a larger sense, we cannot dedicate—we cannot consecrate—we cannot hallow—this ground. The brave men, living and dead, who struggled here, have consecrated it, far above our poor power to add or detract. The world will little note, nor long remember what we say here, but it can never forget what they did here. It is for us the living, rather, to be dedicated here to the unfinished work which they who fought here have thus far so nobly advanced.

It is rather for us to be here dedicated to the great task remaining before us—that from these honored dead we take increased devotion to that cause for which they gave the last full measure of devotion—that we here highly resolve that these dead shall not have died in vain – that this nation, under God, shall have a new birth of freedom—and that government of the people, by the people, for the people, shall not perish from the earth.

Review Questions

1. To what year (and events) does Lincoln ascribe the birth of America?
2. What does it mean to dedicate something? To consecrate it?
3. Why did Lincoln say Americans could not dedicate that ground?
4. What was the cause for which the dead gave their lives?
5. What was the great task of which Lincoln spoke? Has that task been completed today?

Thought Questions

1. Can any nation dedicated to the proposition that "all men are created equal" long endure?
2. Lincoln said, "The world will little note, nor long remember what we say here," yet Lincoln's speech is still famous today. Why?
3. Is our government really "of the people, by the people, [and] for the people"? Explain.
4. Did the Civil War accomplish its purpose? How would our country be different today if the Civil War had never happened?
5. What is the purpose of a memorial? How did the battle of Gettysburg serve as a memorial?

"Atlanta Exposition Address"
Booker T. Washington

Booker Taliaferro Washington (1856–1915) was the son of a white father and a black slave mother in Virginia. He was freed in 1865, after the conclusion of the Civil War, and he and his family moved to West Virginia to work in the coal mines. Washington later left to attend the Hampton Institute in Virginia, and in 1881, he founded the Tuskegee Institute in Alabama on a model of vocational training as well as intellectual study. A savvy politician as well an educator, Washington became a prominent orator and writer on race relations. On September 18, 1895, Washington presented this speech, an excerpt from his autobiography *Up From Slavery*, at the International Exposition in Atlanta. Washington's speech was seen by some to be too conciliatory toward his predominantly white audience, but in contrast with African-American leaders like Frederick Douglass, Washington favored political pragmatism over idealism. For that reason, the speech has also been called the "Atlanta Compromise."

A ship lost at sea for many days suddenly sighted a friendly vessel. From the mast of the unfortunate vessel was seen a signal, "Water, water; we die of thirst!" The answer from the friendly vessel at once came back, "Cast down your bucket where you are." A second time the signal, "Water, water; send us water!" ran up from the distressed vessel, and was answered, "Cast down your bucket where you are." And a third and fourth signal for water was answered, "Cast down your bucket where you are." The captain of the distressed vessel, at last heeding the injunction, cast down his bucket, and it came up full of fresh, sparkling water from the mouth of the Amazon River. To those of my race who depend on bettering their condition in a foreign land or who underestimate the importance of cultivating friendly relations with the Southern white man, who is their next-door neighbor, I would say: "Cast down your bucket where you are"—cast it down in making friends in every manly way of the people of all races by whom we are surrounded.

Cast it down in agriculture, mechanics, in commerce, in domestic service, and in the professions. And in this connection it is well to bear in mind that whatever other sins the South may be called to bear, when it comes to business, pure and simple, it is in the South that the Negro is given a man's chance in the commercial world, and in nothing is this Exposition more eloquent than in emphasizing this chance. Our greatest danger is that in the great leap from slavery to freedom we may overlook the fact that the masses of us are to live by the productions of our hands, and fail to keep in mind that we shall prosper in proportion as we learn to dignify and glorify common labor, and put brains and skill into the common occupations of life; shall prosper in proportion as we learn to draw the line between the superficial and the substantial, the ornamental gewgaws of life and the useful. No race can prosper till it learns that there is as much dignity in tilling a field as in writing a poem. It is at the bottom of life we must begin, and not at the top. Nor should we permit our grievances to overshadow our opportunities.

To those of the white race who look to the incoming of those of foreign birth and strange tongue and habits for the prosperity of the South, were I permitted, I would repeat what I say to my own race, "Cast down your bucket where you are." Cast it down among the eight millions of Negroes whose habits you know, whose fidelity and love you have tested in days when to have proved treacherous meant the ruin of your firesides. Cast down your bucket among these people who have, without strikes and labour wars, tilled your fields, cleared your forests, builded your railroads and cities, and brought forth treasures from the bowels of the earth, and helped make possible this magnificent representation of the progress of the South. Casting down your bucket among my people, helping and encouraging them as you are doing on these grounds, and to education of head, hand, and heart, you will find that they will buy your surplus land, make blossom the waste places in your fields, and run your factories. While doing this, you can be sure in the future, as in the past, that you and your families will be surrounded by the most patient, faithful, law-abiding, and unresentful people that the world has seen. As we have proved our loyalty to you in the past, in nursing your children, watching by the sick-bed of your mothers and fathers, and often following them with tear-dimmed eyes to their graves, so in the future, in our humble way, we shall stand by you with a devotion that no foreigner can approach, ready to lay down our lives, if need be, in defense of yours, interlacing our industrial, commercial, civil, and religious life with yours in a way that shall make the interests of both races one. In all things that are purely social we can be as separate as the fingers, yet one as the hand in all things essential to mutual progress.

There is no defense or security for any of us except in the highest intelligence and development of all. If anywhere there are efforts tending to curtail the fullest growth of the Negro, let these efforts be turned into stimulating, encouraging, and making him the most useful and intelligent citizen. Effort or means so invested will pay a thousand per cent interest. These efforts will be twice blessed — "blessing him that gives and him that takes." There is no escape through law of man or God from the inevitable:

"The laws of changeless justice bind
Oppressor with oppressed;

> And close as sin and suffering joined
> We march to fate abreast."

Nearly sixteen millions of hands will aid you in pulling the load upward, or they will pull against you the load downward. We shall constitute one-third and more of the ignorance and crime of the South, or one-third its intelligence and progress; we shall contribute one-third to the business and industrial prosperity of the South, or we shall prove a veritable body of death, stagnating, depressing, retarding every effort to advance the body politic.

In conclusion, may I repeat that nothing in thirty years has given us more hope and encouragement, and drawn us so near to you of the white race, as this opportunity offered by the Exposition; and here bending, as it were, over the altar that represents the results of the struggles of your race and mine, both starting practically empty-handed three decades ago, I pledge that in your effort to work out the great and intricate problem which God has laid at the doors of the South, you shall have at all times the patient, sympathetic help of my race; only let this be constantly in mind, that, while from representations in these buildings of the product of field, of forest, of mine, of factory, letters, and art, much good will come, yet far above and beyond material benefits will be that higher good, that, let us pray God, will come, in a blotting out of sectional differences and racial animosities and suspicions, in a determination to administer absolute justice, in a willing obedience among all classes to the mandates of law. This, coupled with our material prosperity, will bring into our beloved South a new heaven and a new earth.

Review Questions

1. Why did Washington tell his white audience to "cast down their buckets" among his race?
2. Who did he claim would benefit from this casting down?
3. How do you make sense of Washington's illustration with the bucket?
4. What point was he trying to make? Did it illustrate his point effectively? Why or why not?
5. Washington listed material prosperity and one other thing as the instigators of a new heaven and a new earth for the South. What was the other factor?

Thought Questions

1. What does it mean to allow grievances to overshadow opportunities? Have you ever done so?
2. What occupations are valued highly in American society? What occupations are not valued? What message does this fact send to workers in the unvalued industries?
3. What do you think Washington's purpose was in citing the poem?
4. Can a person oppress another person without feeling the negative effects? Why or why not?
5. Do you think Washington's speech was conciliatory? What do you think he was trying to accomplish? Do you think it is better to achieve political goals or to maintain an ideal? Discuss.

"The Man with the Muck-Rake"
Theodore Roosevelt

Theodore Roosevelt (1858–1919) lived the first part of his life in New York, but after the death of his wife and mother, he moved to the Dakota Territory. As a lieutenant colonel in the Rough Rider Regiment during the Spanish-American War, Roosevelt led a charge at the Battle of San Juan which gave him a reputation as a fierce leader. After the war, Roosevelt returned to New York and was elected governor in 1898. He went on to serve as vice president under William McKinley, and when McKinley was assassinated in 1901, he became the nation's youngest president at the age of forty-three. During his two-term presidency, Roosevelt promoted an active foreign policy as well as reforms at home. Beginning in the 1890s, national politics had become complicated by the rise of exposé journalism, which blended news with sensationalism and used reporting to stir up political sentiments. Roosevelt strongly opposed this movement. This speech, delivered to the House of Representatives on April 14, 1906, articulates his reasons.

Over a century ago Washington laid the corner-stone of the Capitol in what was then little more than a tract of wooded wilderness here beside the Potomac. We now find it necessary to provide great additional buildings for the business of the government. This growth in the need for the housing of the government is but a proof and example of the way in which the nation has grown and the sphere of action of the National Government has grown. We now administer the affairs of a nation in which the extraordinary growth of population has been outstripped by the growth of wealth and the growth in complex interests.

The material problems that face us to-day are not such as they were in Washington's time, but the underlying facts of human nature are the same now as they were then. Under altered external form we war with the same tendencies toward evil that were evident in Washington's time, and are helped by the same tendencies for good.

It is about some of these that I wish to say a word to-day. In Bunyan's "Pilgrim's Progress" you may recall the description of the Man with the Muck-rake, the man who could look no way but downward, with the muck-rake in his hand; who was offered a celestial crown for his muck-rake, but who would neither look up nor regard the crown he was offered, but continued to rake to himself the filth of the floor.

In "Pilgrim's Progress" the Man with the Muck-rake is set forth as the example of him whose vision is fixed on carnal instead of on spiritual things. Yet he also typifies the man who in this life consistently refuses to see aught that is lofty, and fixes his eyes with solemn intentness only on that which is vile and debasing. Now, it is very necessary that we should not flinch from seeing what is vile and debasing. There is filth on the floor and it must be scraped up with the muck-rake; and there are times and places where this service is the most needed of all the services that can be performed. But the man who never does anything else, who never thinks or speaks or writes, save of his feats with the muck-rake, speedily becomes, not a help to society, not an incitement to good, but one of the most potent forces for evil.

There are, in the body politic, economic and social, many and grave evils, and there is urgent necessity for the sternest war upon them. There should be relentless exposure of and attack upon every evil man whether politician or business man, every evil practice, whether in politics, in business, or in social life. I hail as a benefactor every writer or speaker, every man who, on the platform, or in book, magazine, or newspaper, with merciless severity makes such attack, provided always that he in his turn remembers that the attack is of use only if it is absolutely truthful. The liar is no whit better than the thief, and if his mendacity takes the form of slander, he may be worse than most thieves. It puts a premium upon knavery untruthfully to attack an honest man, or even with hysterical exaggeration to assail a bad man with untruth. An epidemic of indiscriminate assault upon character does not good, but very great harm. The soul of every scoundrel is gladdened whenever an honest man is assailed, or even when a scoundrel is untruthfully assailed.

Now, it is easy to twist out of shape what I have just said, easy to affect to misunderstand it, and, if it is slurred over in repetition, not difficult really to misunderstand it. Some persons are sincerely incapable of understanding that to denounce mud-slinging does not mean the endorsement of whitewashing; and both the interested individuals who need whitewashing, and those others who practice mud-slinging, like to encourage such confusion of ideas. One of the chief counts against those who make indiscriminate assault upon men in business or men in public life, is that they invite a reaction which is sure to tell powerfully in favor of the unscrupulous scoundrel who really ought to be attacked, who ought to be exposed, who ought, if possible, to be put in the penitentiary. If Aristides is praised overmuch as just, people get tired of hearing it; and overcensure of the unjust finally and from similar reasons results in their favor.

Any excess is almost sure to invite a reaction; and, unfortunately, the reaction, instead of taking the form of punishment of those guilty of the excess, is very apt to take the form either of punishment of the unoffending or of giving immunity, and even strength, to offenders. The effort to make financial or political profit out of the destruction of character can only result in public calamity. Gross and reckless assaults on character, whether on the stump or in newspaper, magazine, or book, create a morbid and vicious public sentiment, and at the same time act as a profound deterrent to able men of normal sensitiveness and tend to prevent them from entering the public service at any price.

As an instance in point, I may mention that one serious difficulty encountered in getting the right type of men to dig the Panama Canal is the certainty that they will be exposed, both without, and, I am sorry to say, sometimes within, Congress, to utterly reckless assaults on their character and capacity.

At the risk of repetition let me say again that my plea is, not for immunity to but for the most unsparing exposure of the politician who betrays his trust, of the big business man who makes or spends his fortune in illegitimate or corrupt ways. There should be a resolute effort to hunt every such man out of the position he has disgraced. Expose the crime, and hunt down the criminal; but remember that even in the case of crime, if it is attacked in sensational, lurid, and untruthful fashion, the attack may do more damage to the public mind than the crime itself. It is because I feel that there should be no rest in the endless war against the forces of evil that I ask that the war be conducted with sanity as well as with resolution.

The men with the muck-rakes are often indispensable to the well-being of society; but only if they know when to stop raking the muck, and to look upward to the celestial crown above them, to the crown of worthy endeavor.

There are beautiful things above and roundabout them; and if they gradually grow to feel that the whole world is nothing but muck, their power of usefulness is gone. If the whole picture is painted black there remains no hue whereby to single out the rascals for distinction from their fellows. Such painting finally induces a kind of moral color-blindness; and people affected by it come to the conclusion that no man is really black, and no man is really white, but they are all gray. In other words, they neither believe in the truth of the attack, nor in the honesty of the man who is attacked; they grow as suspicious of the accusation as of the offense; it becomes well-nigh hopeless to stir them either to wrath against wrong-doing or to enthusiasm for what is right; and such a mental attitude in the public gives hope to every knave, and is the despair of honest men.

To assail the great and admitted evils of our political and industrial life with such crude and sweeping generalizations as to include decent men in the general condemnation means the searing of the public conscience. There results a general attitude either of cynical belief in and indifference to public corruption or else of a distrustful inability to discriminate between the good and the bad. Either attitude is fraught with untold damage to the country as a whole. The fool who has not sense to discriminate between what is good and what is bad is well-nigh as dangerous as the man who does discriminate and yet chooses the bad. There is nothing more distressing to every good patriot, to every good American, than the hard, scoffing spirit which treats the allegation of dishonesty in a public man as a cause for laughter.

Such laughter is worse than the crackling of thorns under a pot, for it denotes not merely the vacant mind, but the heart in which high emotions have been choked before they could grow to fruition.

There is any amount of good in the world, and there never was a time when loftier and more disinterested work for the betterment of mankind was being done than now. The forces that tend for evil are great and terrible, but the forces of truth and love and courage and honesty and generosity and sympathy are also stronger than ever before. It is a foolish and timid, no less than a wicked, thing to blink the fact that the forces of evil are strong, but it is even worse to fail to take into account the strength of the forces that tell for good.

Hysterical sensationalism is the very poorest weapon wherewith to fight for lasting righteousness. The men who with stern sobriety and truth assail the many evils of our time, whether in the public press or in magazines, or in books, are the leaders and allies of all engaged in the work for social and political betterment. But if they give good reason for distrust of what they say, if they chill the ardor of those who demand truth as a primary virtue, they thereby betray the good cause, and play into the hands of the very men against whom they are nominally at war.

In his "Ecclesiastical Polity" that fine old Elizabethan divine, Bishop Hooker, wrote: "He that goeth about to persuade a multitude that they are not so well governed as they ought to be, shall never want attentive and favorable hearers; because they know the manifold defects whereunto every kind of regimen is subject, but the secret lets and difficulties, which in public proceedings are innumerable and inevitable, they have not ordinarily the judgment to consider."

This truth should be kept constantly in mind by every free people desiring to preserve the sanity and poise indispensable to the permanent success of self-government. Yet, on the other hand, it is vital not to permit this spirit to sanity and self-command to degenerate into mere mental stagnation. Bad though a state of hysterical excitement is, and evil though the results are which come from the violent oscillations such excitement invariably produces, yet a sodden acquiescence in evil is even worse.

At this moment we are passing through a period of great unrest—social, political, and industrial unrest. It is of the utmost importance for our future that this should prove to be not the unrest of mere rebelliousness against life, of mere dissatisfaction with the inevitable inequality of conditions, but the unrest of a resolute and eager ambition to secure the betterment of the individual and the nation. So far as this movement of agitation throughout the country takes the form of a fierce discontent with evil, of a determination to punish the authors of evil, whether in industry or politics, the feeling is to be heartily welcomed as a sign of healthy life.

If, on the other hand, it turns into a mere crusade of appetite against appetite, of a contest between the brutal greed of the "have-nots" and the brutal greed of the "haves," then it has no significance for good, but only for evil. If it seeks to establish a line of cleavage, not along the line which divides good men from bad, but along that other line, running at right angles thereto, which divides those who are well off from those who are less well off, then it will be fraught with immeasurable harm to the body politic.

We can no more and no less afford to condone evil in the man of capital than evil in the man of no capital. The wealthy man who exults because there is a failure of justice in the effort to bring some trust magnate to an account for his misdeeds is as bad as, and no worse than, the so-called labor leader who clamorously strives to excite a foul class feeling on behalf of some other labor leader who is implicated in murder. One attitude is as bad as the other, and no worse; in each case the accused is entitled to exact justice; and in neither case is there need of action by others which can be construed into an expression of sympathy for crime.

It is a prime necessity that if the present unrest is to result in permanent good the emotion shall be translated into action, and that the action shall be marked by honesty, sanity, and self-restraint. There is mighty little good in a mere spasm of reform. The reform that counts is that which comes through steady, continuous growth; violent emotionalism leads to exhaustion.

It is important to this people to grapple with the problems connected with the amassing of enormous fortunes, and the use of those fortunes, both corporate and individual, in business. We should discriminate in the sharpest way between fortunes well-won and fortunes ill-won; between those gained as an incident to performing great services to the community as a whole, and those gained in evil fashion by keeping just within the limits of mere law-honesty.

Of course no amount of charity in spending such fortunes in any way compensates for misconduct in making them. As a matter of personal conviction, and without pretending to discuss the details or formulate the system, I feel that we shall ultimately have to consider the adoption of some such scheme as that of a progressive tax on all fortunes, beyond a certain amount either given in life or devised or bequeathed upon death to any individual—a tax so framed as to put it out of the power of the owner of one of these enormous fortunes to hand on more than a certain amount to any one individual; the tax, of course, to be imposed by the National and not the State Government.

Such taxation should, of course, be aimed merely at the inheritance or transmission in their entirety of those fortunes swollen beyond all healthy limits. Again, the National Government must in some form exercise supervision over corporations engaged in interstate business—and all large corporations are engaged in interstate business—whether by license or otherwise, so as to permit us to deal with the far-reaching evils of overcapitalization.

This year we are making a beginning in the direction of serious effort to settle some of these economic problems by the railway-rate legislation. Such legislation, if so framed, as I am sure it will be, as to secure definite and tangible results, will amount to something of itself; and it will amount to a great deal more in so far as it is taken as a first step in the direction of a policy of superintendence and control over corporate wealth engaged in interstate commerce, this superintendence and control not to be exercised in a spirit of malevolence toward the men who have created the wealth, but with the firm purpose both to do justice to them and to see that they in their turn do justice to the public at large.

The first requisite in the public servants who are to deal in this shape with corporations, whether as legislators or as executives, is honesty. This honesty can be no respecter of persons. There can be no such thing as unilateral honesty. The danger is not really from corrupt corporations; it springs from the corruption itself, whether exercised for or against corporations.

The eighth commandment reads: "Thou shalt not steal." It does not read: "Thou shalt not steal from the rich man." It does not read: "Thou shalt not steal from the poor man." It reads simply and plainly: "Thou shalt not steal."

No good whatever will come from that warped and mock morality which denounces the misdeeds of men of wealth and forgets the misdeeds practiced at their expense; which denounces bribery, but blinds itself to blackmail; which foams with rage if a corporation secures favors by improper methods, and merely leers with hideous mirth if the corporation is itself wronged. The only public servant who can be trusted honestly to protect the rights of the public against the misdeeds of a corporation is that public man who will just as surely protect the corporation itself from wrongful aggression.

If a public man is willing to yield to popular clamor and do wrong to the men of wealth or to rich corporations, it may be set down as certain that if the opportunity comes he will secretly and furtively do wrong to the public in the interest of a corporation.

But, in addition to honesty, we need sanity. No honesty will make public man useful if that man is timid or foolish, if he is a hot-headed zealot or an impracticable visionary.

As we strive for reform we find that it is not at all merely the case of a long up-hill pull. On the contrary, there is almost as much of breeching work as of collar work; to depend only on traces means that there will soon be a runaway and an upset.

The men of wealth who today are trying to prevent the regulation and control of their business in the interest of the public by the proper government authorities will not succeed, in my judgment, in checking the progress of the movement. But if they did succeed they would find that they had sown the wind and would surely reap the whirlwind, for they would ultimately provoke the violent excesses which accompany a reform coming by convulsion instead of by steady and natural growth.

On the other hand, the wild preachers of unrest and discontent, the wild agitators against the entire existing order, the men who act crookedly, whether because of sinister design or from mere puzzle-headedness, the men who preach destruction without proposing any substitute for what they intend to destroy, or who propose a substitute which would be far worse than the existing evils—all these men are the most dangerous opponents of real reform. If they get their way they will lead the people into a deeper pit than any into which they could fall under the present system. If they fail to get their way they will still do incalculable harm by provoking the kind of reaction which, in its revolt against the senseless evil of their teaching, would enthrone more securely than ever the very evils which their misguided followers believe they are attacking.

More important then aught else is the development of the broadest sympathy of man for man. The welfare of the wage-worker, the welfare of the tiller of the soil, upon these depend the welfare of the entire country; their good is not to be sought in pulling down others; but their good must be the prime object of all our statesmanship.

Materially we must strive to secure a broader economic opportunity for all men, so that each shall have a better chance to show the stuff of which he is made.

Spiritually and ethically we must strive to bring about clean living and right thinking. We appreciate also that the things of the soul are immeasurably more important.

The foundation-stone of national life is, and ever must be, the high individual character of the average citizen.

Review Questions

1. What did Roosevelt use as an illustration of the nation's growth?
2. Where did the character the "Man with the Muck-Rake" originate? What did he represent?
3. How did Roosevelt feel about journalists?
4. Roosevelt distinguished between which two ways of gaining wealth? Based on this section of the speech, would you say that Roosevelt thought "the end justifies the means"?
5. Which commandment did Roosevelt cite, and for what reason?

Thought Questions

1. Give an example when you looked down instead of up. Did it help you accomplish anything?
2. Explain: "If the whole picture is painted black, there remains no hue whereby to single out the rascals for distinction from their fellows." Do you agree?
3. Was Roosevelt a pessimist or an optimist? Was he cynical? Can you be both optimistic and cynical at the same time? Support your answer.
4. "Hysterical sensationalism is the very poorest weapon wherewith to fight for lasting righteousness." What is hysterical sensationalism? Have you ever seen it used? How effective was it?
5. Did Roosevelt think moral or economic growth was more important? What would politicians say today? Give examples to support your answer.

"War Message"
Woodrow Wilson

Woodrow Wilson (1856–1924) was born in Virginia and began his career there as an academician. From academics, he made the transition to politics and was elected governor of New Jersey. In 1912, he was elected president. He was reelected in 1916 on the basis of his ability to keep the United States out of World War I. Then, later that year, Germany instituted a policy of unrestricted submarine warfare that called for the attack of neutral countries as well as those taking sides in the war. As a result, in the following speech delivered April 2, 1917, Wilson asked for and subsequently received a declaration of war against Germany. At the conclusion of the war, Wilson went on to be a significant figure in preparations for peace, including his fledgling vision of a League of Nations that would deter future world conflicts by threatening collective punishment of any nation that provoked war. (The League of Nations was the forerunner to the modern United Nations).

Gentlemen of the Congress:

I have called the Congress into extraordinary session because there are serious, very serious, choices of policy to be made, and made immediately, which it was neither right nor constitutionally permissible that I should assume the responsibility of making.

On the third of February last I officially laid before you the extraordinary announcement of the Imperial German Government that on and after the first day of February it was its purpose to put aside all restraints of law or of humanity and use its submarines to sink every vessel that sought to approach either the ports of Great Britain and Ireland or the western coasts of Europe or any of the ports controlled by the enemies of Germany within the Mediterranean. That had seemed to be the object of the German submarine warfare earlier in the war, but since April of last year the Imperial Government had somewhat restrained the commanders of its undersea craft in conformity with its promise then given to us that passenger boats should not be sunk and that due warning would be given to all other vessels which its submarines might seek to destroy, when no resistance was offered or escape attempted, and care taken that their crews were given at least a fair chance to save their lives in their open boats. The precautions taken were meagre and haphazard enough, as was proved in distressing instance after instance in the progress of the cruel and unmanly business, but a certain degree of restraint was observed. The new policy has swept every restriction aside. Vessels of every kind, whatever their flag, their character, their cargo, their destination, their errand, have been ruthlessly sent to the bottom without warning and without thought of help or mercy for those on board, the vessels of friendly neutrals along with those of belligerents. Even hospital ships and ships carrying relief to the sorely bereaved and stricken people of Belgium, though the latter were provided with safe-conduct through the proscribed areas by the German Government itself and were distinguished by unmistakable marks of identity, have been sunk with the same reckless lack of compassion or of principle.

I was for a little while unable to believe that such things would in fact be done by any government that had hitherto subscribed to the humane practices of civilized nations. International law had its origin in the attempt to set up some law which would be respected and observed upon the seas, where no nation had right of dominion and where lay the free highways of the world. By painful stage after stage has that law been built up, with meagre enough results, indeed, after all was accomplished that could be accomplished, but always with a clear view, at least, of what the heart and conscience of mankind demanded. This minimum of right the German Government has swept aside under the plea of retaliation and necessity and because it had no weapons which it could use at sea except these which it is impossible to employ as it is employing them without throwing to the winds all scruples of humanity or of respect for the understandings that were supposed to underlie the intercourse of the world. I am not now thinking of the loss of property involved, immense and serious as that is, but only of the wanton and wholesale destruction of the lives of noncombatants, men, women, and children, engaged in pursuits which have always, even in the darkest periods of modern history, been deemed innocent and legitimate. Property can be paid for; the lives of peaceful and innocent people can not be. The present German submarine warfare against commerce is a warfare against mankind.

It is a war against all nations. American ships have been sunk, American lives taken, in ways which it has stirred us very deeply to learn of, but the ships and people of other neutral and friendly nations have been sunk and overwhelmed in the waters in the same way. There has been no discrimination. The challenge is to all mankind. Each nation must decide for itself how it will meet it. The choice we make for ourselves must be made with a moderation of counsel and a temperateness of judgment befitting our character and our motives as a nation. We must put excited feeling away. Our motive will not be revenge or the victorious assertion of the physical might of the nation, but only the vindication of right, of human right, of which we are only a single champion.

When I addressed the Congress on the twenty-sixth of February last, I thought that it would suffice to assert our neutral rights with arms, our right to use the seas against unlawful interference, our right to keep our people safe against unlawful violence. But armed neutrality, it now appears, is impracticable. Because submarines are in effect outlaws when used as the German submarines have been used against merchant shipping, it is impossible to defend ships against their attacks as the law of nations has assumed that merchantmen would defend themselves against privateers or cruisers, visible craft giving chase upon the open sea. It is common prudence in such circumstances, grim necessity indeed, to endeavour to destroy them before they have shown their own intention. They must be dealt with upon sight, if dealt with at all. The German Government denies the right of neutrals to use arms at all within the areas of the sea which it has proscribed, even in the defense of rights which no modern publicist has ever before questioned their right to defend. The intimation is conveyed that the armed guards which we have placed on our merchant ships will be treated as beyond the pale of law and subject to be dealt with as pirates would be. Armed neutrality is ineffectual enough at best; in such circumstances and in the face of such pretensions it is worse than ineffectual; it is likely only to produce what it was meant to prevent; it is practically certain to draw us into the war without either the rights or the effectiveness of belligerents. There is one choice we can not make, we are incapable of making: we will not choose the path of submission and suffer the most sacred rights of our nation and our people to be ignored or violated. The wrongs against which we now array ourselves are no common wrongs; they cut to the very roots of human life.

With a profound sense of the solemn and even tragic character of the step I am taking and of the grave responsibilities which it involves, but in unhesitating obedience to what I deem my constitutional duty, I advise that the Congress declare the recent course of the Imperial German Government to be in fact nothing less than war against the Government and people of the United States; that it formally accept the status of belligerent which has thus been thrust upon it, and that it take immediate steps not only to put the country in a more thorough state of defense but also to exert all its power and employ all its resources to bring the Government of the German Empire to terms and end the war.

What this will involve is clear. It will involve the utmost practicable cooperation in counsel and action with the governments now at war with Germany, and, as incident to that, the extension to those governments of the most liberal financial credits, in order that our resources may so far as possible be added to theirs. It will involve the organization and mobilization of all the material resources of the country to supply the materials of war and serve the incidental needs of the nation in the most abundant and yet the most economical

and efficient way possible. It will involve the immediate full equipment of the Navy in all respects but particularly in supplying it with the best means of dealing with the enemy's submarines. It will involve the immediate addition to the armed forces of the United States already provided for by law in case of war at least 500,000 men, who should, in my opinion, be chosen upon the principle of universal liability to service, and also the authorization of subsequent additional increments of equal force so soon as they may be needed and can be handled in training. It will involve also, of course, the granting of adequate credits to the Government, sustained, I hope, so far as they can equitably be sustained by the present generation, by well conceived taxation....

While we do these things, these deeply momentous things, let us be very clear, and make very clear to all the world what our motives and our objects are. My own thought has not been driven from its habitual and normal course by the unhappy events of the last two months, and I do not believe that the thought of the nation has been altered or clouded by them I have exactly the same things in mind now that I had in mind when I addressed the Senate on the twenty-second of January last; the same that I had in mind when I addressed the Congress on the third of February and on the twenty-sixth of February. Our object now, as then, is to vindicate the principles of peace and justice in the life of the world as against selfish and autocratic power and to set up amongst the really free and self-governed peoples of the world such a concert of purpose and of action as will henceforth ensure the observance of those principles. Neutrality is no longer feasible or desirable where the peace of the world is involved and the freedom of its peoples, and the menace to that peace and freedom lies in the existence of autocratic governments backed by organized force which is controlled wholly by their will, not by the will of their people. We have seen the last of neutrality in such circumstances. We are at the beginning of an age in which it will be insisted that the same standards of conduct and of responsibility for wrong done shall be observed among nations and their governments that are observed among the individual citizens of civilized states.

We have no quarrel with the German people. We have no feeling towards them but one of sympathy and friendship. It was not upon their impulse that their Government acted in entering this war. It was not with their previous knowledge or approval. It was a war determined upon as wars used to be determined upon in the old, unhappy days when peoples were nowhere consulted by their rulers and wars were provoked and waged in the interest of dynasties or of little groups of ambitious men who were accustomed to use their fellow men as pawns and tools. Self-governed nations do not fill their neighbour states with spies or set the course of intrigue to bring about some critical posture of affairs which will give them an opportunity to strike and make conquest. Such designs can be successfully worked out only under cover and where no one has the right to ask questions. Cunningly contrived plans of deception or aggression, carried, it may be, from generation to generation, can be worked out and kept from the light only within the privacy of courts or behind the carefully guarded confidences of a narrow and privileged class. They are happily impossible where public opinion commands and insists upon full information concerning all the nation's affairs.

A steadfast concert for peace can never be maintained except by a partnership of democratic nations. No autocratic government could be trusted to keep faith within it or observe its covenants. It must be a league of honour, a partnership of opinion. Intrigue would eat its vitals away; the plottings of inner circles who could plan what they would and render account to no one would be a corruption seated at its very heart. Only free peoples can hold their purpose and their honour steady to a common end and prefer the interests of mankind to any narrow interest of their own.

Does not every American feel that assurance has been added to our hope for the future peace of the world by the wonderful and heartening things that have been happening within the last few weeks in Russia? Russia was known by those who knew it best to have been always in fact democratic at heart, in all the vital habits of her thought, in all the intimate relationships of her people that spoke their natural instinct, their habitual attitude towards life. The autocracy that crowned the summit of her political structure, long as it had stood and terrible as was the reality of its power, was not in fact Russian in origin, character, or purpose; and now it has been shaken off and the great, generous Russian people have been added in all their naive majesty and might to the forces that are fighting for freedom in the world, for justice, and for peace. Here is a fit partner for a league of honour.

One of the things that has served to convince us that the Prussian autocracy was not and could never be our friend is that from the very outset of the present war it has filled our unsuspecting communities and even our offices of government with spies and set criminal intrigues everywhere afoot against our national unity of counsel, our peace within and without our industries and our commerce. Indeed it is now evident that its spies were here even before the war began; and it is unhappily not a matter of conjecture but a fact proved in our courts of justice that the intrigues which have more than once come perilously near to disturbing the peace and dislocating the industries of the country have been carried on at the instigation, with the support, and even under the personal direction of official agents of the Imperial Government accredited to the Government of the United States. Even in checking these things and trying to extirpate them we have sought to put the most generous interpretation possible upon them because we knew that their source lay, not in any hostile feeling or purpose of the German people towards us (who were, no doubt, as ignorant of them as we ourselves were), but only in the selfish designs of a Government that did what it pleased and told its people nothing. But they have played their part in serving to convince us at last that that Government entertains no real friendship for us and means to act against our peace and security at its convenience. That it means to stir up enemies against us at our very doors the intercepted note to the German Minister at Mexico City is eloquent evidence.

We are accepting this challenge of hostile purpose because we know that in such a government, following such methods, we can never have a friend; and that in the presence of its organized power, always lying in wait to accomplish we know not what purpose, there can be no assured security for the democratic governments of the world. We are now about to accept gage of battle with this natural foe to liberty and shall, if necessary, spend the whole force of the nation to check and nullify its pretensions and its power. We are glad, now that we see the facts with no veil of false pretence about them, to fight thus for the ultimate peace of the world and for the liberation of its peoples, the German peoples included: for the rights of nations great and small and the privilege of men everywhere to choose their way of life and of obedience. The world must be made safe for democracy. Its peace must be planted upon the tested foundations of political liberty. We have no selfish ends to serve. We desire no conquest, no dominion. We seek no indemnities for ourselves, no material compensation for the sacrifices we shall freely make. We are but one of the champions of the rights of mankind. We shall be satisfied when those rights have been made as secure as the faith and the freedom of nations can make them.

Just because we fight without rancour and without selfish object, seeking nothing for ourselves but what we shall wish to share with all free peoples, we shall, I feel confident, conduct our operations as belligerents without passion and ourselves observe with proud punctilio the principles of right and of fair play we profess to be fighting for.

I have said nothing of the governments allied with the Imperial Government of Germany because they have not made war upon us or challenged us to defend our right and our honour. The Austro-Hungarian Government has, indeed, avowed its unqualified endorsement and acceptance of the reckless and lawless submarine warfare adopted now without disguise by the Imperial German Government, and it has therefore not been possible for this Government to receive Count Tarnowski, the Ambassador recently accredited to this Government by the Imperial and Royal Government of Austria-Hungary; but that

Government has not actually engaged in warfare against citizens of the United States on the seas, and I take the liberty, for the present at least, of postponing a discussion of our relations with the authorities at Vienna. We enter this war only where we are clearly forced into it because there are no other means of defending our rights.

It will be all the easier for us to conduct ourselves as belligerents in a high spirit of right and fairness because we act without animus, not in enmity towards a people or with the desire to bring any injury or disadvantage upon them, but only in armed opposition to an irresponsible government which has thrown aside all considerations of humanity and of right and is running amuck. We are, let me say again, the sincere friends of the German people, and shall desire nothing so much as the early reestablishment of intimate relations of mutual advantage between us — however hard it may be for them, for the time being, to believe that this is spoken from our hearts. We have borne with their present government through all these bitter months because of that friendship — exercising a patience and forbearance which would otherwise have been impossible. We shall, happily, still have an opportunity to prove that friendship in our daily attitude and actions towards the millions of men and women of German birth and native sympathy, who live amongst us and share our life, and we shall be proud to prove it towards all who are in fact loyal to their neighbours and to the Government in the hour of test. They are, most of them, as true and loyal Americans as if they had never known any other fealty or allegiance. They will be prompt to stand with us in rebuking and restraining the few who may be of a different mind and purpose. If there should be disloyalty, it will be dealt with with a firm hand of stern repression; but, if it lifts its head at all, it will lift it only here and there and without countenance except from a lawless and malignant few.

It is a distressing and oppressive duty, gentlemen of the Congress, which I have performed in thus addressing you. There are, it may be, many months of fiery trial and sacrifice ahead of us. It is a fearful thing to lead this great peaceful people into war, into the most terrible and disastrous of all wars, civilization itself seeming to be in the balance. But the right is more precious than peace, and we shall fight for the things which we have always carried nearest our hearts — for democracy, for the right of those who submit to authority to have a voice in their own governments, for the rights and liberties of small nations, for a universal dominion of right by such a concert of free peoples as shall bring peace and safety to all nations and make the world itself at last free. To such a task we can dedicate our lives and our fortunes, everything that we are and everything that we have, with the pride of those who know that the day has come when America is privileged to spend her blood and her might for the principles that gave her birth and happiness and the peace which she has treasured. God helping her, she can do no other.

Review Questions

1. What news came to the president on the third of February? Why was it significant?
2. What were the "free highways of the world"?
3. What type of warfare had Germany initiated?
4. What was "armed neutrality"? Why was it no longer possible?
5. What was the course of war going to mean for the United States?

Thought Questions

1. Do you, like Wilson, have a hard time believing that these acts were committed by a civilized nation? Or does this behavior seem tame compared to warfare today?
2. Was it hypocritical that peace and justice were the objectives of a war?
3. Wilson said, "We have no quarrel with the German people." Is it possible to separate a government from its people? Is this more difficult today?
4. Wilson said, "Only free peoples can […] prefer the interests of mankind to any narrow interest of their own." Do you agree? Why or why not?
5. Explain your response to the phrase "the right is more precious than peace." Do you think this phrase is overused? Misused?

"League of Nations Speech" (excerpt)
Henry Cabot Lodge

Henry Cabot Lodge (1850–1924) grew up in Massachusetts, where he initially pursued a career in the law and academics and wrote extensively on issues of American history and politics. He entered politics himself in the Massachusetts State House of Representatives, and then he went on to serve in both the U.S. House of Representatives and the Senate. After World War I concluded, when President Wilson was forming the League of Nations as part of the Versailles peace treaty, Lodge questioned whether the United States should join the League, or whether it should seek to maintain its traditionally neutral stance. The following is an excerpt from the speech explaining his position, which he presented before the Senate on August 12, 1919.

Mr. President:

The independence of the United States is not only more precious to ourselves but to the world than any single possession. Look at the United States today. We have made mistakes in the past. We have had shortcomings. We shall make mistakes in the future and fall short of our own best hopes. But none the less is there any country today on the face of the earth which can compare with this in ordered liberty, in peace, and in the largest freedom?

I feel that I can say this without being accused of undue boastfulness, for it is the simple fact, and in making this treaty and taking on these obligations all that we do is in a spirit of unselfishness and in a desire for the good of mankind. But it is well to remember that we are dealing with nations every one of which has a direct individual interest to serve, and there is grave danger in an unshared idealism.

Contrast the United States with any country on the face of the earth today and ask yourself whether the situation of the United States is not the best to be found. I will go as far as anyone in world service, but the first step to world service is the maintenance of the United States.

I have always loved one flag and I cannot share that devotion [with] a mongrel banner created for a League.

You may call me selfish if you will, conservative or reactionary, or use any other harsh adjective you see fit to apply, but an American I was born, an American I have remained all my life. I can never be anything else but an American, and I must think of the United States first, and when I think of the United States first in an arrangement like this I am thinking of what is best for the world, for if the United States fails, the best hopes of mankind fail with it.

I have never had but one allegiance—I cannot divide it now. I have loved but one flag and I cannot share that devotion and give affection to the mongrel banner invented for a league. Internationalism, illustrated by the Bolshevik and by the men to whom all countries are alike provided they can make money out of them, is to me repulsive.

National I must remain, and in that way I like all other Americans can render the amplest service to the world. The United States is the world's best hope, but if you fetter her in the interests and quarrels of other nations, if you tangle her in the intrigues of Europe, you will destroy her power for good and endanger her very existence. Leave her to march freely through the centuries to come as in the years that have gone.

Strong, generous, and confident, she has nobly served mankind. Beware how you trifle with your marvellous inheritance, this great land of ordered liberty, for if we stumble and fall, freedom and civilization everywhere will go down in ruin.

We are told that we shall "break the heart of the world" if we do not take this league just as it stands. I fear that the hearts of the vast majority of mankind would beat on strongly and steadily and without any quickening if the league were to perish altogether. If it should be effectively and beneficently changed the people who would lie awake in sorrow for a single night could be easily gathered in one not very large room but those who would draw a long breath of relief would reach to millions.

We hear much of visions and I trust we shall continue to have visions and dream dreams of a fairer future for the race. But visions are one thing and visionaries are another, and the mechanical appliances of the rhetorician designed to give a picture of a present which does not exist and of a future which no man can predict are as unreal and short-lived as the steam or canvas clouds, the angels suspended on wires and the artificial lights of the stage.

They pass with the moment of effect and are shabby and tawdry in the daylight. Let us at least be real. Washington's entire honesty of mind and his fearless look into the face of all facts are qualities which can never go out of fashion and which we should all do well to imitate.

Ideals have been thrust upon us as an argument for the league until the healthy mind which rejects cant revolts from them. Are ideals confined to this deformed experiment upon a noble purpose, tainted, as it is, with bargains and tied to a peace treaty which might have been disposed of long ago to the great benefit of the world if it had not been compelled to carry this rider on its back? *"Post equitem sedet atra cura,"* Horace tells us, but no blacker care ever sat behind any rider than we shall find in this covenant of doubtful and disputed interpretation as it now perches upon the treaty of peace.

No doubt many excellent and patriotic people see a coming fulfillment of noble ideals in the words "League for Peace." We all respect and share these aspirations and desires, but some of us see no hope, but rather defeat, for them in this murky covenant. For we, too, have our ideals, even if we differ from those who have tried to establish a monopoly of idealism.

Our first ideal is our country, and we see her in the future, as in the past, giving service to all her people and to the world. Our ideal of the future is that she should continue to render that service of her own free will. She has great problems of her own to solve, very grim and perilous problems, and a right solution, if we can attain to it, would largely benefit mankind.

We would have our country strong to resist a peril from the West, as she has flung back the German menace from the East. We would not have our politics distracted and embittered by the dissensions of other lands. We would not have our country's vigour exhausted or her moral force abated, by everlasting meddling and muddling in every quarrel, great and small, which afflicts the world.

Our ideal is to make her ever stronger and better and finer, because in that way alone, as we believe, can she be of the greatest service to the world's peace and to the welfare of mankind.

Review Questions

1. What was more precious to the United States than any possession?
2. What was the occasion of Lodge's speech? What was its purpose?
3. According to Lodge, what would destroy the power of the United States?
4. What would "break the heart of the world"? Did Lodge agree?
5. Who said, *"Post equitem sedet atra cura"*? What did it mean?

Thought Questions

1. Why did Lodge think he could make these claims without boasting? Were his boasts justified?
2. Do you agree with Lodge's statement, "If the United States fails, the best hopes of mankind fail with it"? Be prepared to explain your answer.
3. How did Lodge distinguish between visions and visionaries? Did he think one was better?
4. In your opinion, what was the purpose of Lodge's illustration of the stage?
5. Were Lodge's ideals valid, in your opinion? Do you agree with his reasoning?

"Pearl Harbor Address"
Franklin D. Roosevelt

Franklin Delano Roosevelt (1882–1945), the fifth cousin of President Theodore Roosevelt, was also born in New York. This Roosevelt entered politics by serving in the state senate. In 1921, Roosevelt fell ill with polio, which left him crippled, but did not diminish his career in politics. He was elected president in 1932, in the midst of the Great Depression, and died during his fourth term. His "New Deal" was a set of reforms designed to restore jobs and boost the economy by allowing the federal government to regulate the economy. As World War II developed, Roosevelt kept the United States out of direct involvement in the war, instead providing supplies to Britain and France. Then, on December 7, 1941, the Japanese bombed American naval stations in Hawaii and other Pacific islands, and in the following speech, Roosevelt asked Congress to declare war. These events proved to be a turning point in the war, and they also led to the first use of the atom bomb. After the war, Roosevelt was instrumental in developing the United Nations out of the failed League of Nations.

Mr. Vice President, Mr. Speaker, Members of the Senate, and of the House of Representatives:

Yesterday, December 7th, 1941–a date which will live in infamy—the United States of America was suddenly and deliberately attacked by naval and air forces of the Empire of Japan.

The United States was at peace with that nation and, at the solicitation of Japan, was still in conversation with its government and its emperor looking toward the maintenance of peace in the Pacific. Indeed, one hour after

Japanese air squadrons had commenced bombing in the American island of Oahu, the Japanese ambassador to the United States and his colleagues delivered to our Secretary of State a formal reply to a recent American message. And while this reply stated that it seemed useless to continue the existing diplomatic negotiations, it contained no threat or hint of war or of armed attack.

It will be recorded that the distance of Hawaii from Japan makes it obvious that the attack was deliberately planned many days or even weeks ago. During the intervening time, the Japanese government has deliberately sought to deceive the United States by false statements and expressions of hope for continued peace.

The attack yesterday on the Hawaiian Islands has caused severe damage to American naval and military forces. I regret to tell you that very many American lives have been lost. In addition, American ships have been reported torpedoed on the high seas between San Francisco and Honolulu.

Yesterday, the Japanese government also launched an attack against Malaya. Last night, Japanese forces attacked Hong Kong. Last night, Japanese forces attacked Guam. Last night, Japanese forces attacked the Philippine Islands. Last night, the Japanese attacked Wake Island. And this morning, the Japanese attacked Midway Island. Japan has, therefore, undertaken a surprise offensive extending throughout the Pacific area.

The facts of yesterday and today speak for themselves. The people of the United States have already formed their opinions and well understand the implications to the very life and safety of our nation. As commander in chief of the Army and Navy, I have directed that all measures be taken for our defense.

But always will our whole nation remember the character of the onslaught against us. No matter how long it may take us to overcome this premeditated invasion, the American people in their righteous might will win through to absolute victory. I believe that I interpret the will of the Congress and of the people when I assert that we will not only defend ourselves to the uttermost, but will make it very certain that this form of treachery shall never again endanger us.

Hostilities exist. There is no blinking at the fact that our people, our territory, and our interests are in grave danger. With confidence in our armed forces, with the unbounding determination of our people, we will gain the inevitable triumph – so help us God.

I ask that the Congress declare that since the unprovoked and dastardly attack by Japan on Sunday, December 7th, 1941, a state of war has existed between the United States and the Japanese empire.

Review Questions

1. What happened on December 7, 1941?
2. Why did FDR believe the attack was deliberately planned much earlier?
3. What damage did the attack cause?
4. Which Pacific islands did Japan attack?
5. What action was FDR hoping to provoke with this speech?

Thought Questions

1. What events in your lifetime (personal or national) stick out in your memory? What makes you remember the specific date of an event?
2. What happened after the Japanese air squadrons began to bomb Hawaii? Why was it ironic?
3. What opinion would you have formed if you had been listening to the news? Would FDR's speech have altered your opinion at all?
4. What did FDR mean when he said we would always remember "the character of the onslaught against us"? What was the character of the onslaught? Was there something unique about it?
5. What were the national implications of Pearl Harbor? The international implications?

"The Marshall Plan"
George C. Marshall

George Catlett Marshall (1880–1959) was born in Pennsylvania but enrolled in the Virginia Military Institute on his way to a career in the military. Marshall served in France during World War I, and served as chief of staff for the General Staff during World War II. After retiring from the military in 1945, Marshall worked as a diplomat, and then in 1947, he was named secretary of state under President Truman. While serving in that capacity, Marshall delivered the following speech as the commencement address at Harvard in the spring of 1947. His speech, later termed "The Marshall Plan," outlined a policy of reconstruction for post-WWII Europe that would benefit all Europe, not just democratic nations. In 1953, Marshall was honored for his efforts with the Nobel Peace Prize.

I need not tell you gentlemen that the world situation is very serious. That must be apparent to all intelligent people. I think one difficulty is that the problem is one of such enormous complexity that the very mass of facts presented to the public by press and radio make it exceedingly difficult for the man in the street to reach a clear appraisement of the situation. Furthermore, the people of this country are distant from the troubled areas of the earth, and it is hard for them to comprehend the plight and consequent reaction of the long-suffering peoples and the effect of those reactions on their governments in connection with our efforts to promote peace in the world.

In considering the requirements for the rehabilitation of Europe, the physical loss of life, the visible destruction of cities, factories, mines, and railroads was correctly estimated, but it has become obvious during recent months that this visible destruction was probably less serious than the dislocation of the entire fabric of European economy. For the past ten years conditions have been highly abnormal. The feverish maintenance of the war effort engulfed all aspects of national economics. Machinery has fallen into disrepair or is entirely obsolete. Under the arbitrary and destructive Nazi rule, virtually every possible enterprise was geared into the German war machine. Long-standing commercial ties, private institutions, banks, insurance companies and shipping companies disappeared, through the loss of capital, absorption through nationalization, or by simple destruction. In many countries, confidence in the local currency has been severely shaken. The breakdown of the business structure of Europe during the war was complete. Recovery has been seriously retarded by the fact that two years after the close of hostilities a peace settlement with Germany and Austria has not been agreed upon. But even given a more prompt solution of these difficult problems, the rehabilitation of the economic structure of Europe quite evidently will require a much longer time and greater effort than had been foreseen.

There is a phase of this matter which is both interesting and serious. The farmer has always produced the foodstuffs to exchange with the city dweller for the other necessities of life. This division of labor is the basis of modern civilization. At the present time it is threatened with breakdown. The town and city industries are not producing adequate goods to exchange with the food-producing farmer. Raw materials and fuel are in short supply. Machinery is lacking or worn out. The farmer or the peasant cannot find the goods for sale which he desires to purchase. So the sale of his farm produce for money which he cannot use seems to him an unprofitable transaction. He, therefore, has withdrawn many fields from crop cultivation and is using them for grazing. He feeds more grain to stock and finds for himself and his family an ample supply of food, however short he may be on clothing and the other ordinary gadgets of civilization. Meanwhile, people in the cities are short of food and fuel. So the governments are forced to use their foreign money and credits to procure these necessities abroad. This process exhausts funds which are urgently needed for reconstruction. Thus a very serious situation is rapidly developing which bodes no good for the world. The modern system of the division of labor upon which the exchange of products is based is in danger of breaking down.

The truth of the matter is that Europe's requirements for the next three or four years of foreign food and other essential products—principally from America—are so much greater than her present ability to pay that she must have substantial additional help, or face economic, social, and political deterioration of a very grave character.

The remedy lies in breaking the vicious circle and restoring the confidence of the European people in the economic future of their own countries and of Europe as a whole. The manufacturer and the farmer throughout wide areas must be able and willing to exchange their products for currencies the continuing value of which is not open to question.

Aside from the demoralizing effect on the world at large and the possibilities of disturbances arising as a result of the desperation of the people concerned, the consequences to the economy of the United States should be apparent to all. It is logical that the United States should do whatever it is able to do to assist in the return of normal economic health in the world, without which there can be no political stability and no assured peace. Our policy is directed not against any country or doctrine but against hunger, poverty, desperation, and chaos. Its purpose should be the revival of working economy in the world so as to permit the emergence of political and social conditions in which free institutions can exist. Such assistance, I am convinced, must not be on a piecemeal basis as various crises develop. Any assistance that this Government may render in the future should provide a cure rather than a mere palliative. Any government that is willing to assist in the task of recovery will find full cooperation, I am sure, on the part of the United States Government. Any government which maneuvers to block the recovery of other countries cannot expect help from us. Furthermore, governments, political parties, or groups which seek to perpetuate human misery in order to profit therefrom politically or otherwise, will encounter the opposition of the United States.

It is already evident that, before the United States Government can proceed much further in its efforts to alleviate the situation and help start the European world on its way to recovery, there must be some agreement among the countries of Europe as to the requirements of the situation and the part those countries themselves will take in order to give proper effect to whatever action might be undertaken by this Government. It would be neither fitting nor efficacious for this Government to undertake to draw up unilaterally a program designed to place Europe on its feet economically. This is the business of the Europeans. The initiative, I think, must come from Europe. The role of this country should consist of friendly aid in the drafting of a European program so far as it may be practical for us to do so. The program should be a joint one, agreed to by a number, if not all European nations.

An essential part of any successful action on the part of the United States is an understanding on the part of the people of America of the character of the problem and the remedies to be applied. Political passion and prejudice should have no part. With foresight, and a willingness on the part of our people to face up to the vast responsibilities which history has clearly placed upon our country, the difficulties I have outlined can and will be overcome.

Review Questions

1. Why was it difficult "for the man in the street to reach a clear appraisement of the situation"?
2. What factor undermined the recovery of Europe's business structure, according to Marshall?
3. What kind of division of labor is "the basis of modern civilization"? What threatened it?
4. What was Marshall's remedy for the current situation?
5. Why did Marshall say the United States should get involved with Europe's problem?

Thought Questions

1. Is it difficult to empathize with people in other parts of the world?
2. What do you think Marshall meant by the "fabric of European economy"?
3. Why was a division of labor so important to the modern economy?
4. Should America care about the economic problems of other nations? If not, why not?
5. Marshall said America could not fix Europe. Why would that approach have been a bad idea?

"Inaugural Address"
John F. Kennedy

John Fitzgerald Kennedy (1917–1963) was born to an Irish family in Massachusetts. After college, he entered the Navy and served on a PT boat in World War II. He returned and entered state-level politics before reaching the Senate. In 1960, he was elected president. While in office, in domestic affairs, Kennedy was active in his support of equal rights and his campaign against poverty. International affairs, meanwhile, were complicated by the rivalry between the United States and the Soviet Union. In October 1962, after the failed Bay of Pigs invasion (an attempt to remove Cuban leader Fidel Castro from power), intelligence discovered a Russian plan to place nuclear missiles in Cuba. In the ensuing Cuban Missile Crisis, Kennedy prevented ships carrying weapons from entering Cuban waters until he could negotiate a Russian concession. On November 22, 1963, just a few months after passing a partial ban on further nuclear tests, Kennedy was assassinated. The phrase he coined in his inaugural address, "Ask not what your country can do for you—ask what you can do for your country," remains a byword for the Kennedy administration.

Vice President Johnson, Mr. Speaker, Mr. Chief Justice, President Eisenhower, Vice President Nixon, President Truman, reverend clergy, fellow citizens;

We observe today not a victory of party, but a celebration of freedom—symbolizing an end, as well as a beginning—signifying renewal, as well as change. For I have sworn before you and Almighty God the same solemn oath our forebears prescribed nearly a century and three-quarters ago.

The world is very different now. For man holds in his mortal hands the power to abolish all forms of human poverty and all forms of human life. And yet the same revolutionary beliefs for which our forebears fought are still at issue around the globe—the belief that the rights of man come not from the generosity of the state, but from the hand of God.

We dare not forget today that we are the heirs of that first revolution. Let the word go forth from this time and place, to friend and foe alike, that the torch has been passed to a new generation of Americans—born in this century, tempered by war, disciplined by a hard and bitter peace, proud of our ancient heritage—and unwilling to witness or permit the slow undoing of those human rights to which this Nation has always been committed, and to which we are committed today at home and around the world.

Let every nation know, whether it wishes us well or ill, that we shall pay any price, bear any burden, meet any hardship, support any friend, oppose any foe, in order to assure the survival and the success of liberty.

This much we pledge—and more.

To those old allies whose cultural and spiritual origins we share, we pledge the loyalty of faithful friends. United, there is little we cannot do in a host of cooperative ventures. Divided, there is little we can do—for we dare not meet a powerful challenge at odds and split asunder.

To those new States whom we welcome to the ranks of the free, we pledge our word that one form of colonial control shall not have passed away merely to be replaced by a far more iron tyranny. We shall not always expect to find them supporting our view. But we shall always hope to find them strongly supporting their own freedom—and to remember that, in the past, those who foolishly sought power by riding the back of the tiger ended up inside.

To those peoples in the huts and villages across the globe struggling to break the bonds of mass misery, we pledge our best efforts to help them help themselves, for whatever period is required—not because the Communists may be doing it, not because we seek their votes, but because it is right. If a free society cannot help the many who are poor, it cannot save the few who are rich.

To our sister republics south of our border, we offer a special pledge—to convert our good words into good deeds—in a new alliance for progress—to assist free men and free governments in casting off the chains of poverty. But this peaceful revolution of hope cannot become the prey of hostile powers. Let all our neighbors know that we shall join with them to oppose aggression or subversion anywhere in the Americas. And let every other power know that this Hemisphere intends to remain the master of its own house.

To that world assembly of sovereign states, the United Nations, our last best hope in an age where the instruments of war have far outpaced the instruments of peace, we renew our pledge of support—to prevent it from becoming merely a forum for invective—to strengthen its shield of the new and the weak—and to enlarge the area in which its writ may run.

Finally, to those nations who would make themselves our adversary, we offer not a pledge but a request: that both sides begin anew the quest for peace, before the dark powers of destruction unleashed by science engulf all humanity in planned or accidental self-destruction.

We dare not tempt them with weakness. For only when our arms are sufficient beyond doubt can we be certain beyond doubt that they will never be employed.

But neither can two great and powerful groups of nations take comfort from our present course—both sides overburdened by the cost of modern weapons, both rightly alarmed by the steady spread of the deadly atom, yet both racing to alter that uncertain balance of terror that stays the hand of mankind's final war.

So let us begin anew—remembering on both sides that civility is not a sign of weakness, and sincerity is always subject to proof. Let us never negotiate out of fear. But let us never fear to negotiate.

Let both sides explore what problems unite us instead of belaboring those problems which divide us.

Let both sides, for the first time, formulate serious and precise proposals for the inspection and control of arms—and bring the absolute power to destroy other nations under the absolute control of all nations.

Let both sides seek to invoke the wonders of science instead of its terrors. Together let us explore the stars, conquer the deserts, eradicate disease, tap the ocean depths, and encourage the arts and commerce.

Let both sides unite to heed in all corners of the earth the command of Isaiah—to "undo the heavy burdens…and to let the oppressed go free."

And if a beachhead of cooperation may push back the jungle of suspicion, let both sides join in creating a new endeavor, not a new balance of power, but a new world of law, where the strong are just and the weak secure and the peace preserved.

All this will not be finished in the first 100 days. Nor will it be finished in the first 1,000 days, nor in the life of this Administration, nor even perhaps in our lifetime on this planet. But let us begin. In your hands, my fellow citizens, more than in mine, will rest the final success or failure of our course. Since this country was founded, each generation of Americans has been summoned to give testimony to its national loyalty. The graves of young Americans who answered the call to service surround the globe.

Now the trumpet summons us again—not as a call to bear arms, though arms we need; not as a call to battle, though embattled we are—but a call to bear the burden of a long twilight struggle, year in and year out, "rejoicing in hope, patient in tribulation"—a struggle against the common enemies of man: tyranny, poverty, disease, and war itself.

Can we forge against these enemies a grand and global alliance, North and South, East and West, that can assure a more fruitful life for all mankind? Will you join in that historic effort? In the long history of the world, only a few generations have been granted the role of defending freedom in its hour of maximum danger. I do not shrink from this responsibility—I welcome it. I do not believe that any of us would exchange places with any other people or any other generation. The energy, the faith, the devotion which we bring to this endeavor will light our country and all who serve it—and the glow from that fire can truly light the world.

And so, my fellow Americans: ask not what your country can do for you—ask what you can do for your country.

My fellow citizens of the world: ask not what America will do for you, but what together we can do for the freedom of man.

Finally, whether you are citizens of America or citizens of the world, ask of us the same high standards of strength and sacrifice which we ask of you. With a good conscience our only sure reward, with history the final judge of our deeds, let us go forth to lead the land we love, asking His blessing and His help, but knowing that here on earth God's work must truly be our own.

Review Questions

1. What was the audience observing, according to Kennedy? What were they not observing?
2. How was the world different from the time of the forbearers that Kennedy mentioned? How was it the same?
3. How much did Kennedy pledge to the cause of liberty?
4. Explain Kennedy's example: "Those who foolishly sought power by riding the back of the tiger ended up inside."
5. To what did the "dark powers of destruction unleashed by science" refer?

Thought Questions

1. What difference does it make to believe that the rights of man come from God rather than man?
2. Does a country have more responsibility to maintain its own wealth or to raise other countries to its level? (Keep in mind that if a country loses its wealth, it will be unable to help others).
3. What does it mean to "remain master of [one's] own house"?
4. "Instruments of war" refer to weapons. What are "weapons of peace"?
5. Is the United Nations "merely a forum of invective"? Why or why not? What does this mean?
6. "Only when our arms are sufficient […] can we be certain […] that they will never be employed." Is this rationale for the arms race logical? Explain your answer.

"First Inaugural Address"
Ronald Reagan

Ronald Reagan (1911–2004) was born in Illinois, but he moved to California as a young man to begin a career as an actor. He became active in politics while serving as the president of the Screen Actors Guild, and in 1966, he was elected governor of California. In 1980, he was elected president. Reagan entered office during a period in the Cold War when Americans were disillusioned about the future of capitalism. His inaugural address responded to these concerns and set the tone for his presidency. He went on to enact policies designed to decrease inflation, increase frugality, and restore balance to the economy. In his second term, Reagan continued his domestic reforms of tax policy and government spending. In foreign policy, he negotiated the 1987 Intermediate Nuclear Force Treaty with Mikhail Gorbachev of the Soviet Union, which eliminated intermediate-range nuclear missiles.

Senator Hatfield, Mr. Chief Justice, Mr. President, Vice President Bush, Vice President Mondale, Senator Baker, Speaker O'Neill, Reverend Moomaw, and my fellow citizens:

To a few of us here today this is a solemn and most momentous occasion, and yet in the history of our nation it is a commonplace occurrence. The orderly transfer of authority as called for in the Constitution routinely takes place as it has for almost two centuries, and few of us stop to think how unique we really are. In the eyes of many in the world, this every-four-year ceremony we accept as normal is nothing less than a miracle.

Mr. President, I want our fellow citizens to know how much you did to carry on this tradition. By your gracious cooperation in the transition process, you have shown a watching world that we are a united people pledged to maintaining a political system which guarantees individual liberty to a greater degree than any other, and I thank you and your people for all your help in maintaining the continuity which is the bulwark of our Republic.

The business of our nation goes forward. These United States are confronted with an economic affliction of great proportions. We suffer from the longest and one of the worst sustained inflations in our national history. It distorts our economic decisions, penalizes thrift, and crushes the struggling young and the fixed-income elderly alike. It threatens to shatter the lives of millions of our people.

Idle industries have cast workers into unemployment, human misery, and personal indignity. Those who do work are denied a fair return for their labor by a tax system which penalizes successful achievement and keeps us from maintaining full productivity.

But great as our tax burden is, it has not kept pace with public spending. For decades, we have piled deficit upon deficit, mortgaging our future and our children's future for the temporary convenience of the present. To continue this long trend is to guarantee tremendous social, cultural, political, and economic upheavals.

You and I, as individuals, can, by borrowing, live beyond our means, but for only a limited period of time. Why, then, should we think that collectively, as a nation, we are not bound by that same limitation? We must act today in order to preserve tomorrow. And let there be no misunderstanding: We are going to begin to act, beginning today.

The economic ills we suffer have come upon us over several decades. They will not go away in days, weeks, or months, but they will go away. They will go away because we as Americans have the capacity now, as we've had in the past, to do whatever needs to be done to preserve this last and greatest bastion of freedom.

In this present crisis, government is not the solution to our problem; government is the problem. From time to time, we've been tempted to believe that society has become too complex to be managed by self-rule, that government by an elite group is superior to government for, by, and of the people. Well, if no one among us is capable of governing himself, then who among us has the capacity to govern someone else? All of us together, in and out of government, must bear the burden. The solutions we seek must be equitable, with no one group singled out to pay a higher price.

We hear much of special interest groups. Well, our concern must be for a special interest group that has been too long neglected. It knows no sectional boundaries or ethnic and racial divisions, and it crosses political party lines. It is made up of men and women who raise our food, patrol our streets, man our mines and factories, teach our children, keep our homes, and heal us when we are sick—professionals, industrialists, shopkeepers, clerks, cabbies, and truck drivers. They are, in short, "We the people," this breed called Americans.

Well, this administration's objective will be a healthy, vigorous, growing economy that provides equal opportunities for all Americans with no barriers born of bigotry or discrimination. Putting America back to work means putting all Americans back to work. Ending inflation means freeing all Americans from the terror of runaway living costs. All must share in the productive work of this "new beginning" and all must share in the bounty of a revived economy. With the idealism and fair play which are the core of our system and our strength, we can have a strong and prosperous America, at peace with itself and the world.

So, as we begin, let us take inventory. We are a nation that has a government—not the other way around. And this makes us special among the nations of the Earth. Our government has no power except that granted it by the people. It is time to check and reverse the growth of government, which shows signs of having grown beyond the consent of the governed.

It is my intention to curb the size and influence of the Federal establishment and to demand recognition of the distinction between the powers granted to the Federal Government and those reserved to the States or to the people. All of us need to be reminded that the Federal Government did not create the States; the States created the Federal Government.

Now, so there will be no misunderstanding, it's not my intention to do away with government. It is rather to make it work—work with us, not over us; to stand by our side, not ride on our back. Government can and must provide opportunity, not smother it; foster productivity, not stifle it.

If we look to the answer as to why for so many years we achieved so much, prospered as no other people on Earth, it was because here in this land we unleashed the energy and individual genius of man to a greater extent than has ever been done before. Freedom and the dignity of the individual have been more available and assured here than in any other place on Earth. The price for this freedom at times has been high, but we have never been unwilling to pay that price.

It is no coincidence that our present troubles parallel and are proportionate to the intervention and intrusion in our lives that result from unnecessary and excessive growth of government. It is time for us to realize that we're too great a nation to limit ourselves to small dreams. We're not, as some would have us believe, doomed to an inevitable decline. I do not believe in a fate that will fall on us no matter what we do. I do believe in a fate that will fall on us if we do nothing. So, with all the creative energy at our command, let us begin an era of national renewal. Let us renew our determination, our courage, and our strength. And let us renew our faith and our hope.

We have every right to dream heroic dreams. Those who say that we're in a time when there are no heroes, they just don't know where to look. You can see heroes every day going in and out of factory gates. Others, a handful in number, produce enough food to feed all of us and then the world beyond. You meet heroes across a counter, and they're on both sides of that counter. There are entrepreneurs with faith in themselves and faith in an idea who create new jobs, new wealth and opportunity. They're individuals and families whose taxes support the government and whose voluntary gifts support church, charity, culture, art, and education. Their patriotism is quiet, but deep. Their values sustain our national life.

I have used the words "they" and "their" in speaking of these heroes. I could say "you" and "your," because I'm addressing the heroes of whom I speak—you, the citizens of this blessed land. Your dreams, your hopes, your goals are going to be the dreams, the hopes, and the goals of this administration, so help me God.

We shall reflect the compassion that is so much a part of your makeup. How can we love our country and not love our countrymen, and loving them, reach out a hand when they fall, heal them when they're sick, and provide opportunity to make them self-sufficient so they will be equal in fact and not just in theory?

Can we solve the problems confronting us? Well, the answer is an unequivocal and emphatic "yes." To paraphrase Winston Churchill, I did not take the oath I have just taken with the intention of presiding over the dissolution of the world's strongest economy.

In the days ahead I will propose removing the roadblocks that have slowed our economy and reduced productivity. Steps will be taken aimed at restoring the balance between the various levels of government. Progress may be slow, measured in inches and feet, not miles, but we will progress. Is it time to reawaken this industrial giant, to get government back within its means, and to lighten our punitive tax burden. And these will be our first priorities, and on these principles, there will be no compromise.

On the eve of our struggle for independence a man who might have been one of the greatest among the Founding Fathers, Dr. Joseph Warren, president of the Massachusetts Congress, said to his fellow Americans, "Our country is in danger, but not to be despaired of…On you depend the fortunes of America. You are to decide the important questions upon which rests the happiness and the liberty of millions yet unborn. Act worthy of yourselves."

Well, I believe we, the Americans of today, are ready to act worthy of ourselves, ready to do what must be done to ensure happiness and liberty for ourselves, our children and our children's children. And as we renew ourselves here in our own land, we will be seen as having greater strength throughout the world. We will again be the exemplar of freedom and a beacon of hope for those who do not now have freedom.

To those neighbors and allies who share our freedom, we will strengthen our historic ties and assure them of our support and firm commitment. We will match loyalty with loyalty. We will strive for mutually beneficial relations. We will not use our friendship to impose on their sovereignty, for our own sovereignty is not for sale.

As for the enemies of freedom, those who are potential adversaries, they will be reminded that peace is the highest aspiration of the American people. We will negotiate for it, sacrifice for it; we will not surrender for it, now or ever.

Our forbearance should never be misunderstood. Our reluctance for conflict should not be misjudged as a failure of will. When action is required to preserve our national security, we will act. We will maintain sufficient strength to prevail if need be, knowing that if we do so we have the best chance of never having to use that strength.

Above all, we must realize that no arsenal or no weapon in the arsenals of the world is so formidable as the will and moral courage of free men and women. It is a weapon our adversaries in today's world do not have. It is a weapon that we as Americans do have. Let that be understood by those who practice terrorism and prey upon their neighbors.

I am told that tens of thousands of prayer meetings are being held on this day, and for that I'm deeply grateful. We are a nation under God, and I believe God intended for us to be free. It would be fitting and good, I think, if on each Inaugural Day in future years it should be declared a day of prayer.

This is the first time in our history that this ceremony has been held, as you have been told, on this West Front of the Capitol. Standing here, one faces a magnificent vista, opening up on this city's special beauty and history. At the end of this open mall are those shrines to the giants on whose shoulders we stand.

Directly in front of me, the monument to a monumental man, George Washington, father of our country. A man of humility who came to greatness reluctantly. He led America out of revolutionary victory into infant nationhood. Off to one side, the stately memorial to Thomas Jefferson. The Declaration of Independence flames with his eloquence. And then beyond the Reflecting Pool, the dignified columns of the Lincoln Memorial. Whoever would understand in his heart the meaning of America will find it in the life of Abraham Lincoln.

Beyond those monuments to heroism is the Potomac River, and on the far shore the sloping hills of Arlington National Cemetery, with its row upon row of simple white markers bearing crosses or Stars of David. They add up to only a tiny fraction of the price that has been paid for our freedom.

Each one of those markers is a monument to the kind of hero I spoke of earlier. Their lives ended in places called Belleau Wood, The Argonne, Omaha Beach, Salerno, and halfway around the world on Guadalcanal, Tarawa, Pork Chop Hill, the Chosin Reservoir, and in a hundred rice paddies and jungles of a place called Vietnam.

Under one such marker lies a young man, Martin Treptow, who left his job in a small town barber shop in 1917 to go to France with the famed Rainbow Division. There, on the western front, he was killed trying to carry a message between battalions under heavy artillery fire.

We are told that on his body was found a diary. On the flyleaf under the heading, "My Pledge," he had written these words: "America must win this war. Therefore, I will work, I will save, I will sacrifice, I will endure, I will fight cheerfully and do my utmost, as if the issue of the whole struggle depended on me alone."

The crisis we are facing today does not require of us the kind of sacrifice that Martin Treptow and so many thousands of others were called upon to make. It does require, however, our best effort, and our willingness to believe in ourselves and to believe in our capacity to perform great deeds, to believe that together, with God's help, we can and will resolve the problems which now confront us.

And, after all, why shouldn't we believe that? We are Americans.

God bless you, and thank you.

Review Questions

1. What did Americans think of as ordinary that other countries might have seen as miraculous?
2. What large problem was the United States dealing with at the time of this speech?
3. Why did Reagan argue that government was not the solution to the problem?
4. What special interest group did Reagan advocate?
5. Which Founding Father did Reagan quote? What point did the quote reinforce?

Thought Questions

1. What does inflation mean to you? Does it have any personal impact on your life? Explain.
2. Have you ever lived beyond your means? How long were you able to avoid the consequences? What happened when that period of avoidance ended?
3. Some have said, "it is better to be ruled by a wise few than a foolish multitude." How would Reagan answer this? How would you?
4. What did Reagan mean, "We are a nation that has a government—not the other way around"?
5. What is the significance of the various monuments Reagan mentioned? Would this speech have been different if given somewhere else? Does location impact the power of a speech?

SPEECHES

Writing Practice

Now that you have finished reading and studying a number of important speeches in American history, you should have a better sense of what makes a speech powerful and persuasive. Some of the features you may have noticed include memorable phrases, repetition, clear verbal cues for transitions, and vivid language.

Now it is your turn to put those techniques into practice. Below is a paragraph from *The Federalist Papers,* Number 47 (an article which you will read in full, later in this book).

> "The accumulation of all powers, legislative, executive, and judiciary, in the same hands, whether of one, a few, or many, and whether hereditary, self-appointed, or elective, may justly be pronounced the very definition of tyranny. Were the federal Constitution, therefore, really chargeable with the accumulation of power, or with a mixture of powers, having a dangerous tendency to such an accumulation, no further arguments would be necessary to inspire a universal reprobation of the system. I persuade myself, however, that it will be made apparent to every one, that the charge cannot be supported, and that the maxim on which it relies has been totally misconceived and misapplied. In order to form correct ideas on this important subject, it will be proper to investigate the sense in which the preservation of liberty requires that the three great departments of power should be separate and distinct."

Read it several times to make sure you understand it. Then, keeping the same basic ideas and some of the wording, rewrite this paragraph in your own words to turn it into a speech. Think about using simpler sentences and more colloquial language, but also feel free to add rhetorical flourishes and devices like those you've seen in the speeches you have just read.

Is it Time to Rhyme?
POETRY

Poetry may not seem political, but even literature can actively discuss and challenge history. Sometimes literature gives new life to a historic event or reminds readers that historical figures were also humans; sometimes it memorializes or critiques a historical event or situation.

Poetry is one of the oldest forms of literature and one of the most varied and complex. Although people often think of rhyming verses when they think of poetry, not all poetry has to rhyme. Pay particular attention to the following questions:

- Does the poem tell a story, describe something, or do a combination of both?
- Is the poem based on fiction or fact?
- What is the poem's focus?
- How is the poem structured? Does the poet use rhyme or meter (regular rhythm)?
- What is the tone of the poem in relation to its subject?
- What kind of images does the poet use?

Each poem in this section creatively portrays and gives a personal perspective to a large-scale historic event that played a role in American history or in the formation of American government. As you read, look for the devices each poet uses to accomplish his or her desired effect. Ask yourself what sets poetry apart from other genres of writing about history.

Poetry is a very versatile genre. Several of the poems in this section were later used for other purposes. For example, "Defence of Fort McHenry" is now the American national anthem, and several lines from "The New Colossus" were inscribed as a quote on the base of the Statue of Liberty. Think carefully about the use of poetry for patriotic purposes. Consider potential advantages, disadvantages, and ethical considerations.

"Pocahontas"
William M. Thackeray

William Makepeace Thackeray (1811–1863) was born in India, where his father was an administrator for the East India Company, but he moved to England when he was five years old. Thackeray did freelance and travel writing in various parts of Europe for ten years; then, in 1847, he began serialization of Vanity Fair, which would give him greater financial stability. Thackeray traveled widely, including a lecture tour of the United States in 1852 and 1853. The information he gathered during his travels informed his later work, including this poem, "Pocahontas," which was published in 1855 as part of the collection *Ballads*. The historical figure Pocahontas (c. 1595-1617) was the daughter of the Algonquian chief Powhatan of Virginia. When European explorers came to the Americas in 1607, according to reports, Pocahontas saved the life of Captain John Smith in what may have been an Indian ritual of introduction. Pocahontas later married a settler named John Rolfe, and he accompanied her on a trip to England, where she was presented to King James I.

Wearied arm and broken sword
Wage in vain the desperate fight;
Round him press a countless horde,
He is but a single knight.
Hark! a cry of triumph shrill
Through the wilderness resounds,
As, with twenty bleeding wounds,
Sinks the warrior, fighting still.

Now they heap the funeral pyre,
And the torch of death they light;
Ah! 'tis hard to die by fire!
Who will shield the captive knight?
Round the stake with fiendish cry
Wheel and dance the savage crowd;
Cold the victim's mien and proud,
And his breast is bared to die.

Who will shield the fearless heart?
Who avert the murderous blade?
From the throng with sudden start,
See, there springs an Indian maid.
Quick she stands before the knight:
"Loose the chain, unbind the ring!
I am daughter of the king,
And I claim the Indian right!"

Dauntlessly aside she flings
Lifted axe and thirsty knife;
Fondly to his heart she clings,
And her bosom guards his life!
Still 'tis told by Indian fires
How a daughter of their sires
Saved a captive Englishman.

Review Questions

1. What happened in this poem?
2. Did the poem say why the Englishman was a captive? Why or why not?
3. What was the warrior's attitude as he was about to be killed?
4. What was the Indian right? Did the poem explicitly say? Did it need to?
5. Where did the legend of Pocahontas come from, according to the poem?

Thought Questions

1. How did the poem differ from other popular media versions of this story?
2. Explain the statement: "Ah, 'tis hard to die by fire!" Why might this be true?
3. Why did the poet call the Englishman a knight? What sort of mental images does that evoke?
4. What precedent, if any, did this act set for relations between Native Americans and settlers?
5. Have English/Native American relations changed significantly? What are they like now?

"Five Kernels of Corn"
Hezekiah Butterworth

Hezekiah Butterworth (1839–1905) was born in Rhode Island into an old New England family. As a writer, Butterworth produced religious novels, short stories, and poetry as well as travel accounts. Butterworth was also a prolific speaker for various social organizations. The poem "Five Kernels of Corn" was published in 1895, in the collection *In Old New England: The Romance of a Colonial Fireside*. The poem commemorates the first difficult winters spent by the Pilgrims, who arrived in New England in 1620 under the leadership of Governor William Bradford (1590–1657).

'Twas the year of the famine in Plymouth of old,
The ice and the snow from the thatched roofs had rolled;
Through the warm purple skies steered the geese o'er the seas,
And the woodpeckers tapped in the clocks of the trees;
And the boughs on the slopes to the south winds lay bare,
and dreaming of summer, the buds swelled in the air.
The pale Pilgrims welcomed each reddening morn;
There were left but for rations Five Kernels of Corn.
Five Kernels of Corn!
Five Kernels of Corn!
But to Bradford a feast were Five Kernels of Corn!

"Five Kernels of Corn! Five Kernels of Corn!
Ye people, be glad for Five Kernels of Corn!"
So Bradford cried out on bleak Burial Hill,
And the thin women stood in their doors, white and still.
"Lo, the harbor of Plymouth rolls bright in the Spring,
The maples grow red, and the wood robins sing,
The west wind is blowing, and fading the snow,
And the pleasant pines sing, and arbutuses blow.
Five Kernels of Corn!
Five Kernels of Corn!
To each one be given Five Kernels of Corn!"

O Bradford of Austerfield hast on thy way,
The west winds are blowing o'er Provincetown Bay,
The white avens bloom, but the pine domes are chill,
And new graves have furrowed Precisioners' Hill!
"Give thanks, all ye people, the warm skies have come,
The hilltops are sunny, and green grows the holm,
And the trumpets of winds, and the white March is gone,
Five Kernels of Corn!
Five Kernels of Corn!
Ye have for Thanksgiving Five Kernels of Corn!

"The raven's gift eat and be humble and pray,
A new light is breaking and Truth leads your way;
One taper a thousand shall kindle; rejoice
That to you has been given the wilderness voice!"
O Bradford of Austerfield, daring the wave,
And safe through the sounding blasts leading the brave,
Of deeds such as thine was the free nation born,
And the festal world sings the "Five Kernels of Corn."
Five Kernels of Corn!
Five Kernels of Corn!
The nation gives thanks for Five Kernels of Corn!
To the Thanksgiving Feast bring Five Kernels of Corn!

Review Questions

1. Where did this poem take place?
2. What was the situation in which the poem was set?
3. What was the name of the family for whom "a feast were Five Kernels of Corn"?
4. From the poem, in what season would you guess this Thanksgiving took place?
5. What did "one taper a thousand shall kindle" mean?

Thought Questions

1. The phrase "Five Kernels of Corn" was repeated numerous times throughout the poem, always capitalized. What made this phrase significant?
2. Think about it: how much food are five kernels of corn? How long could you live on them?
3. What is the longest amount of time you have gone without food? How did you feel afterward? Do you remember what was the first food you ate afterward?
4. Did you ever think about the fact that going without food was a deed "of […] such […] was the free nation born"? Of what kinds of deeds do you picture America being born?
5. For what are you thankful? Why are these things important to you?

"Nathan Hale"
Francis M. Finch

Francis Miles Finch (1827–1907), born in New York, earned a degree in law and worked for Internal Revenue before he became a judge of the New York Court of Appeals. From his college days at Yale, he also frequently wrote poetry. Because he considered it only incidental, most of his poetry was not published until after his death. Finch presented the poem "Nathan Hale" at the centenary of the Linonian society at Yale in 1853. The poem is based on the life of Captain Nathan Hale (1755–1776), a Revolutionary War spy for the American army who was captured and subsequently hanged by the British. At his execution, Hale uttered the soon-to-be famous line, "I only regret that I have but one life to lose for my country."

To drum-beat and heart-beat,
A soldier marches by:
There is color in his cheek,
There is courage in his eye,
Yet to drum-beat and heart-beat
In a moment he must die.

By starlight and moonlight,
He seeks the Briton's camp;
He hears the rustling flag,
And the armed sentry's tramp;
And the starlight and moonlight
His silent wanderings lamp.

With slow tread and still tread,
He scans the tented line;
And he counts the battery guns
By the gaunt and shadowy pine;
And his slow tread and still tread
Gives no warning sign.

The dark wave, the plumed wave,
It meets his eager glance;
And it sparkles 'neath the stars,
Like the glimmer of a lance
A dark wave, a plumed wave,
On an emerald expanse.

A sharp clang, a steel clang,
And terror in the sound!
For the sentry, falcon-eyed,
In the camp a spy hath found;
With a sharp clang, a steel clang,
The patriot is bound.

With calm brow, steady brow,
He listens to his doom;
In his look there is no fear,
Nor a shadow-trace of gloom;
But with calm brow and steady brow
He robes him for the tomb.

In the long night, the still night,
He kneels upon the sod;
And the brutal guards withhold
E'en the solemn Word of God!
In the long night, the still night,
He walks where Christ hath trod.

'Neath the blue morn, the sunny morn,
He dies upon the tree;
And he mourns that he can lose
But one life for Liberty;
And in the blue morn, the sunny morn,
His spirit-wings are free.

But his last words, his message-words,
They burn, lest friendly eye
Should read how proud and calm
A patriot could die,
With his last words, his dying words,
A soldier's battle-cry.

From the Fame-leaf and Angel-leaf,
From monument and urn,
The sad of earth, the glad of heaven,
His tragic fate shall learn;

POETRY : *"Nathan Hale"*

And on Fame-leaf and Angel-leaf
The name of Hale shall burn.

Review Questions

1. Who was Nathan Hale? What was his role in the American army?
2. What were "fame-leaf" and "angel-leaf"?
3. What was Nathan Hale doing when he was captured?
4. What were the famous last words of Nathan Hale?
5. How does the repeated phrase, "to drum-beat and heart-beat" influence the poem's mood?

Thought Questions

1. Explain: "In the long night, the still night, he walks where Christ hath trod." With which Bible story does this create a connection?
2. What is the overall mood of the poem? Triumphant? Tragic? What creates that impression?
3. Why do you think Finch chose to repeat strategic words in the poem? Does this influence the flow of the poem? Its meaning?
4. Why do you think Finch noted that Hale's eyes burned "lest friendly eye / should read how proud and calm / a patriot could die"? What does this statement mean?
5. Faced with death, as Hale was, do you think you would be as calm? Why or why not? What last words would you want to say?

"Valley Forge" (excerpt)
Thomas B. Read

Thomas Buchanan Read (1822–1872) was born in a rural part of Pennsylvania, but in pursuit of a career in art, he moved from Cincinnati to Boston, where he began to publish poetry, and from there to Philadelphia. In his studies as an artist, Read also traveled to London and spent several years in Italy. Read's poetry alternated in topic between American and Italian subjects. The following piece is an excerpt from section two, part six ("Headquarters") of a longer patriotic poem entitled "The Wagoner of the Alleghanies," which was published in 1863. The poem describes the conditions of the winter of 1777, which the Continental Army spent in Valley Forge, Pennsylvania. It was one of the lowest points for General Washington's army, who faced starvation, desertion, and bitter cold. However, due in part to Washington's resolve, and in part to the training and drilling of German military volunteers, the Continental Army emerged from Valley Forge a stronger, more unified fighting force that went on to win key victories against the British.

O'er town and cottage, vale and height,
Down came Winter, fierce and white,
And shuddering wildly, as distraught
At horrors his own hand had wrought.

His child, the young Year, newly born,
   Cheerless, cowering, and affrighted,
Wailed with a shivering voice forlorn,
   As on a frozen heath benighted.
In vain the hearths were set aglow,
   In vain the evening lamps were lighted,
To cheer the dreary realm of snow:
Old Winter's brow would not be smoothed,
Nor the young Year's wailing soothed.

How sad the wretch at morn or eve
Compelled his starving home to leave,
Who, plunged breast-deep from drift to drift,
Toils slowly on from rift to rift,

Still hearing in his aching ear
The cry his fancy whispers near,
Of little ones who weep for bread
Within an ill-provided shed!

But wilder, fiercer, sadder still,
   Freezing the tear it caused to start,
Was the inevitable chill
   Which pierced a nation's agued heart,—
A nation with its naked breast
Against the frozen barriers prest,
Heaving its tedious way and slow
Through shifting gulfs and drifts of woe,
Where every blast that whistled by
Was bitter with its children's cry.

Such was the winter's awful sight
For many a dreary day and night,
What time our country's hope forlorn,
Of every needed comfort shorn,
Lay housed within a hurried tent,
Where every keen blast found a rent,
And oft the snow was seen to sift
Along the floor its piling drift,
Or, mocking the scant blanket's fold,
Across the night-couch frequent rolled;
Where every path by a soldier beat,
   Or every track where a sentinel stood,
Still held the print of naked feet,
   And oft the crimson stains of blood;
Where Famine held her spectral court,
   And joined by all her fierce allies:
She ever loved a camp or fort

> Beleaguered by the wintry skies,—
> But chiefly when Disease is by,
> To sink the frame and dim the eye,
> Until, with seeking forehead bent,
>   In martial garments cold and damp,
> Pale Death patrols from tent to tent,
>   To count the charnels of the camp.
>
> Such was the winter that prevailed
>   Within the crowded, frozen gorge;
> Such were the horrors that assailed
>   The patriot band at Valley Forge.
> It was a midnight storm of woes
>   To clear the sky for Freedom's morn;
> And such must ever be the throes
>   The hour when Liberty is born.

Review Questions

1. Name the "characters" in the poem.
2. Who was the wretch in stanza 3? With what problem was he wrestling (implied)?
3. Who were Famine's companions? How were they described?
4. To what did the "night-couch" probably refer?
5. How did the phrases "Old Winter" and "the young Year" set the time frame of the poem?

Thought Questions

1. The poem referred to winter as "shuddering wildly, as distraught / At horrors his own hand had wrought." Does winter have feelings? Why do you think Read used this imagery?
2. Compare the feelings of the wretch in stanza 3 with the feelings of the nation in stanza 4.
3. Explain: "And such must ever be the throes / The hour when Liberty is born." Do you agree?
4. This section of the poem ends on a positive note. Is the overall mood positive, or do the negative images last longer in your memory?
5. Why do you think Read wrote this poem about the Revolutionary War during the Civil War? What message do you think the poem might have sent to Union soldiers reading it?

"Defence of Fort McHenry"
"The Star-Spangled Banner"
Francis Scott Key

Francis Scott Key (c. 1780–1843) was born in Maryland and began to practice law there before he became the district attorney for the District of Columbia. During the War of 1812, he was sent to arrange the release of a prisoner of war from a British ship anchored outside Fort McHenry in Baltimore, Maryland. While he was there, on September 13, 1814, the fort was attacked by the British navy. The American defenses held, and what is more, the American flag flying over the fort was still hanging when morning came and the attack ceased. The flag is now on display at the Smithsonian Museum of American History. In response to these events, Key wrote the following poem, initially published as "Defence of Fort McHenry." The poem was soon set to music, and over a hundred years later, in 1931, it became the United States' national anthem.

O say can you see, by the dawn's early light,
    What so proudly we hail'd at the twilight's last gleaming,
Whose broad stripes and bright stars, through the perilous fight,
    O'er the ramparts we watch'd, were so gallantly streaming?
    And the rockets' red glare, the bombs bursting in air,
    Gave proof thro' the night that our flag was still there.
O say, does that star-spangled banner yet wave
O'er the land of the free and the home of the brave?

On the shore dimly seen through the mists of the deep,
    Where the foe's haughty host in dread silence reposes,
What is that which the breeze, o'er the towering steep,
    As it fitfully blows, half conceals, half discloses?
    Now it catches the gleam of the morning's first beam,
    In full glory reflected now shines on the stream,
'Tis the star-spangled banner—O long may it wave
O'er the land of the free and the home of the brave!

And where is that band who so vauntingly swore,
    That the havoc of war and the battle's confusion
A home and a Country should leave us no more?
     Their blood has wash'd out their foul footsteps' pollution.
     No refuge could save the hireling and slave
   From the terror of flight or the gloom of the grave,
And the star-spangled banner in triumph doth wave
O'er the land of the free and the home of the brave.

O thus be it ever when freemen shall stand
    Between their lov'd home and the war's desolation,
Blest with vict'ry and peace may the heav'n-rescued land
    Praise the power that hath made and preserv'd us a nation!
    Then conquer we must, when our cause it is just,
    And this be our motto— "In God is our trust,"
And the star-spangled banner in triumph shall wave
O'er the land of the free and the home of the brave.

POETRY : *"Defence of Fort McHenry"*

Review Questions
1. To what does the "Star-Spangled Banner" refer?
2. How did the narrator know that the flag had lasted through the night?
3. To what was the poem referring in this line: "the breeze, o'er the towering steep, / As it fitfully blows, half conceals, half discloses?"?
4. This poem was written during the war of 1812. In that historical context, to whom does "that band who so vauntingly swore / That the havoc of war and the battle's confusion, / A home and a country should leave us no more" refer?
5. What are the circumstances under which Key justifies conquering?

Thought Questions
1. Why would a flag, an inanimate object, have so much power? What larger force or emotion does the flag represent?
2. Why do you think flag burning and flag desecration are illegal? Do you agree with this law?
3. Could our nation today still be classified as "free and brave"? Give arguments for each side.
4. Where else have you seen a similar motto to the one expressed in the fourth stanza? Why would this particular motto be chosen?
5. Why do you think this poem was chosen to be the national anthem?

"Defense of the Alamo"
Joaquin Miller

Cincinnatus Hiner Miller (c. 1841–1913) was born into a Quaker family in Indiana. In 1852, following the Oregon Trail, Miller's family moved to Oregon. Miller's personal wanderings began while he was still young; during the Gold Rush, Miller traveled to California to work in the mines. Over the course of his life, he wrote for a newspaper, served as a judge, and wrote extensively using the name Joaquin, after the California bandit Joaquin Murietta (c. 1829–1853). Although initially unpopular, Miller later became known as "The Poet of the Sierras." The following poem was published in 1898 in the collection *Poems of American Patriotism 1776–1898*. Miller used for his subject the events of February 1836, when a Franciscan mission in San Antonio, Texas was the site of a battle between Texan freedom fighters and the Mexican National Army. Although the Texans were vastly outnumbered, they chose to fight to the death rather than surrender.

Santa Ana came storming, as a storm might come;
There was rumble of cannon; there was rattle of blade;
There was cavalry, infantry, bugle and drum —
Full seven thousand in pomp and parade.
The chivalry, flower of Mexico;
And a gaunt two hundred in the Alamo!
And thirty lay sick, and some were shot through;
For the siege had been bitter, and bloody, and long.
"Surrender, or die!" — "Men, what will you do?"
And Travis, great Travis, drew sword, quick and strong;
Drew a line at his feet …"Will you come — Will you go?
I die with my wounded, in the Alamo."
Then Bowie gasped, "Lead me over that line!"
Then Crockett, one hand to the sick, one hand to his gun,
Crossed with him; then never a word or a sign
Till all, sick or well, all, all save but one,
One man. Then a woman stepped, praying, and slow
Across; to die at her post in the Alamo.
Then that one coward fled, in the night, in that night

When all men silently prayed and thought
Of home; of to-morrow; of God and the right,
Till dawn; and with dawn came Travis's cannon-shot,
In answer to insolent Mexico,
From the old bell-tower of the Alamo.
Then came Santa Ana; a crescent of flame!
Then the red escalade; then the fight hand to hand;
Such an unequal fight as never had name
Since the Persian hordes butchered that doomed Spartan band.
All day – all day and all night; and the morning? so slow,
Through the battle smoke mantling the Alamo.
Now silence! Such silence! Two thousand lay dead
In a crescent outside! And within? Not a breath
Save the gasp of a woman, with gory gashed head,
All alone, all alone there, waiting for death;
And she but a nurse. Yet when shall we know
Another like this of the Alamo?
Shout "Victory, victory, victory ho!"
I say 'tis not always to the hosts that win!
I say that the victory, high or low,
Is given the hero who grapples with sin,
Or legion or single; just asking to know
When duty fronts death in his Alamo.

Review Questions

1. Who was the leader of the Mexicans? How large was the Mexican army?
2. How numerous were the Texans and Americans?
3. Which American and Texan heroes were mentioned by name in the poem?
4. What caused the one coward to flee?
5. What did the men in the Alamo do the night before the final combat?

Thought Questions

1. Explain: "[Victory] 'tis not always to the hosts that win." Having heard the end result of the battle, would you agree?
2. Why do you think Miller emphasized the death of the nurse more than the others who died?
3. How does the fact that the fight was unequal change the way that the Alamo is remembered?
4. Do you think the men and women in the Alamo knew their struggle was hopeless? Why did they continue to fight? If you had been in their place, would you have done the same?
5. Miller concluded: "I say that the victory, high or low, / Is given the hero who grapples with sin." Do you agree? Can you think of another situation that might illustrate this quote?

"Liberty for All"
William L. Garrison

William Lloyd Garrison (1805–1879) was born in Massachusetts, where, as an adult, he worked as a newspaperman. In 1831, he started his own paper called *The Liberator*, which emphasized and promoted the abolition of slavery as a practice. *The Liberator* ran until 1865, when the Thirteenth Amendment was adopted, abolishing slavery. A noted orator for the abolitionist cause, Garrison worked closely at various times with the American Anti-Slavery Society and other advocates like Frederick Douglass. Garrison wrote the following poem for *The Liberator* in 1831. Despite the small size of the paper and the humble nature of both the poem and its author, "Liberty for All" became a rallying cry of the abolitionist movement. Until his death, Garrison remained active in social reform movements including the fight for women's rights.

They tell me, Liberty! that in thy name
I may not plead for all the human race;
That some are born to bondage and disgrace,
Some to a heritage of woe and shame,
And some to power supreme, and glorious fame:
With my whole soul I spurn the doctrine base,
And, as an equal brotherhood, embrace
All people, and for all fair freedom claim!
Know this, O man! whate'er thy earthly fate—
God never made a tyrant nor a slave:
Woe, then, to those who dare to desecrate
His glorious image!—for to all He gave
Eternal rights, which none may violate;
And, by a mighty hand, the oppressed He yet shall save!

Review Questions
1. To which (he believed, erroneous) concept was Garrison speaking?
2. What was the "doctrine base" to which Garrison referred?
3. How, according to the poem, do men "desecrate / [God's] glorious image"?
4. Did Garrison believe that God designates tyrant and slave?
5. What did Garrison say would save the oppressed?

Thought Questions
1. Why did Garrison refer to Liberty as a person? What other poem used this technique?
2. How was this poem similar to the one mentioned in Thought Question 1? How was it different? Did giving an idea a personality have the same impact in both poems?
3. Do you believe God designates some men to be greater than others? Why or why not?
4. Did Garrison seem to think the salvation of the oppressed was the responsibility of man or God? Do you agree? Why or why not?
5. In one way or another, everyone is born into a particular situation. Is there something wrong with this, or is it natural? Explain your answer.

"The New Colossus"
Emma Lazarus

Emma Lazarus (1849–1887) grew up in a Jewish family living in New York and Rhode Island, where she privately published her first collection of poetry at the age of seventeen. Lazarus's poetry and essays advocated for immigrants' and women's rights and for Jewish nationalism. She was active in American literary communities, and also traveled to Europe several times during her writing career. Lazarus wrote the following poem, a sonnet, in 1883 as part of an auction to raise funds for the construction of the Statue of Liberty's pedestal. The poem's subject spoke to the refugees who had settled in the United States and rebuked those who preferred to close the nation's gates to the needy. In 1903, a plaque with the text of the poem was mounted inside the completed pedestal.

Not like the brazen giant of Greek fame
With conquering limbs astride from land to land;
Here at our sea-washed, sunset gates shall stand
A mighty woman with a torch, whose flame
Is the imprisoned lightning, and her name
Mother of Exiles. From her beacon-hand
Glows world-wide welcome; her mild eyes command
The air-bridged harbor that twin cities frame,
"Keep, ancient lands, your storied pomp!" cries she
With silent lips. "Give me your tired, your poor,
Your huddled masses yearning to breathe free,
The wretched refuse of your teeming shore,
Send these, the homeless, tempest-tossed to me,
I lift my lamp beside the golden door!"

Review Questions

1. To what do you think the "brazen giant of Greek fame" referred?
2. Look at Act 1, Scene 2 in William Shakespeare's *Julius Caesar*. In Cassius' speech to Brutus, how does the image of a "Colossus" compare to Lazarus' description?
3. What contrast did Lazarus make between the "brazen giant" and the "mighty woman"?
4. Why did Lazarus use the imagery of "imprisoned lightning" for the woman's torch? What connections does this image evoke in your mind?
5. This poem was written in 1883. Do you think the "huddled masses" look different today?

Thought Questions

1. Does world-wide welcome gleam from the United States now? Should it? Explain.
2. Does the "storied pomp" of the ancient lands have a place in American society today?
3. What do you picture when you think of a homeless person? Is your impression positive or negative? What two words come to mind? What experiences have created this impression?
4. Our nation once had an open immigration policy. Many of your relatives probably came from other nations. Would you support an open immigration policy today? Why or why not?
5. What does the Statue of Liberty mean to you? What do you think it meant to the immigrants coming to America?

"The Men of the Maine"
Clinton Scollard

Clinton Scollard (1860–1932) was born in New York and returned there as an adult to become a professor of literature. Also a poet, Scollard published "The Men of the *Maine*" in 1903 in the collection *Ballads of Valor and Victory*. The poem describes an important but controversial moment at the outset of the Spanish-American War. In 1898, there was an explosion on board an American battleship, the U.S.S. *Maine*, which was stationed in a harbor in Cuba. Although the explosion was initially attributed to a mine, the source was not identified. However, at that time, William Randolph Hearst, the owner of the *New York Journal*, was competing with Joseph Pulitzer's *New York World* for dominance in news production. Both men employed questionable tactics geared more toward sensationalism than accuracy. (This style was called "yellow journalism" after "the yellow kid," a character in the Hogan's Alley comic strip—another point of competition between the two papers.) When the *Maine* sank, Hearst's paper blamed the Spanish and raised public outcry for a United States response. Later findings called into question this explanation of the explosion, but in the meantime, the United States was already moving toward war with Spain.

Not in the dire, ensanguined front of war,
Conquered or conqueror,
'Mid the dread battle-peal, did they go down
To the still under-seas, with fair Renown
To weave for them the hero-martyr's crown.
They struck no blow
'Gainst an embattled foe;
With valiant-hearted Saxon hardihood
They stood not as the Essex sailors stood,
So sore bestead in that far Chilian bay;
Yet no less faithful they,
These men who, in a passing of the breath,
Were hurtled upon death.
No warning the salt-scented sea-wind bore,
No presage whispered from the Cuban shore
Of the appalling fate
That in the tropic night-time lay in wait

To bear them whence they shall return no more.
Some lapsed from dreams of home and love's clear star
Into a realm where dreams eternal are;
And some into a world of wave and flame
Wherethrough they came
To living agony that no words can name.
Tears for them all,

And the low-tuned dirge funereal!
Their place is now
With those who wear, green-set about the brow,
The deathless immortelles, —
The heroes torn and scarred
Whose blood made red the barren ocean dells,
Fighting with him the gallant Ranger bore,
Daring to do what none had dared before, —
To wave the New World banner, freedom-starred,
At England's very door!
Yea, with such noble ones their names shall stand
As those who heard the dying Lawrence speak
His burning words upon the Chesapeake,
And grappled in the hopeless hand-to-hand;
With those who fell on Erie and Champlain
Beneath the pouring, pitiless battle-rain:

With such as these, our lost men of the *Maine*!

What though they faced no storm of iron hail
That freedom and the right might still prevail?
The path of duty it was theirs to tread
To death's dark vale through ways of travail led,
And they are ours,—our dead!
If it be true that each loss holds a gain,
It must be ours through saddened eyes to see
From out this tragic holocaust of pain
The whole land bound in closer amity!

Review Questions

1. According to the poem, did the men of the *Maine* have any warning of the attack?
2. List two names by which Scollard called the sailors. What images do these names bring to your mind? Why do you think he chose them?
3. What had "none […] dared [to do] before"?
4. To whom did Scollard compare the men of the *Maine*?
5. What gain resulted from this loss, according to Scollard?

Thought Questions

1. What does it mean to be a hero? Is a hero always active, or is there such a thing as a passive hero (heroic for inaction rather than for actions)?
2. When you hear the word "duty," what does it make you think? Do you have a positive or a negative reaction to the word? Why? Since death was not a choice for the men of the *Maine*, why do you think that Scollard refers to them as treading this path of duty?
3. Is death ever glorious? Think well before you answer, and explain your response.
4. In the opening lines of the poem, Scollard paints a contrast between death in battle and the silent, defenseless death of the men of the *Maine*. Why do you think this contrast is important?
5. Discuss the concept of sensation journalism and its impact on national history. Do you think this poem is similarly sensational because it memorializes the event?

"Panama"
James J. Roche

James Jeffrey Roche (1847–1908) was born in Ireland but grew up in Prince Edward Island, Canada, and then moved to Boston as a young man. In Boston, Roche worked as a journalist, eventually becoming editor of the Boston Pilot, an Irish Nationalist paper. In addition to his political and journalistic writing, Roche was also a poet. The following poem about the Panama Canal was published in *Scribner's Magazine* in 1904. The idea of a canal across the Isthmus of Panama, to replace railroads as the major link between the Atlantic and Pacific Oceans, had been raised in the 1870s by a French company, but the company went bankrupt before the canal was completed. President Theodore Roosevelt re-initiated the project after the Hay-Bunau-Varilla Treaty of 1903 granted the Canal Zone to the United States. The canal, which represented an important engineering feat for the United States, but a source of conflict with Panama, opened in 1914, ten years after Roche's poem was published.

Here the oceans twain have waited
All the ages to be mated, —
Waited long and waited vainly,
Though the script was written plainly:
"This, the portal of the sea,
Open for him who holds the key;
Here the empire of the earth
Waits in patience for its birth."

But the Spanish monarch, dimly
Seeing little, answered grimly:
"North and South the land is Spain's;
As God gave it, it remains.
He who seeks to break the tie,
By mine honor, he shall die!"

So the centuries rolled on,
And the gift of great Colòn,
Like a spendthrift's heritage,
Dwindled slowly, age by age,
Till the flag of red and gold
Fell from hands unnerved and old
And the granite-pillared gate
Waited still the key of fate.

Who shall hold that magic key
But the child of destiny,
In whose veins has mingled long
All the best blood of the strong?
He who takes his place by grace
Of no single tribe or race,
But by many a rich bequest
From the bravest and the best.
Sentinel of duty, here
Must he guard a hemisphere.

Let the old world keep its ways;
Naught to him its blame or praise;
Naught its greed, or hate, or fear;
For all swords be sheathèd here.

Yea, the gateway shall be free
Unto all, from sea to sea;
And no fratricidal slaughter
Shall defile its sacred water;
But—the hand that ope'd the gate shall
    forever hold the key!

POETRY : *"Panama"*

Review Questions
1. Which two oceans were joined by the Panama Canal?
2. To what did the "empire of the earth" refer?
3. Who, according to the poem, initially contested the creation of the canal?
4. Who ultimately was the "child of destiny" who held the magic key?
5. What does the section "He who takes…and the best" mean?

Thought Questions
1. Why was the phrase, "For all swords be sheathed here," important?
2. Roche said Roosevelt was not from one race or culture. Why did Roche make this distinction?
3. Look up the history of "Cristóbal Colón." Why did Roche bring up this particular figure?
4. Explain: "the hand that opened the gate shall forever hold the key." Given that jurisdiction over the Panama Canal became a source of conflict between the United States and Panama, do you agree with the sentiment Roche is expressing?
5. How might Roche's perspective in this poem have been influenced by the fact that the canal was still under construction while he was writing? Who do you think was his audience?

POETRY

Writing Practice

As you have now seen, poetry is a diverse genre with a wide range of styles and devices, but it can also serve a political purpose. The best way to understand the difference between this genre and others you are reading is to practice taking the same material and putting it in different forms, paying attention to what changes you have to make in order to accommodate the demands of each genre.

First, look at the following lines from Miller's "Defense of the Alamo":

> All day — all day and all night; and the morning? so slow,
> Through the battle smoke mantling the Alamo.
> Now silence! Such silence! Two thousand lay dead
> In a crescent outside! And within? Not a breath
> Save the gasp of a woman, with gory gashed head,
> All alone, all alone there, waiting for death;
> And she but a nurse. Yet when shall we know
> Another like this of the Alamo?

Write a few sentences describing the events in prose, as if you were writing a newspaper account. Now compare the two versions. What do you lose when you turn poetry into prose?

Second, look at this passage from Patrick Henry's "Liberty or Death" speech:

> "The battle, sir, is not to the strong alone; it is to the vigilant, the active, the brave. Besides, sir, we have no election. If we were base enough to desire it, it is now too late to retire from the contest. There is no retreat but in submission and slavery! Our chains are forged! Their clanking may be heard on the plains of Boston! The war is inevitable—and let it come! I repeat it, sir, let it come!"

Try your hand at turning this passage into poetry. Begin by identifying the images Henry uses (hint: one is a competition or contest). What key words from the speech would you want to emphasize in a poem? Does the speech have rhythm? How might that rhythm translate into lines of poetry? Experiment with rhyme, lines of varying length, alliteration (words that begin with the same sound), and inverted sentence order. Look back at the poems you have read for other possible techniques.

Can You Write That Down?
ARTICLES and ESSAYS

The written word is a powerful vehicle for persuasion and information. Like speechmaking, writing allows the author to guide the reader toward a certain conclusion. Yet writing, particularly writing articles, also works within a set of conventions, advantages, and disadvantages.

Without the immediacy and physical presence of a speaker, an article must keep the reader's attention through words, so the reader does not set down the unfinished article and move on to something more interesting. The language may be more formal, but the author may provide more description or background information, because readers can skip over passages that don't interest them.

As you read the articles in this section, pay particular attention to the following questions:

- How is the article organized?
- How much background information does the author provide?
- What other works or historical figures does the article reference?
- Who seems to be the intended audience?
- What is the tone of the article?

Each of these articles had a significant impact on the formation of American government. As you read, look for the tools that each writer uses to accomplish his objectives.

In some ways, an article has greater permanence than a speech, because its form does not have to change in order for it to be preserved. However, each article was written in a specific context, and it is important to keep those historical factors in mind when studying the text. Think about how you might have responded differently to these articles if you had read them when they were written. Finally, ask yourself about the risks and benefits of applying historical documents to contemporary situations.

"Apologia" (excerpt)
Christopher Columbus

Cristoforo Colombo (1451–1506), or Christopher Columbus, was a native of Italy who showed early interest in sailing and navigation. After sailing with several expeditions around Europe, he devised a scheme for reaching the Indies by sailing west across the Atlantic Ocean. In 1492, he finally received funding for a voyage from King Ferdinand and Queen Isabella of Spain, and later that year he landed his three ships in the Bahamas, on an island he named "San Salvador." Although Columbus thought he had reached the West Indies, his discovery opened up a new phase in western exploration. Columbus went on to complete three more voyages to the Caribbean before retiring to Spain. "Apologia" is a selection from Columbus's reflections on his journeys, called *El Libro de las Profecías* (*Book of Prophecies*), which he probably composed between 1501 and 1502.

At a very early age I went to sea and have continued navigating until today. The art of sailing is favorable for anyone who wants to pursue knowledge of this world's secrets. I have already been at this business for forty years. I have sailed all the waters which up to now, have been navigated. I have had dealings and conversations with learned people — clergymen and laymen, Latins and Greeks, Jews and Moors, and with many others of other sects. I found our Lord very well disposed toward this desire, and he gave me the spirit for it. He prospered me in seamanship and supplied me with the necessary tools of astronomy, as well as geometry and arithmetic and ingenuity of manual skill to draw spherical maps which show cities, rivers and mountains, islands and ports — everything in its proper place.

I have seen and put into study to look into all the Scriptures, cosmography, histories, chronicles, philosophy, and other arts, which our Lord has opened to understanding, so that it became clear to me that it was feasible to navigate from here to the Indies; and He unlocked within me the determination to execute the idea. And I came to the Sovereigns of Castile and Aragon with this ardor. All those who heard about my enterprise rejected it with laughter, scoffing at me. Neither the sciences which I mentioned, nor the authoritative citations from them, were of any avail. In only the sovereigns remained faith and constancy. Who doubts that this illumination was from the Holy Spirit? I attest that He, with marvelous rays of light, consoled me through the holy and sacred Scriptures, a strong and clear testimony, with forty-four books of the Old Testament, and four Gospels with twenty-three Epistles of those blessed Apostles, encouraging me to proceed, and, continually, without ceasing for a moment, they inflame me with a sense of great urgency.

Our Lord wished to perform the clearest work of providence in this matter—the voyage to the Indies—to console me and others in this matter of the Holy Temple: I have spent seven years in the royal court arguing the case with many persons of such authority and learned in all the arts, and in the end they concluded that all was idle nonsense, and with this they gave up the enterprise; yet the outcome was to be the fulfillment of what our Redeemer Jesus Christ said beforehand through the mouth of the prophets.

And so the prophesy has been made manifest.

Review Questions

1. Why was Columbus in favor of sailing as a profession?
2. What were some of the skills Columbus connected with a career in sailing?
3. To what source did Columbus credit the fact that he had those skills?
4. Which sovereigns did Columbus ask for aid?
5. Where was Columbus' desired destination?

Thought Questions

1. What did Columbus believe about the role of providence in his explorations? How do you think this influenced his view of his trip?
2. Do you believe God points you toward a career? Is it possible to choose the wrong one?
3. Why weren't the sovereigns willing to back Columbus? Would you have been willing?
4. Why was Columbus' accidental discovery so important to history?
5. Do you think Columbus' religious views influenced the foundations of the New World?

"The Federalist: Number 30"

Alexander Hamilton

Alexander Hamilton (1755–1804) was born in the British West Indies and moved to New York at the age of seventeen. During the Revolutionary War, he served as an aide to General Washington, and after the war, Hamilton was one of the leaders in calling for a constitutional convention. As Secretary of the Treasury, Hamilton established a federal monetary system that is still influential. *The Federalist Papers* were a series of eighty-five newspaper articles written by Hamilton, James Madison, and John Jay between October 1787 and May 1788 to support the proposed Constitution. They were published primarily in two New York newspapers, *The New York Packet* and *The Independent Journal*. All of the essays were published under the name "Publius." Number 30, "Concerning the General Power of Taxation," discusses the authority of the federal government to tax citizens. This paper, published December 28, 1787 in the *New York Packet*, is one of fifty-two written by Hamilton.

To the People of the State of New York:

It has been already observed that the federal government ought to possess the power of providing for the support of the national forces; in which proposition was intended to be included the expense of raising troops, of building and equipping fleets, and all other expenses in any wise connected with military arrangements and operations. But these are not the only objects to which the jurisdiction of the Union, in respect to revenue, must necessarily be empowered to extend. It must embrace a provision for the support of the national civil list; for the payment of the national debts contracted, or that may be contracted; and, in general, for all those matters which will call for disbursements out of the national treasury. The conclusion is, that there must be interwoven, in the frame of the government, a general power of taxation, in one shape or another.

Money is, with propriety, considered as the vital principle of the body politic; as that which sustains its life and motion, and enables it to perform its most essential functions. A complete power, therefore, to procure a regular and adequate supply of it, as far as the resources of the community will permit, may be regarded as an indispensable ingredient in every constitution. From a deficiency in this particular, one of two evils must ensue; either the people must be subjected to continual plunder, as a substitute for a more eligible mode of supplying the public wants, or the government must sink into a fatal atrophy, and, in a short course of time, perish.

In the Ottoman or Turkish empire, the sovereign, though in other respects absolute master of the lives and fortunes of his subjects, has no right to impose a new tax. The consequence is that he permits the bashaws or governors of provinces to pillage the people without mercy; and, in turn, squeezes out of them the sums of which he stands in need, to satisfy his own exigencies and those of the state. In America, from a like cause, the government of the Union has gradually dwindled into a state of decay, approaching nearly to annihilation. Who can doubt, that the happiness of the people in both countries would be promoted by competent authorities in the proper hands, to provide the revenues which the necessities of the public might require?

The present Confederation, feeble as it is intended to repose in the United States, an unlimited power of providing for the pecuniary wants of the Union. But proceeding upon an erroneous principle, it has been done in such a manner as entirely to have frustrated the intention. Congress, by the articles which compose that compact (as has already been stated), are authorized to ascertain and call for any sums of money necessary, in their judgment, to the service of the United States; and their requisitions, if conformable to the rule of apportionment, are in every constitutional sense obligatory upon the States. These have no right to question the propriety of the demand; no discretion beyond that of devising the ways and means of furnishing the sums demanded. But though this be strictly and truly the case; though the assumption of such a right would be an infringement of the articles of Union; though it may seldom or never have been avowedly claimed, yet in practice it has been constantly exercised, and would continue to be so, as long as the revenues of the Confederacy should remain dependent on the intermediate agency of its members. What the consequences of this system have been, is within the knowledge of every man the least conversant in our public affairs, and has been amply unfolded in different parts of these inquiries. It is this which has chiefly contributed to reduce us to a situation, which affords ample cause both of mortification to ourselves, and of triumph to our enemies.

What remedy can there be for this situation, but in a change of the system which has produced it in a change of the fallacious and delusive system of quotas and requisitions? What substitute can there be imagined for this *ignis fatuus* in finance, but that of permitting the national government to raise its own revenues by the ordinary methods of taxation authorized in every well-ordered constitution of civil government? Ingenious men may declaim with plausibility on any subject; but no human ingenuity can point out any other expedient to rescue us from the inconveniences and embarrassments naturally resulting from defective supplies of the public treasury.

The more intelligent adversaries of the new Constitution admit the force of this reasoning; but they qualify their admission by a distinction between what they call internal and external taxation. The former they would reserve to the State governments; the latter, which they explain into commercial imposts, or rather duties on imported articles, they declare themselves willing to concede to the federal head. This distinction, however, would violate the maxim of good sense and sound policy, which dictates that every power ought to be in proportion to its object; and would still leave the general government in a kind of tutelage to the State governments, inconsistent with every idea of vigor or efficiency. Who can pretend that commercial imposts are, or would be, alone equal to the present and future exigencies of the Union? Taking into the account the existing debt, foreign and domestic, upon any plan of extinguishment which a man moderately impressed with the importance of public justice and public credit could approve, in addition to the establishments which all parties will acknowledge to be necessary, we could not reasonably flatter ourselves, that this resource alone, upon the most improved scale, would even suffice for its present necessities. Its future necessities admit not of calculation or limitation; and upon the principle, more than once adverted to, the power of making provision for them as they arise ought to be equally unconfined. I believe it may be regarded as a position warranted by the history of mankind, that, in the usual progress of things, the necessities of a nation, in every stage of its existence, will be found at least equal to its resources.

To say that deficiencies may be provided for by requisitions upon the States, is on the one hand to acknowledge that this system cannot be depended upon, and on the other hand to depend upon it for every thing beyond a certain limit. Those who have carefully attended to its vices and deformities as they have been exhibited by experience or delineated in the course of these papers, must feel invincible repugnancy to trusting the national interests in any degree to its operation. Its inevitable tendency, whenever it is brought into activity, must be to enfeeble the Union, and sow the seeds of discord and contention between the federal head and its members, and between the members themselves. Can it be expected that the deficiencies would be better supplied in this mode than the total wants of the Union have heretofore been supplied in the same mode? It ought to be recollected that if less will be required from the States, they will have proportionally less means to answer the demand.

If the opinions of those who contend for the distinction which has been mentioned were to be received as evidence of truth, one would be led to conclude that there was some known point in the economy of national affairs at which it would be safe to stop and to say: Thus far the ends of public happiness will be promoted by supplying the wants of government, and all beyond this is unworthy of our care or anxiety. How is it possible that a government half supplied and always necessitous, can fulfill the purposes of its institution, can provide for the security, advance the prosperity, or support the reputation of the commonwealth? How can it ever possess either energy or stability, dignity or credit, confidence at home or respectability abroad? How can its administration be any thing else than a succession of expedients temporizing, impotent, disgraceful? How will it be able to avoid a frequent sacrifice of its engagements to immediate necessity? How can it undertake or execute any liberal or enlarged plans of public good?

Let us attend to what would be the effects of this situation in the very first war in which we should happen to be engaged. We will presume, for argument's sake, that the revenue arising from the impost duties answers the purposes of a provision for the public debt and of a peace establishment for the Union. Thus circumstanced, a war breaks out. What would be the probable conduct of the government in such an emergency? Taught by experience that proper dependence could not be placed on the success of requisitions, unable by its own authority to lay hold of fresh resources, and urged by considerations of national danger, would it not be driven to the expedient of diverting the funds already appropriated from their proper objects to the defense of the State? It is not easy to see how a step of this kind could be avoided; and if it should be taken, it is evident that it would prove the destruction of public credit at the very moment that it was becoming essential to the public safety. To imagine that at such a crisis credit might be dispensed with, would be the extreme of infatuation. In the modern system of war, nations the most wealthy are obliged to have recourse to large loans. A country so little opulent as ours must feel this necessity in a much stronger degree. But who would lend to a government that prefaced its overtures for borrowing by an act which demonstrated that no reliance could be placed on the steadiness of its measures for paying? The loans it might be able to procure would be as limited in their extent as burdensome in their conditions. They would be made upon the same principles that usurers commonly lend to bankrupt and fraudulent debtors, with a sparing hand and at enormous premiums.

It may perhaps be imagined that, from the scantiness of the resources of the country, the necessity of diverting the established funds in the case supposed would exist, though the national government should possess an unrestrained power of taxation. But two considerations will serve to quiet all apprehension on this head: one is, that we are sure the resources of the community, in their full extent, will be brought into activity for the benefit of the Union; the other is, that whatever deficiencies there may be, can without difficulty be supplied by loans.

The power of creating new funds upon new objects of taxation, by its own authority, would enable the national government to borrow as far as its necessities might require. Foreigners, as well as the citizens of America, could then reasonably repose confidence in its engagements; but to depend upon a government that must itself depend upon thirteen other governments for the means of fulfilling its contracts, when once its situation is clearly understood, would require a degree of credulity not often to be met with in the pecuniary transactions of mankind, and little reconcilable with the usual sharp-sightedness of avarice.

Reflections of this kind may have trifling weight with men who hope to see realized in America the halcyon scenes of the poetic or fabulous age; but to those who believe we are likely to experience a common portion of the vicissitudes and calamities which have fallen to the lot of other nations, they must appear entitled to serious attention. Such men must behold the actual situation of their country with painful solicitude, and deprecate the evils which ambition or revenge might, with too much facility, inflict upon it.

Review Questions

1. What did Hamilton say were the financial needs of the federal government? What were the government's financial responsibilities?
2. What, according to Hamilton, "sustains [the] life and motion" of the body politic?
3. What was the difference between internal and external taxation?
4. Did Hamilton think imposts and duties would raise sufficient revenue to support the Union?
5. How did Hamilton say this means of taxation would affect America's standing in the world?

Thought Questions

1. What is the purpose of taxation? How well do you think it meets this goal?
2. Is taxation necessary for a successful government?
3. Can an under-funded government accomplish anything?
4. Explain, in your own words, Hamilton's concluding thought (last paragraph). Do you agree?
5. What are the responsibilities of the government? What are its rights?

"The Federalist: Number 47"

James Madison

This *Federalist Paper* is attributed to James Madison, the eventual fourth president of the United States. Madison contributed a total of twenty-eight essays to *The Federalist Papers*. Number 47, "The Particular Structure of the New Government and the Distribution of Power Among Its Different Parts," addresses the question of separation of powers. Originally written to refute arguments raised against the Constitution after the Philadelphia Convention of 1787, it was published in the *New York Packet* on February 1, 1788.

To the People of the State of New York:

Having reviewed the general form of the proposed government and the general mass of power allotted to it, I proceed to examine the particular structure of this government, and the distribution of this mass of power among its constituent parts.

One of the principal objections inculcated by the more respectable adversaries to the Constitution, is its supposed violation of the political maxim, that the legislative, executive, and judiciary departments ought to be separate and distinct. In the structure of the federal government, no regard, it is said, seems to have been paid to this essential precaution in favor of liberty. The several departments of power are distributed and blended in such a manner as at once to destroy all symmetry and beauty of form, and to expose some of the essential parts of the edifice to the danger of being crushed by the disproportionate weight of other parts.

No political truth is certainly of greater intrinsic value, or is stamped with the authority of more enlightened patrons of liberty, than that on which the objection is founded. The accumulation of all powers, legislative, executive, and judiciary, in the same hands, whether of one, a few, or many, and whether hereditary, self-appointed, or elective, may justly be pronounced the very definition of tyranny. Were the federal Constitution, therefore, really chargeable with the accumulation of power, or with a mixture of powers, having a dangerous tendency to such an accumulation, no further arguments would be necessary to inspire a universal reprobation of the system. I persuade myself, however, that it will be made apparent to every one, that the charge cannot be supported, and that the maxim on which it relies has been totally misconceived and misapplied. In order to form correct ideas on this important subject, it will be proper to investigate the sense in which the preservation of liberty requires that the three great departments of power should be separate and distinct.

The oracle who is always consulted and cited on this subject is the celebrated Montesquieu. If he be not the author of this invaluable precept in the science of politics, he has the merit at least of displaying and recommending it most effectually to the attention of mankind. Let us endeavor, in the first place, to ascertain his meaning on this point.

The British Constitution was to Montesquieu what Homer has been to the didactic writers on epic poetry. As the latter have considered the work of the immortal bard as the perfect model from which the principles and rules of the epic art were to be drawn, and by which all similar works were to be judged, so this great political critic appears to have viewed the Constitution of England as the standard, or to use his own expression, as the mirror of political liberty; and to have delivered, in the form of elementary truths, the several characteristic principles of that particular system. That we may be sure, then, not to mistake his meaning in this case, let us recur to the source from which the maxim was drawn.

On the slightest view of the British Constitution, we must perceive that the legislative, executive, and judiciary departments are by no means totally separate and distinct from each other. The executive magistrate forms an integral part of the legislative authority. He alone has the prerogative of making treaties with foreign sovereigns, which, when made, have, under certain limitations, the force of legislative acts. All the members of the judiciary department are appointed by him, can be removed by him on the address of the two Houses of Parliament, and form, when he pleases to consult them, one of his constitutional councils. One branch of the legislative department forms also a great constitutional council to the executive chief, as, on another hand, it is the sole depositary of judicial power in cases of impeachment, and is invested with the supreme appellate jurisdiction in all other cases. The judges, again, are so far connected with the legislative department as often to attend and participate in its deliberations, though not admitted to a legislative vote.

From these facts, by which Montesquieu was guided, it may clearly be inferred that, in saying "There can be no liberty where the legislative and executive powers are united in the same person, or body of magistrates," or, "if the power of judging be not separated from the legislative and executive powers," he did not mean that these departments ought to have no partial agency in, or no control over, the acts of each other. His meaning, as his own words import, and still more conclusively as illustrated by the example in his eye, can amount to no more than this, that where the whole power of one department is exercised by the same hands which possess the whole power of another department, the fundamental principles of a free constitution are subverted. This would have been the case in the constitution examined by him, if the king, who is the sole executive magistrate, had possessed also the complete legislative power, or the supreme administration of justice; or if the entire legislative body had possessed the supreme judiciary, or the supreme executive authority. This, however, is not among the vices of that constitution. The magistrate in whom the whole executive power resides cannot of himself make a law, though he can put a negative on every law; nor administer justice in person, though he has the appointment of those who do administer it. The judges can exercise no executive prerogative, though they are shoots from the executive stock; nor any legislative function, though they may be advised with by the legislative councils. The entire legislature can perform no judiciary act, though by the joint act of two of its branches the judges may be removed from their offices, and though one of its branches is possessed of the judicial power in the last resort. The entire legislature, again, can exercise no executive prerogative, though one of its branches constitutes the supreme executive magistracy, and another, on the impeachment of a third, can try and condemn all the subordinate officers in the executive department.

The reasons on which Montesquieu grounds his maxim are a further demonstration of his meaning. "When the legislative and executive powers are united in the same person or body," says he, "there can be no liberty, because apprehensions may arise lest the same monarch or senate should enact tyrannical laws to execute them in a tyrannical manner." Again: "Were the power of judging joined with the legislative, the life and liberty of the subject would be exposed to arbitrary control, for the judge would then be the legislator. Were it joined to the executive power, the judge might behave with all the violence of an oppressor."

Some of these reasons are more fully explained in other passages; but briefly stated as they are here, they sufficiently establish the meaning which we have put on this celebrated maxim of this celebrated author.

If we look into the constitutions of the several States, we find that, notwithstanding the emphatical and, in some instances, the unqualified terms in which this axiom has been laid down, there is not a single instance in which the several departments of power have been kept absolutely separate and distinct. New Hampshire, whose constitution was the last formed, seems to have been fully aware of the impossibility and inexpediency of avoiding any mixture whatever of these departments, and has qualified the doctrine by declaring "that the legislative, executive, and judiciary powers ought to be kept as separate from, and independent of, each other as the nature of a free government will admit; or as is consistent with that chain of connection that binds the whole fabric of the constitution in one indissoluble bond of unity and amity." Her constitution accordingly mixes these departments in several respects. The Senate, which is a branch of the legislative department, is also a judicial tribunal for the trial of impeachments. The president, who is the head of the executive department, is the presiding member also of the Senate; and, besides an equal vote in all cases, has a casting vote in case of a tie. The executive head is himself eventually elective every year by the legislative department, and his council is every year chosen by and from the members of the same department. Several of the officers of state are also appointed by the legislature. And the members of the judiciary department are appointed by the executive department.

The constitution of Massachusetts has observed a sufficient though less pointed caution, in expressing this fundamental article of liberty. It declares "that the legislative department shall never exercise the executive and judicial powers, or either of them; the executive shall never exercise the legislative and judicial powers, or either of them; the judicial shall never exercise the legislative and executive powers, or either of them." This declaration corresponds precisely with the doctrine of Montesquieu, as it has been explained, and is not in a single point violated by the plan of the convention. It goes no farther than to prohibit any one of the entire departments from exercising the powers of another department. In the very Constitution to which it is prefixed, a partial mixture of powers has been admitted. The executive magistrate has a qualified negative on the legislative body, and the Senate, which is a part of the legislature, is a court of impeachment for members both of the executive and judiciary departments. The members of the judiciary department, again, are appointable by the executive department, and removable by the same authority on the address of the two legislative branches. Lastly, a number of the officers of government are annually appointed by the legislative department. As the appointment to offices, particularly executive offices, is in its nature an executive function, the compilers of the Constitution have, in this last point at least, violated the rule established by themselves.

I pass over the constitutions of Rhode Island and Connecticut, because they were formed prior to the Revolution, and even before the principle under examination had become an object of political attention.

The constitution of New York contains no declaration on this subject; but appears very clearly to have been framed with an eye to the danger of improperly blending the different departments. It gives, nevertheless, to the executive magistrate, a partial control over the legislative department; and, what is more, gives a like control to the judiciary department; and even blends the executive and judiciary departments in the exercise of this control. In its council of appointment members of the legislative are associated with the executive authority, in the appointment of officers, both executive and judiciary. And its court for the trial of impeachments and correction of errors is to consist of one branch of the legislature and the principal members of the judiciary department.

The constitution of New Jersey has blended the different powers of government more than any of the preceding. The governor, who is the executive magistrate, is appointed by the legislature; is chancellor and ordinary, or surrogate of the State; is a member of the Supreme Court of Appeals, and president, with a casting vote, of one of the legislative branches. The same legislative branch acts again as executive council of the governor, and with him constitutes the Court of Appeals. The members of the judiciary department are appointed by the legislative department and removable by one branch of it, on the impeachment of the other.

According to the constitution of Pennsylvania, the president, who is the head of the executive department, is annually elected by a vote in which the legislative department predominates. In conjunction with an executive council, he appoints the members of the judiciary department, and forms a court of impeachment for trial of all officers, judiciary as well as executive. The judges of the Supreme Court and justices of the peace seem also to be removable by the legislature; and the executive power of pardoning in certain cases, to be referred to the same department. The members of the executive council are made *ex-officio* justices of peace throughout the State.

In Delaware, the chief executive magistrate is annually elected by the legislative department. The speakers of the two legislative branches are vice-presidents in the executive department. The executive chief, with six others, appointed, three by each of the legislative branches constitutes the Supreme Court of Appeals; he is joined with the legislative department in the appointment of the other judges. Throughout the States, it appears that the members of the legislature may at the same time be justices of the peace; in this State, the members of one branch of it are *ex-officio* justices of the peace; as are also the members of the executive council. The principal officers of the executive department are appointed by the legislative; and one branch of the latter forms a court of impeachments. All officers may be removed on address of the legislature.

Maryland has adopted the maxim in the most unqualified terms; declaring that the legislative, executive, and judicial powers of government ought to be forever separate and distinct from each other. Her constitution, notwithstanding, makes the executive magistrate appointable by the legislative department; and the members of the judiciary by the executive department.

The language of Virginia is still more pointed on this subject. Her constitution declares, "that the legislative, executive, and judiciary departments shall be separate and distinct; so that neither exercise the powers properly belonging to the other; nor shall any person exercise the powers of more than one of them at the same time, except that the justices of county courts shall be eligible to either House of Assembly." Yet we find not only this express exception, with respect to the members of the inferior courts, but that the chief magistrate, with his executive council, are appointable by the legislature; that two members of the latter are triennially displaced at the pleasure of the legislature; and that all the principal offices, both executive and judiciary, are filled by the same department. The executive prerogative of pardon, also, is in one case vested in the legislative department.

The constitution of North Carolina, which declares "that the legislative, executive, and supreme judicial powers of government ought to be forever separate and distinct from each other," refers, at the same time, to the legislative department, the appointment not only of the executive chief, but all the principal officers within both that and the judiciary department.

In South Carolina, the constitution makes the executive magistracy eligible by the legislative department. It gives to the latter, also, the appointment of the members of the judiciary department, including even justices of the peace and sheriffs; and the appointment of officers in the executive department, down to captains in the army and navy of the State.

In the constitution of Georgia, where it is declared "that the legislative, executive, and judiciary departments shall be separate and distinct, so that neither exercise the powers properly belonging to the other," we find that the executive department is to be filled by appointments of the legislature; and the executive prerogative of pardon to be finally exercised by the same authority. Even justices of the peace are to be appointed by the legislature.

In citing these cases, in which the legislative, executive, and judiciary departments have not been kept totally separate and distinct, I wish not to be regarded as an advocate for the particular organizations of the several State governments. I am fully aware that among the many excellent principles which they exemplify, they carry strong marks of the haste, and still stronger of the inexperience, under which they were framed. It is but too obvious that in some instances the fundamental principle under consideration has been violated by too great a mixture, and even an actual consolidation, of the different powers; and that in no instance has a competent provision been made for maintaining in practice the separation delineated on paper. What I have wished to evince is, that the charge brought against the proposed Constitution, of violating the sacred maxim of free government, is warranted neither by the real meaning annexed to that maxim by its author, nor by the sense in which it has hitherto been understood in America. This interesting subject will be resumed in the ensuing paper.

Review Questions

1. What was one of the main arguments against the Constitution?
2. What was the "political truth" on which this opposition was founded? Who was the founder?
3. Did Madison reject this political doctrine?
4. How did Madison argue against complete separation between the branches of government?
5. What disclaimer did Madison make after using state governments as evidence?

Thought Questions

1. Madison used past precedent and current usage to make his argument. Would these have been sufficient to convince you? What other arguments could he have used?
2. Montesquieu is quoted as saying, "Where the whole power of one department is exercised by the same hands which possess the whole power of another department, the fundamental principles of a free constitution are subverted." Explain. Do you agree? Why or why not?
3. How does separation of power protect the government from tyranny? Is it always effective?
4. How does tyranny happen? What factors allow it to continue?
5. Can you find any logical or practical flaws in Madison's argument? What are they?

"Farewell Address"
George Washington

Washington served two terms as president, from 1789 to 1797, before he voluntarily retired from the position. As president, Washington had advocated for a neutral foreign policy and unified domestic politics, but by his second term, political parties were already beginning to emerge, and international conflicts following the French Revolution (1789–1799) were challenging the United States' neutrality. Leaving politics behind, Washington retired to his home at Mount Vernon, Virginia. In his farewell address, which was printed in the *American Daily Advertiser* on September 19, 1796, Washington charged the leaders of the country to seek a new administrator who would love his country, honor God, and always seek the advancement of the people of the United States.

Friends and Citizens:

The period for a new election of a citizen to administer the executive government of the United States being not far distant, and the time actually arrived when your thoughts must be employed in designating the person who is to be clothed with that important trust, it appears to me proper, especially as it may conduce to a more distinct expression of the public voice, that I should now apprise you of the resolution I have formed, to decline being considered among the number of those out of whom a choice is to be made.

I beg you, at the same time, to do me the justice to be assured that this resolution has not been taken without a strict regard to all the considerations appertaining to the relation which binds a dutiful citizen to his country; and that in withdrawing the tender of service, which silence in my situation might imply, I am influenced by no diminution of zeal for your future interest, no deficiency of grateful respect for your past kindness, but am supported by a full conviction that the step is compatible with both.

The acceptance of, and continuance hitherto in, the office to which your suffrages have twice called me have been a uniform sacrifice of inclination to the opinion of duty and to a deference for what appeared to be your desire. I constantly hoped that it would have been much earlier in my power, consistently with motives which I was not at liberty to disregard, to return to that retirement from which I had been reluctantly drawn. The strength of my inclination to do this, previous to the last election, had even led to the preparation of an address to declare it to you; but mature reflection on the then perplexed and critical posture of our affairs with foreign nations, and the unanimous advice of persons entitled to my confidence, impelled me to abandon the idea.

I rejoice that the state of your concerns, external as well as internal, no longer renders the pursuit of inclination incompatible with the sentiment of duty or propriety, and am persuaded, whatever partiality may be retained for my services, that, in the present circumstances of our country, you will not disapprove my determination to retire.

The impressions with which I first undertook the arduous trust were explained on the proper occasion. In the discharge of this trust, I will only say that I have, with good intentions, contributed towards the organization and administration of the government the best exertions of which a very fallible judgment was capable. Not unconscious in the outset of the inferiority of my qualifications, experience in my own eyes, perhaps still more in the eyes of others, has strengthened the motives to diffidence of myself; and every day the increasing weight of years admonishes me more and more that the shade of retirement is as necessary to me as it will be welcome. Satisfied that if any circumstances have given peculiar value to my services, they were temporary, I have the consolation to believe that, while choice and prudence invite me to quit the political scene, patriotism does not forbid it.

In looking forward to the moment which is intended to terminate the career of my public life, my feelings do not permit me to suspend the deep acknowledgment of that debt of gratitude which I owe to my beloved country for the many honors it has conferred upon me; still more for the steadfast confidence with which it has supported me; and for the opportunities I have thence enjoyed of manifesting my inviolable attachment, by services faithful and persevering, though in usefulness unequal to my zeal. If benefits have resulted to our country from these services, let it always be remembered to your praise, and as an instructive example in our annals, that under circumstances in which the passions, agitated in every direction, were liable to mislead, amidst appearances sometimes dubious, vicissitudes of fortune often discouraging, in situations in which not infrequently want of success has countenanced the spirit of criticism, the constancy of your support was the essential prop of the efforts, and a guarantee of the plans by which they were effected. Profoundly penetrated with this idea, I shall carry it with me to my grave, as a strong incitement to unceasing vows that Heaven may continue to you the choicest tokens of its beneficence; that your union and brotherly affection may be perpetual; that the free Constitution, which is the work of your hands, may be sacredly maintained; that its administration in every department may be stamped with wisdom and virtue; that, in fine, the happiness of the people of these States, under the auspices of liberty, may be made complete by so careful a preservation and so prudent a use of this blessing as will acquire to them the glory of recommending it to the applause, the affection, and adoption of every nation which is yet a stranger to it.

Here, perhaps, I ought to stop. But a solicitude for your welfare, which cannot end but with my life, and the apprehension of danger, natural to that solicitude, urge me, on an occasion like the present, to offer to your solemn contemplation, and to recommend to your frequent review, some sentiments which are the result of much reflection, of no inconsiderable observation, and which appear to me all-important to the permanency of your felicity as a people. These will be offered to you with the more freedom, as you can only see in them the disinterested warnings of a parting friend, who can possibly have no personal motive to bias his counsel. Nor can I forget, as an encouragement to it, your indulgent reception of my sentiments on a former and not dissimilar occasion.

Interwoven as is the love of liberty with every ligament of your hearts, no recommendation of mine is necessary to fortify or confirm the attachment.

The unity of government which constitutes you one people is also now dear to you. It is justly so, for it is a main pillar in the edifice of your real independence, the support of your tranquility at home, your peace abroad; of your safety; of your prosperity; of that very liberty which you so highly prize. But as it is easy to foresee that, from different causes and from different quarters, much pains will be taken, many artifices employed to weaken in your minds the conviction of this truth; as this is the point in your political fortress against which the batteries of internal and external enemies will be most constantly and actively (though often covertly and insidiously) directed, it is of infinite moment that you should properly estimate the immense value of your national union to your collective and individual happiness; that you should cherish a cordial, habitual, and immovable attachment to it; accustoming yourselves to think and speak of it as of the palladium of your political safety and prosperity; watching for its preservation with jealous anxiety; discountenancing whatever may suggest even a suspicion that it can in any event be abandoned; and indignantly frowning upon the first dawning of every attempt to alienate any portion of our country from the rest, or to enfeeble the sacred ties which now link together the various parts.

For this you have every inducement of sympathy and interest. Citizens, by birth or choice, of a common country, that country has a right to concentrate your affections. The name of American, which belongs to you in your national capacity, must always exalt the just pride of patriotism more than any appellation derived from local discriminations. With slight shades of difference, you have the same religion, manners, habits, and political principles. You have in a common cause fought and triumphed together; the independence and liberty you possess are the work of joint counsels, and joint efforts of common dangers, sufferings, and successes.

But these considerations, however powerfully they address themselves to your sensibility, are greatly outweighed by those which apply more immediately to your interest. Here every portion of our country finds the most commanding motives for carefully guarding and preserving the union of the whole.

The North, in an unrestrained intercourse with the South, protected by the equal laws of a common government, finds in the productions of the latter great additional resources of maritime and commercial enterprise and precious materials of manufacturing industry. The South, in the same intercourse, benefiting by the agency of the North, sees its agriculture grow and its commerce expand. Turning partly into its own channels the seamen of the North, it finds its particular navigation invigorated; and, while it contributes, in different ways, to nourish and increase the general mass of the national navigation, it looks forward to the protection of a maritime strength, to which itself is unequally adapted. The East, in a like intercourse with the West, already finds, and in the progressive improvement of interior communications by land and water, will more and more find a valuable vent for the commodities which it brings from abroad, or manufactures at home. The West derives from the East supplies requisite to its growth and comfort, and, what is perhaps of still greater consequence, it must of necessity owe the secure enjoyment of indispensable outlets for its own productions to the weight, influence, and the future maritime strength of the Atlantic side of the Union, directed by an indissoluble community of interest as one nation. Any other tenure by which the West can hold this essential advantage, whether derived from its own separate strength, or from an apostate and unnatural connection with any foreign power, must be intrinsically precarious.

While, then, every part of our country thus feels an immediate and particular interest in union, all the parts combined cannot fail to find in the united mass of means and efforts greater strength, greater resource, proportionally greater security from external danger, a less frequent interruption of their peace by foreign nations; and, what is of inestimable value, they must derive from union an exemption from those broils and wars between themselves, which so frequently afflict neighboring countries not tied together by the same governments, which their own rival ships alone would be sufficient to produce, but which opposite foreign alliances, attachments, and intrigues would stimulate and embitter. Hence, likewise, they will avoid the necessity of those overgrown military establishments which, under any form of government, are inauspicious to liberty, and which are to be regarded as particularly hostile to republican liberty. In this sense it is that your union ought to be considered as a main prop of your liberty, and that the love of the one ought to endear to you the preservation of the other.

These considerations speak a persuasive language to every reflecting and virtuous mind, and exhibit the continuance of the Union as a primary object of patriotic desire. Is there a doubt whether a common government can embrace so large a sphere? Let experience solve it. To listen to mere speculation in such a case were criminal. We are authorized to hope that a proper organization of the whole with the auxiliary agency of governments for the respective subdivisions, will afford a happy issue to the experiment. It is well worth a fair and full experiment. With such powerful and obvious motives to union, affecting all parts of our country, while experience shall not have demonstrated its impracticability, there will always be reason to distrust the patriotism of those who in any quarter may endeavor to weaken its bands.

In contemplating the causes which may disturb our Union, it occurs as matter of serious concern that any ground should have been furnished for characterizing parties by geographical discriminations, Northern and Southern, Atlantic and Western; whence designing men may endeavor to excite a belief that there is a real difference of local interests and views. One of the expedients of party to acquire influence within particular districts is to misrepresent the opinions and aims of other districts. You cannot shield yourselves too much against the jealousies and heartburnings which spring from these misrepresentations; they tend to render alien to each other those who ought to be bound together by fraternal affection. The inhabitants of our Western country have lately had a useful lesson on this head; they have seen, in the negotiation by the Executive, and in the unanimous ratification by the Senate, of the treaty with Spain, and in the universal satisfaction at that event, throughout the United States, a decisive proof how unfounded were the suspicions propagated among them of a policy in the General Government and in the Atlantic States unfriendly to their interests in regard to the Mississippi; they have been witnesses to the formation of two treaties, that with Great Britain, and that with Spain, which secure to them everything they could desire, in respect to our foreign relations, towards confirming their prosperity. Will it not be their wisdom to rely for the preservation of these advantages on the Union by which they were procured? Will they not henceforth be deaf to those advisers, if such there are, who would sever them from their brethren and connect them with aliens?

To the efficacy and permanency of your Union, a government for the whole is indispensable.

No alliance, however strict, between the parts can be an adequate substitute; they must inevitably experience the infractions and interruptions which all alliances in all times have experienced. Sensible of this momentous truth, you have improved upon your first essay, by the adoption of a constitution of government better calculated than your former for an intimate union, and for the efficacious management of your common concerns. This government, the offspring of our own choice, uninfluenced and unawed, adopted upon full investigation and mature deliberation, completely free in its principles, in the distribution of its powers, uniting security with energy, and containing within itself a provision for its own amendment, has a just claim to your confidence and your support. Respect for its authority, compliance with its laws, acquiescence in its measures, are duties enjoined by the fundamental maxims of true liberty. The basis of our political systems is the right of the people to make and to alter their constitutions of government. But the Constitution which at any time exists, till changed by an explicit and authentic act of the whole people, is sacredly obligatory upon all. The very idea of the power and the right of the people to establish government presupposes the duty of every individual to obey the established government.

All obstructions to the execution of the laws, all combinations and associations, under whatever plausible character, with the real design to direct, control, counteract, or awe the regular deliberation and action of the constituted authorities, are destructive of this fundamental principle, and of fatal tendency. They serve to organize faction, to give it an artificial and extraordinary force; to put, in the place of the delegated will of the nation the will of a party, often a small but artful and enterprising minority of the community; and, according to the alternate triumphs of different parties, to make the public administration the mirror of the ill-concerted and incongruous projects of faction, rather than the organ of consistent and wholesome plans digested by common counsels and modified by mutual interests.

However combinations or associations of the above description may now and then answer popular ends, they are likely, in the course of time and things, to become potent engines, by which cunning, ambitious, and unprincipled men will be enabled to subvert the power of the people and to usurp for themselves the reins of government, destroying afterwards the very engines which have lifted them to unjust dominion.

Towards the preservation of your government, and the permanency of your present happy state, it is requisite, not only that you steadily discountenance irregular oppositions to its acknowledged authority, but also that you resist with care the spirit of innovation upon its principles, however specious the pretexts. One method of assault may be to effect, in the forms of the Constitution, alterations which will impair the energy of the system, and thus to undermine what cannot be directly overthrown. In all the changes to which you may be invited, remember that time and habit are at least as necessary to fix the true character of governments as of other human institutions; that experience is the surest standard by which to test the real tendency of the existing constitution of a country; that facility in changes, upon the credit of mere hypothesis and opinion, exposes to perpetual change, from the endless variety of hypothesis and opinion; and remember, especially, that for the efficient management of your common interests, in a country so extensive as ours, a government of as much vigor as is consistent with the perfect security of liberty is indispensable. Liberty itself will find in such a government, with powers properly distributed and adjusted, its surest guardian. It is, indeed, little else than a name, where the government is too feeble to withstand the enterprises of faction, to confine each member of the society within the limits prescribed by the laws, and to maintain all in the secure and tranquil enjoyment of the rights of person and property.

I have already intimated to you the danger of parties in the State, with particular reference to the founding of them on geographical discriminations. Let me now take a more comprehensive view, and warn you in the most solemn manner against the baneful effects of the spirit of party generally.

This spirit, unfortunately, is inseparable from our nature, having its root in the strongest passions of the human mind. It exists under different shapes in all governments, more or less stifled, controlled, or repressed; but, in those of the popular form, it is seen in its greatest rankness, and is truly their worst enemy.

The alternate domination of one faction over another, sharpened by the spirit of revenge, natural to party dissension, which in different ages and countries has perpetrated the most horrid enormities, is itself a frightful despotism. But this leads at length to a more formal and permanent despotism. The disorders and miseries which result gradually incline the minds of men to seek security and repose in the absolute power of an individual; and sooner or later the chief of some prevailing faction, more able or more fortunate than his competitors, turns this disposition to the purposes of his own elevation, on the ruins of public liberty.

Without looking forward to an extremity of this kind (which nevertheless ought not to be entirely out of sight), the common and continual mischiefs of the spirit of party are sufficient to make it the interest and duty of a wise people to discourage and restrain it.

It serves always to distract the public councils and enfeeble the public administration. It agitates the community with ill-founded jealousies and false alarms, kindles the animosity of one part against another, foments occasionally riot and insurrection. It opens the door to foreign influence and corruption, which finds a facilitated access to the government itself through the channels of party passions. Thus the policy and the will of one country are subjected to the policy and will of another.

There is an opinion that parties in free countries are useful checks upon the administration of the government and serve to keep alive the spirit of liberty. This within certain limits is probably true; and in governments of a monarchical cast, patriotism may look with indulgence, if not with favor, upon the spirit of party. But in those of the popular character, in governments purely elective, it is a spirit not to be encouraged. From their natural tendency, it is certain there will always be enough of that spirit for every salutary purpose. And there being constant danger of excess, the effort ought to be by force of public opinion, to mitigate and assuage it. A fire not to be quenched, it demands a uniform vigilance to prevent its bursting into a flame, lest, instead of warming, it should consume.

It is important, likewise, that the habits of thinking in a free country should inspire caution in those entrusted with its administration, to confine themselves within their respective constitutional spheres, avoiding in the exercise of the powers of one department to encroach upon another. The spirit of encroachment tends to consolidate the powers of all the departments in one, and thus to create, whatever the form of government, a real despotism. A just estimate of that love of power, and proneness to abuse it, which predominates in the human heart, is sufficient to satisfy us of the truth of this position. The necessity of reciprocal checks in the exercise of political power, by dividing and distributing it into different depositaries, and constituting each the guardian of the public weal against invasions by the others, has been evinced by experiments ancient and modern; some of them in our country and under our own eyes. To preserve them must be as necessary as to institute them. If, in the opinion of the people, the distribution or modification of the constitutional powers be in any particular wrong, let it be corrected by an amendment in the way which the Constitution designates. But let there be no change by usurpation; for though this, in one instance, may be the instrument of good, it is the customary weapon by which free governments are destroyed. The precedent must always greatly overbalance in permanent evil any partial or transient benefit, which the use can at any time yield.

Of all the dispositions and habits which lead to political prosperity, religion and morality are indispensable supports. In vain would that man claim the tribute of patriotism, who should labor to subvert these great pillars of human happiness, these firmest props of the duties of men and citizens. The mere politician, equally with the pious man, ought to respect and to cherish them. A volume could not trace all their connections with private and public felicity. Let it simply be asked: Where is the security for property, for reputation, for life, if the sense of religious obligation desert the oaths which are the instruments of investigation in courts of justice? And let us with caution indulge the supposition that morality can be maintained without religion. Whatever may be conceded to the influence of refined education on minds of peculiar structure, reason and experience both forbid us to expect that national morality can prevail in exclusion of religious principle.

It is substantially true that virtue or morality is a necessary spring of popular government. The rule, indeed, extends with more or less force to every species of free government. Who that is a sincere friend to it can look with indifference upon attempts to shake the foundation of the fabric?

Promote then, as an object of primary importance, institutions for the general diffusion of knowledge. In proportion as the structure of a government gives force to public opinion, it is essential that public opinion should be enlightened.

As a very important source of strength and security, cherish public credit. One method of preserving it is to use it as sparingly as possible, avoiding occasions of expense by cultivating peace, but remembering also that timely disbursements to prepare for danger frequently prevent much greater disbursements to repel it, avoiding likewise the accumulation of debt, not only by shunning occasions of expense, but by vigorous exertion in time of peace to discharge the debts which unavoidable wars may have occasioned, not ungenerously throwing upon posterity the burden which we ourselves ought to bear. The execution of these maxims belongs to your representatives, but it is necessary that public opinion should co-operate. To facilitate to them the performance of their duty, it is essential that you should practically bear in mind that towards the payment of debts there must be revenue; that to have revenue there must be taxes; that no taxes can be devised which are not more or less inconvenient and unpleasant; that the intrinsic embarrassment, inseparable from the selection of the proper objects (which is always a choice of difficulties), ought to be a decisive motive for a candid construction of the conduct of the government in making it, and for a spirit of acquiescence in the measures for obtaining revenue, which the public exigencies may at any time dictate.

Observe good faith and justice towards all nations; cultivate peace and harmony with all. Religion and morality enjoin this conduct; and can it be, that good policy does not equally enjoin it? It will be worthy of a free, enlightened, and at no distant period, a great nation, to give to mankind the magnanimous and too novel example of a people always guided by an exalted justice and benevolence. Who can doubt that, in the course of time and things, the fruits of such a plan would richly repay any temporary advantages which might be lost by a steady adherence to it? Can it be that Providence has not connected the permanent felicity of a nation with its virtue? The experiment, at least, is recommended by every sentiment which ennobles human nature. Alas! is it rendered impossible by its vices?

In the execution of such a plan, nothing is more essential than that permanent, inveterate antipathies against particular nations, and passionate attachments for others, should be excluded; and that, in place of them, just and amicable feelings towards all should be cultivated. The nation which indulges towards another a habitual hatred or a habitual fondness is in some degree a slave. It is a slave to its animosity or to its affection, either of which is sufficient to lead it astray from its duty and its interest. Antipathy in one nation against another disposes each more readily to offer insult and injury, to lay hold of slight causes of umbrage, and to be haughty and intractable, when accidental or trifling occasions of dispute occur. Hence, frequent collisions, obstinate, envenomed, and bloody contests. The nation, prompted by ill-will and resentment, sometimes impels to war the government, contrary to the best calculations of policy. The government sometimes participates in the national propensity, and adopts through passion what reason would reject; at other times it makes the animosity of the nation subservient to projects of hostility instigated by pride, ambition, and other sinister and pernicious motives. The peace often, sometimes perhaps the liberty, of nations, has been the victim.

So likewise, a passionate attachment of one nation for another produces a variety of evils. Sympathy for the favorite nation, facilitating the illusion of an imaginary common interest in cases where no real common interest exists, and infusing into one the enmities of the other, betrays the former into a participation in the quarrels and wars of the latter without adequate inducement or justification. It leads also to concessions to the favorite nation of privileges denied to others which is apt doubly to injure the nation making the concessions; by unnecessarily parting with what ought to have been retained, and by exciting jealousy, ill-will, and a disposition to retaliate, in the parties from whom equal privileges are withheld. And it gives to ambitious, corrupted, or deluded citizens (who devote themselves to the favorite nation), facility to betray or sacrifice the interests of their own country, without odium, sometimes even with popularity; gilding, with the appearances of a virtuous sense of obligation, a commendable deference for public opinion, or a laudable zeal for public good, the base or foolish compliances of ambition, corruption, or infatuation.

As avenues to foreign influence in innumerable ways, such attachments are particularly alarming to the truly enlightened and independent patriot. How many opportunities do they afford to tamper with domestic factions, to practice the arts of seduction, to mislead public opinion, to influence or awe the public councils? Such an attachment of a small or weak towards a great and powerful nation dooms the former to be the satellite of the latter.

Against the insidious wiles of foreign influence (I conjure you to believe me, fellow-citizens) the jealousy of a free people ought to be constantly awake, since history and experience prove that foreign influence is one of the most baneful foes of republican government. But that jealousy to be useful must be impartial; else it becomes the instrument of the very influence to be avoided, instead of a defense against it. Excessive partiality for one foreign nation and excessive dislike of another cause those whom they actuate to see danger only on one side, and serve to veil and even second the arts of influence on the other. Real patriots who may resist the intrigues of the favorite are liable to become suspected and odious, while its tools and dupes usurp the applause and confidence of the people, to surrender their interests.

The great rule of conduct for us in regard to foreign nations is in extending our commercial relations, to have with them as little political connection as possible. So far as we have already formed engagements, let them be fulfilled with perfect good faith. Here let us stop. Europe has a set of primary interests which to us have none or a very remote relation. Hence she must be engaged in frequent controversies, the causes of which are essentially foreign to our concerns. Hence, therefore, it must be unwise in us to implicate ourselves by artificial ties in the ordinary vicissitudes of her politics, or the ordinary combinations and collisions of her friendships or enmities.

Our detached and distant situation invites and enables us to pursue a different course. If we remain one people under an efficient government, the period is not far off when we may defy material injury from external annoyance; when we may take such an attitude as will cause the neutrality we may at any time resolve upon to be scrupulously respected; when belligerent nations, under the impossibility of making acquisitions upon us, will not lightly hazard the giving us provocation; when we may choose peace or war, as our interest, guided by justice, shall counsel.

Why forego the advantages of so peculiar a situation? Why quit our own to stand upon foreign ground? Why, by interweaving our destiny with that of any part of Europe, entangle our peace and prosperity in the toils of European ambition, rivalship, interest, humor or caprice?

It is our true policy to steer clear of permanent alliances with any portion of the foreign world; so far, I mean, as we are now at liberty to do it; for let me not be understood as capable of patronizing infidelity to existing engagements. I hold the maxim no less applicable to public than to private affairs, that honesty is always the best policy. I repeat it, therefore, let those engagements be observed in their genuine sense. But, in my opinion, it is unnecessary and would be unwise to extend them.

Taking care always to keep ourselves by suitable establishments on a respectable defensive posture, we may safely trust to temporary alliances for extraordinary emergencies.

Harmony, liberal intercourse with all nations, are recommended by policy, humanity, and interest. But even our commercial policy should hold an equal and impartial hand; neither seeking nor granting exclusive favors or preferences; consulting the natural course of things; diffusing and diversifying by gentle means the streams of commerce, but forcing nothing; establishing (with powers so disposed, in order to give trade a stable course, to define the rights of our merchants, and to enable the government to support them) conventional rules of intercourse, the best that present circumstances and mutual opinion will permit, but temporary, and liable to be from time to time abandoned or varied, as experience and circumstances shall dictate; constantly keeping in view that it is folly in one nation to look for disinterested favors from another; that it must pay with a portion of its independence for whatever it may accept under that character; that, by such acceptance, it may place itself in the condition of having given equivalents for nominal favors, and yet of being reproached with ingratitude for not giving more. There can be no greater error than to expect or calculate upon real favors from nation to nation. It is an illusion, which experience must cure, which a just pride ought to discard.

In offering to you, my countrymen, these counsels of an old and affectionate friend, I dare not hope they will make the strong and lasting impression I could wish; that they will control the usual current of the passions, or prevent our nation from running the course which has hitherto marked the destiny of nations. But, if I may even flatter myself that they may be productive of some partial benefit, some occasional good; that they may now and then recur to moderate the fury of party spirit, to warn against the mischiefs of foreign intrigue, to guard against the impostures of pretended patriotism; this hope will be a full recompense for the solicitude for your welfare, by which they have been dictated.

How far in the discharge of my official duties I have been guided by the principles which have been delineated, the public records and other evidences of my conduct must witness to you and to the world. To myself, the assurance of my own conscience is, that I have at least believed myself to be guided by them.

In relation to the still subsisting war in Europe, my proclamation of the twenty-second of April, 1793, is the index of my plan. Sanctioned by your approving voice, and by that of your representatives in both houses of Congress, the spirit of that measure has continually governed me, uninfluenced by any attempts to deter or divert me from it.

After deliberate examination, with the aid of the best lights I could obtain, I was well satisfied that our country, under all the circumstances of the case, had a right to take, and was bound in duty and interest to take, a neutral position. Having taken it, I determined, as far as should depend upon me, to maintain it, with moderation, perseverance, and firmness.

The considerations which respect the right to hold this conduct, it is not necessary on this occasion to detail. I will only observe that, according to my understanding of the matter, that right, so far from being denied by any of the belligerent powers, has been virtually admitted by all.

The duty of holding a neutral conduct may be inferred, without anything more, from the obligation which justice and humanity impose on every nation, in cases in which it is free to act, to maintain inviolate the relations of peace and amity towards other nations.

The inducements of interest for observing that conduct will best be referred to your own reflections and experience. With me a predominant motive has been to endeavor to gain time to our country to settle and mature its yet recent institutions, and to progress without interruption to that degree of strength and consistency which is necessary to give it, humanly speaking, the command of its own fortunes.

Though, in reviewing the incidents of my administration, I am unconscious of intentional error, I am nevertheless too sensible of my defects not to think it probable that I may have committed many errors. Whatever they may be, I fervently beseech the Almighty to avert or mitigate the evils to which they may tend. I shall also carry with me the hope that my country will never cease to view them with indulgence; and that, after forty-five years of my life dedicated to its service with an upright zeal, the faults of incompetent abilities will be consigned to oblivion, as myself must soon be to the mansions of rest.

Relying on its kindness in this as in other things, and actuated by that fervent love towards it, which is so natural to a man who views in it the native soil of himself and his progenitors for several generations, I anticipate with pleasing expectation that retreat in which I promise myself to realize, without alloy, the sweet enjoyment of partaking, in the midst of my fellow-citizens, the benign influence of good laws under a free government, the ever-favorite object of my heart, and the happy reward, as I trust, of our mutual cares, labors, and dangers.

WASHINGTON AT MOUNT VERNON 1797

Review Questions

1. Washington indicated that he took the presidency from a sense of duty, not of desire. How many times have you been faced with a choice between what you wanted to do and what you knew you should do? What choice did you make?
2. Why had Washington not stepped down at the last election?
3. What was the "debt of gratitude" Washington owed to his country?
4. What did Washington say was "a main pillar in the edifice of your real independence, the support of your tranquility at home, your peace abroad; of your safety; of your prosperity; of that very liberty which you so highly prize"?
5. According to Washington, how were the East and West connected? The North and South? Why were these connections important?

Thought Questions

1. What did Washington use to create an image of similarity between Americans? Do these characteristics separate Americans from other peoples, in your opinion?
2. "The name of American, which belongs to you in your national capacity, must always exalt the just pride of patriotism more than any appellation [name] derived from local discriminations." Do you agree? Why or why not? Is there any danger in this philosophy?
3. How do you think Washington would have responded to the Civil War?
4. How did Washington view the Constitution in relation to the people? Do you agree?
5. Washington spoke firmly against favoritism between nations. How does this compare to your personal ideas about alliances? Do you think Washington's advice is reasonable? Logical?

"The American Language" (preface)
H. L. Mencken

Henry Louis Mencken (1880–1956) spent most of his life in Maryland working as a journalist and literary critic. Mencken wrote for several Baltimore newspapers and also edited or co-edited literary journals like the *Smart Set* and *American Mercury*. He was a provocative writer about a wide range of cultural topics, and he eventually became one of the foremost experts on American English. In 1919, he first published *The American Language*, a collection of American idioms and terms; the book was subsequently reissued multiple times with updates and additions. The preface details Mencken's reasons for taking on this daunting project and provides background information about his quest to understand the role of language in culture.

The aim of this book is best exhibited by describing its origin. I am, and have been since early manhood, an editor of newspapers and books, and a critic of the last named. These occupations have forced me into a pretty wide familiarity with current literature, both periodical and within covers, and in particular into familiarity with the current literature of England and America. It was part of my daily work, for a number of years, to read the principal English newspapers and reviews; it has been part of my work, all the time, to read the more important English novels, essays, poetry and criticism. An American born and bred, I early noted, as everyone else in like case must note, certain salient differences between the English of England and the English of America as practically spoken and written—differences in vocabulary, in syntax, in the shade and habits of idiom, and even, coming to the common speech, in grammar. And I noted too, of course, partly during visits to England but more largely by a somewhat wide and intimate intercourse with English people in the United States, the obvious differences between English and American pronunciation and intonation.

Greatly interested in these differences—some of them so great that they led me to seek exchanges of light with Englishmen—I looked for some work that would describe and account for them with a show of completeness, and perhaps depict the process of their origin. I soon found that no such work existed, in either England or America—that the whole literature of the subject was astonishingly meagre and unsatisfactory. There were several dictionaries of Americanisms, true enough, but only one of them made any pretension to scientific method, and even that one was incomplete. The solitary general treatise on the American dialect, the work of a man foreign to both England and America in race and education, was more than 40 years old, and full of palpable errors. For the rest, there was only a fugitive and inconsequential literature—an almost useless mass of notes and essays, chiefly by the minor sort of pedagogues, seldom illuminating, save in small details, and often incredibly ignorant and inaccurate. On the large and important subject of American pronunciation, for example, I could find nothing save a few casual essays. On American spelling, with its wide and constantly visible divergences from English usages, there was little more. On American grammar there was nothing whatsoever. Worse, an important part of the poor literature that I unearthed was devoted to absurd efforts to prove that no such thing as an American variety of English existed—that the differences I constantly encountered in English and that my English friends encountered in American were chiefly imaginary, and to be explained away by denying them.

Still interested in the subject, and despairing of getting any illumination from such theoretical masters of it, I began a collection of materials for my own information and amusement, and gradually it took on a rather formidable bulk. My employment being made known by various articles in the newspapers and magazines, I began also to receive contributions from other persons of the same taste, both English and American, and gradually my collection fell into a certain order, and I saw the workings of general laws in what, at first, had appeared to be mere chaos. The present book then began to take form—its preparation a sort of recreation from other and far different labor. It is anything but an exhaustive treatise upon the subject; it is not even an exhaustive examination of the materials. All it pretends to do is to articulate some of those materials—to get some approach to order and coherence into them, and so pave the way for a better work by some more competent man. That work calls for the equipment of a first-rate philologist, which I am surely not. All I have done here is to stake out the field, sometimes borrowing suggestions from other inquirers and sometimes, as in the case of popular American grammar, attempting to run the lines myself.

That it should be regarded as an anti-social act to examine and exhibit the constantly growing differences between English and American, as certain American pedants argue sharply—this doctrine is quite beyond my understanding. All it indicates, stripped of sophistry, is a somewhat childish effort to gain the approval of Englishmen—a belated efflorescence of the colonial spirit, often commingled with fashionable aspiration. The plain fact is that the English themselves are not deceived, nor do they grant the approval so ardently sought for. On the contrary, they are keenly aware of the differences between the two dialects, and often discuss them, as the following pages show. Perhaps one dialect, in the long run, will defeat and absorb the other; if the two nations continue to be partners in great adventures it may very well happen. But even in that case, something may be accomplished by examining the differences which exist today. In some ways, as in intonation, English usage is plainly better than American. In others, as in spelling, American usage is as plainly better than English. But in order to develop usages that the people of both nations will accept, it is necessary to study the differences now visible. This study thus shows a certain utility. But its chief excuse is its human interest, for it prods deeply into national idiosyncrasies and ways of mind, and that sort of prodding is always entertaining.

I am thus neither teacher, nor prophet, nor reformer, but merely inquirer. The exigencies of my vocation make me almost completely bilingual; moreover, I have a hand for a compromise dialect which embodies the common materials of both languages, and is thus free from offense on both sides of the water—as befits the editor of a magazine published in both countries. But that compromise dialect is the living speech of neither. What I have tried to do here is to make a first sketch of the living speech of these States. The work is confessedly incomplete, and in places very painfully so, but in such enterprises a man must put an arbitrary term to his labors, lest some mischance, after years of diligence, take him from them too suddenly for them to be closed, and his laborious accumulations, as Ernest Weekly says in his book on English surnames, be "doomed to the waste-basket by harassed executors."

If the opportunity offers in future I shall undoubtedly return to the subject. For one thing, I am eager to attempt a more scientific examination of the grammar of the American vulgar speech, here discussed briefly in Chapter VI. For another thing, I hope to make further inquiries into the subject of American surnames of non-English origin. Various other fields invite. No historical study of American pronunciation exists; the influence of German, Irish-English, Yiddish and other such immigrant dialects upon American has never been fully investigated; there is no adequate treatise on American geographical names. Contributions of materials and suggestions for a possible revised edition of the present book will reach me if addressed to me in care of the publisher at 220 West Forty-second Street, New York. I shall also be very grateful for the correction of errors, some perhaps typographical, but others due to faulty information or mistaken judgment.

In conclusion, I borrow a plea in confession and avoidance from Ben Jonson's pioneer grammar of English, published in incomplete form after his death. "We have set down," he said, "that that in our judgment agreeth best with reason and good order. Which notwithstanding, if it seem to any to be too rough hewed, let him plane it out more smoothly, and I shall not only not envy it, but in the behalf of my country most heartily thank him for so great a benefit; hoping that I shall be thought sufficiently to have done my part if in tolling this bell I may draw others to a deeper consideration of the matter; for, touching myself, I must needs confess that after much painful churning this only would come which here we have devised."

Review Questions

1. Why did Mencken write his book?
2. What differences did Mencken mention between England's English and America's English?
3. What specific examples did Mencken cite about the lack of current literature on this topic?
4. How did Mencken refute the argument that his work was anti-social?
5. Did Mencken see the work that he had done as unchanging or infallible?

Thought Questions

1. Other nations have adapted languages and renamed them as their own throughout history. Why do you think our language was never renamed "American"?
2. What is a *philologist*? Why is their work important?
3. Is the English language better than the American language? What did Mencken conclude?
4. Have you ever spoken with someone from England or another British-influenced nation? What, if any, misunderstandings occurred as a result of language differences?
5. What role does language play in a society? Why is it important to study language systems?

ARTICLES and ESSAYS

Writing Practice

Articles employ yet another set of techniques, different from those used in poetry or oratory. Because they are designed to be read—possibly multiple times—they can include longer, more complex ideas and sentence structure, formal language, and references or quotations from other sources. They are also subject to closer scrutiny and side-by-side comparison with other documents, so their arguments require more support from logic or other types of evidence.

For practice, look at the following paragraph from Washington's Atlanta Exposition Address:

> There is no defense or security for any of us except in the highest intelligence and development of all. If anywhere there are efforts tending to curtail the fullest growth of the Negro, let these efforts be turned into stimulating, encouraging, and making him the most useful and intelligent citizen. Effort or means so invested will pay a thousand per cent interest. These efforts will be twice blessed—"blessing him that gives and him that takes." There is no escape through law of man or God from the inevitable:
>
> "The laws of changeless justice bind
>
> Oppressor with oppressed;
>
> And close as sin and suffering joined
>
> We march to fate abreast."

Begin by rewriting the passage in your own words, but as you do so, imagine you were going to publish it as an article, and make changes accordingly. Think about adding evidence, developing ideas more fully, and using formal language and varied sentence structure. If you get stuck, look back at some of the articles and essays you have just read and imitate the techniques they use to make an argument that will stand up to scrutiny.

Where's the Evidence?
LEGAL DOCUMENTS

The law is a contract between government and the people. Although the law can be changed, in American culture it is much less flexible than informal or verbal agreements. Putting something in a legal document indicates that the signers take it seriously and believe it should be binding for everyone in their jurisdiction.

Legal documents are a very different genre than essays, poetry, or speeches because they are designed to be clear, precise, and unambiguous. Nonetheless, legal documents frequently use language that is open to interpretation. As you read these legal documents, pay particular attention to the following questions:

- To what situation (a court case, a dispute) does this document respond?
- What type of facts does the author use to build his or her argument?
- What is the purpose of the document? What is its immediate effect?
- Where does the document get its authority?
- Does this legal document still have authority today?

These legal documents from American history contain some of the basic principles and fundamental statements that America's founders developed and considered worthy of preserving. As you read, pay attention to the values and visions for the United States that are represented in these legal documents.

Remember, the U.S. legal system is based on precedent (how the issue has been handled in the past). The same is often true for the laws and policies of a government. Decisions made today still refer back to legal precedent set in previous Supreme Court cases and in the Constitution. While reading these documents, think carefully about not only the immediate impact of the document, but also the kind of precedent each one sets for future laws.

The Mayflower Compact

In November 1620, The *Mayflower* arrived in New Plymouth, in what is now Massachusetts, near Cape Cod. The settlers on board were a group of Separatists from the Church of England who had fled to Holland in 1607 and 1608 to avoid religious persecution, before deciding to venture to the New World. The *Mayflower Compact* was written in an effort to avoid the fate of earlier colonies that had failed due to a lack of internal structure and government. For this reason, the covenant was signed by all forty-one adult males on board the *Mayflower*, and as the founding charter of their settlement, it was treated as the governing authority until 1691. The text of the (now lost) document was found in William Bradford's journal *Of Plymouth Plantation* and corroborated by Edward Winslow's *Mourt's Relation: A Journal of the Pilgrims at Plymouth*.

IN The Name of God, Amen.

We, whose names are underwritten, the Loyal Subjects of our dread Sovereign Lord King James, by the Grace of God, of Great Britain, France, and Ireland, King, Defender of the Faith, &c. Having undertaken for the Glory of God, and Advancement of the Christian Faith, and the Honor of our King and Country, a Voyage to plant the first colony in the northern Parts of Virginia; Do by these Presents, solemnly and mutually in the Presence of God and one another, covenant and combine ourselves together into a civil Body Politick, for our better Ordering and Preservation, and Furtherance of the Ends aforesaid; And by Virtue hereof do enact, constitute, and frame, such just and equal Laws, Ordinances, Acts, Constitutions, and Offices, from time to time, as shall be thought most meet and convenient for the general Good of the Colony; unto which we promise all due Submission and Obedience.

In WITNESS whereof we have hereunto subscribed our names at Cape Cod the eleventh of November, in the Reign of our Sovereign Lord King James of England, France, and Ireland, the eighteenth and of Scotland, the fifty-fourth. Anno Domini, 1620.

Edward Tilley
John Tilley
Francis Cooke
Thomas Rogers
Thomas Tinker
John Rigdale
Richard Warren
Edward Fuller
John Turner
Francis Eaton
James Chilton
John Howland
Stephen Hopkins
John Goodman
Degory Priest
Thomas Williams
Gilbert Winslow
Edmund Margeson
Peter Browne
Richard Britteridge
George Soule
Richard Clarke

Richard Gardiner
John Allerton
John Crackston
John Billington
Moses Fletcher

John Carver
William Bradford
Edward Winslow
William Brewster
Issac Allterton
Myles Standish
John Alden

Samuel Fuller
Christopher Martin
William Mullins
William White
Thomas English
Edward Dotey
Edward Leister

Review Questions

1. Why did the signers of the *Mayflower Compact* form a civil body?
2. Why had they made this voyage?
3. Who was going to be responsible for making the laws?
4. For what equivalent modern state were the pilgrims bound?
5. How many sets of relatives signed the compact?

Thought Questions

1. What does the term "dread sovereign" mean?
2. Are any of the names on this compact familiar to you? What happened after they landed?
3. What is a compact? How is it different from a law?
4. Does a compact have a different meaning if it is made under/dedicated to God, as this one was?
5. What would it have been like to be on board the *Mayflower*? To be related to the signers? Is your family descended from the first colonists, or did they immigrate later?

The Declaration of Independence

On June 28, 1776, a committee made up of Thomas Jefferson, John Adams, Benjamin Franklin, Roger Sherman, and Robert Livingston brought a document, originally drafted by Jefferson, before the Continental Congress for debate and revision. The document proclaimed the colonies' independence from England on the basis of the king's disregard for their natural rights. A revised version of the Declaration of Independence was adopted by Congress on July 4, and it was signed by delegates from all thirteen states then recognized. At this point, the Revolutionary War was already underway. It had been a year since the first shots were fired at Lexington and Concord on April 19, 1775, but the Declaration announced "to a candid world" the formal disintegration of the relationship between England and the United States.

The unanimous Declaration of the thirteen united States of America

When in the Course of human events it becomes necessary for one people to dissolve the political bands which have connected them with another and to assume among the powers of the earth, the separate and equal station to which the Laws of Nature and of Nature's God entitle them, a decent respect to the opinions of mankind requires that they should declare the causes which impel them to the separation.

We hold these truths to be self-evident, that all men are created equal, that they are endowed by their Creator with certain unalienable Rights, that among these are Life, Liberty and the pursuit of Happiness. –That to secure these rights, Governments are instituted among Men, deriving their just powers from the consent of the governed, –That whenever any Form of Government becomes destructive of these ends, it is the Right of the People to alter or to abolish it, and to institute new Government, laying its foundation on such principles and organizing its powers in such form, as to them shall seem most likely to effect their Safety and Happiness. Prudence, indeed, will dictate that Governments long established should not be changed for light and transient causes; and accordingly all experience hath shewn that mankind are more disposed to suffer, while evils are sufferable than to right themselves by abolishing the forms to which they are accustomed. But when a long train of abuses and usurpations, pursuing invariably the same Object evinces a design to reduce them under absolute Despotism, it is their right, it is their duty, to throw off such Government, and to provide new Guards for their future security. —Such has been the patient sufferance of these Colonies; and such is now the necessity which constrains them to alter their former Systems of Government. The history of the present King of Great Britain is a history of repeated injuries and usurpations, all having in direct object the establishment of an absolute Tyranny over these States.

To prove this, let Facts be submitted to a candid world.

He has refuted his Assent to Laws, the most wholesome and necessary for the public good.

He has forbidden his Governors to pass Laws of immediate and pressing importance, unless suspended in their operation till his Assent should be obtained; and when so suspended, he has utterly neglected to attend to them.

He has refused to pass other Laws for the accommodation of large districts of people, unless those people would relinquish the right of Representation in the Legislature, a right inestimable to them and formidable to tyrants only.

He has called together legislative bodies at places unusual, uncomfortable, and distant from the depository of their Public Records, for the sole purpose of fatiguing them into compliance with his measures.

He has dissolved Representative Houses repeatedly, for opposing with manly firmness his invasions on the rights of the people.

He has refused for a long time, after such dissolutions, to cause others to be elected, whereby the Legislative Powers, incapable of Annihilation, have returned to the People at large for their exercise; the State remaining in the mean time exposed to all the dangers of invasion from without, and convulsions within.

He has endeavored to prevent the population of these States; for that purpose obstructing the Laws for Naturalization of Foreigners; refusing to pass others to encourage their migrations hither, and raising the conditions of new Appropriations of Lands.

He has obstructed the Administration of Justice by refusing his Assent to Laws for establishing Judiciary Powers.

He has made Judges dependent on his Will alone for the tenure of their offices, and the amount and payment of their salaries.

He has erected a multitude of New Offices, and sent hither swarms of Officers to harass our people and eat out their substance.

He has kept among us, in times of peace, Standing Armies without the Consent of our legislatures.

He has affected to render the Military independent of and superior to the Civil Power.

He has combined with others to subject us to a jurisdiction foreign to our constitution, and unacknowledged by our laws; giving his Assent to their Acts of pretended Legislation:

For quartering large bodies of armed troops among us:

For protecting them, by a mock Trial from punishment for any Murders which they should commit on the Inhabitants of these States:

For cutting off our Trade with all parts of the world:

For imposing Taxes on us without our Consent:

For depriving us in many cases, of the benefit of Trial by Jury:

For transporting us beyond Seas to be tried for pretended offences:

For abolishing the free System of English Laws in a neighbouring Province, establishing therein an Arbitrary government, and enlarging its Boundaries so as to render it at once an example and fit instrument for introducing the same absolute rule into these Colonies:

For taking away our Charters, abolishing our most valuable Laws and altering fundamentally the Forms of our Governments:

For suspending our own Legislatures, and declaring themselves invested with power to legislate for us in all cases whatsoever.

He has abdicated Government here, by declaring us out of his Protection and waging War against us.

He has plundered our seas, ravaged our Coasts burnt our towns, and destroyed the lives of our people.

He is at this time transporting large Armies of foreign Mercenaries to compleat the works of death, desolation, and tyranny, already begun with circumstances of Cruelty & perfidy scarcely paralleled in the most barbarous ages, and totally unworthy the Head of a civilized nation.

He has constrained our fellow Citizens taken Captive on the high Seas to bear Arms against their Country, to become the executioners of their friends and Brethren, or to fall themselves by their Hands.

He has excited domestic insurrections amongst us, and has endeavoured to bring on the inhabitants of our frontiers, the merciless Indian Savages whose known rule of warfare, is an undistinguished destruction of all ages, sexes and conditions.

In every stage of these Oppressions We have Petitioned for Redress in the most humble terms: Our repeated Petitions have been answered only by repeated injury. A Prince, whose character is thus marked by every act which may define a Tyrant, is unfit to be the ruler of a free people.

Nor have we been wanting in attentions to our British brethren. We have warned them from time to time of attempts by their legislature to extend an unwarrantable jurisdiction over us. We have reminded them of the circumstances of our emigration and settlement here. We have appealed to their native justice and magnanimity, and we have conjured them by the ties of our common kindred to disavow these usurpations, which would inevitably interrupt our connections and correspondence. They too have been deaf to the voice of justice and of consanguinity. We must, therefore, acquiesce in the necessity, which denounces our Separation, and hold them, as we hold the rest of mankind, Enemies in War, in Peace Friends.

We, therefore, the Representatives of the United States of America, in General Congress, Assembled, appealing to the Supreme Judge of the world for the rectitude of our intentions, do, in the Name, and by Authority of the good People of these Colonies, solemnly publish and declare, That these United Colonies are, and of Right ought to be Free and Independent States, that they are Absolved from all Allegiance to the British Crown, and that all political connection between them and the State of Great Britain, is and ought to be totally dissolved; and that as Free and Independent States, they have full Power to levy War, conclude Peace contract Alliances, establish Commerce, and to do all other Acts and Things which Independent States may of right do.—And for the support of this Declaration, with a firm reliance on the protection of Divine Providence, we mutually pledge to each other our Lives, our Fortunes and our sacred Honor.

Review Questions

1. Why did the people feel obligated to say why they were separating from England?
2. From where do governments derive their power, according to this document?
3. Were the Americans eager to separate from the British? Cite the passage that answers this.
4. What had the king's "injuries and usurpations," been designed to accomplish?
5. What rights did the colonists claim after their separation from Britain? (See the last paragraph).

Thought Questions

1. Of the causes listed, which one seems the most significant to you? Why?
2. Do you think Congress was overreacting or being too hasty? Explain your answer.
3. Why do you think King George "endeavored to prevent the population of [the] states"?
4. What was the main problem? (Be specific; avoid using general words such as "freedom.")
5. Can you really hold someone as "enemies in war, in peace, friends"?

The Articles of the Confederation

The first constitution of the United States, called the Articles of the Confederation, was ratified on March 1, 1781, and signed by representatives of all thirteen states. The Articles were developed by the Third Continental Congress to give specific, permanent powers to the federal government and to the states. Developed in the midst of the Revolutionary War, the Articles represent the first attempt to create a sense of permanency and stability in the early government. The Articles were replaced in 1788 by the current Constitution. Some of the major changes that went into the new document were the division of Congress into the House of Representatives and the Senate, a different method of allocating Congressmen to each state, the addition of an executive branch consisting of president and vice president, and the transfer of select powers from the states to the federal government.

Agreed to by Congress November 15, 1777; ratified and in force, March 1, 1781.

To all to whom these Presents shall come, we the undersigned Delegates of the States affixed to our Names send greeting.

Whereas the Delegates of the United States of America in Congress assembled did on the fifteenth day of November in the Year of our Lord One Thousand Seven Hundred and Seventy seven, and in the Second Year of the Independence of America, agree to certain articles of Confederation and perpetual Union between the States of New-hampshire, Massachusetts-bay, Rhodeisland and Providence Plantations, Connecticut, New York, New Jersey, Pennsylvania, Delaware, Maryland, Virginia, North Carolina, South Carolina and Georgia, in the words following, viz:

Articles of Confederation and perpetual Union between the States of New-hampshire, Massachusetts bay, Rhodeisland and Providence Plantations, Connecticut, New York, New Jersey, Pennsylvania, Delaware, Maryland, Virginia, North Carolina, South Carolina and Georgia.

Article I. The Stile of this Confederacy shall be "The United States of America."

Article II. Each state retains its sovereignty, freedom, and independence, and every Power, Jurisdiction, and right, which is not by this confederation expressly delegated to the United States, in Congress assembled.

Article III. The said states hereby severally enter into a firm league of friendship with each other, for their common defence, the security of their Liberties, and their mutual and general welfare, binding themselves to assist each other, against all force offered to, or attacks made upon them, or any of them, on account of religion, sovereignty, trade, or any other pretence whatever.

Article IV. The better to secure and perpetuate mutual friendship and intercourse among the people of the different states in this union, the free inhabitants of each of these states, paupers, vagabonds, and fugitives from justice excepted, shall be entitled to all privileges and immunities of free citizens in the several states; and the people of each state shall have free ingress and regress to and from any other state, and shall enjoy therein all the privileges of trade and commerce, subject to the same duties, impositions, and restrictions as the inhabitants thereof respectively, provided that such restrictions shall not extend so far as to prevent the removal of property imported into any state, to any other state, of which the Owner is an inhabitant; provided also that no imposition, duties or restriction shall be laid by any state, on the property of the united states, or either of them.

If any Person guilty of, or charged with treason, felony, or other high misdemeanor in any state, shall flee from Justice, and be found in any of the united states, he shall, upon demand of the Governor or executive power, of the state from which he fled, be delivered up and removed to the state having jurisdiction of his offence.

Full faith and credit shall be given in each of these states to the records, acts and judicial proceedings of the courts and magistrates of every other state.

Article V. For the most convenient management of the general interests of the united states, delegates shall be annually appointed in such manner as the legislatures of each state shall direct, to meet in Congress on the first Monday in November, in every year, with a power reserved to each state to recal its delegates, or any of them, at any time within the year, and to send others in their stead for the remainder of the Year.

No state shall be represented in Congress by less than two, nor by more than seven Members; and no person shall be capable of being a delegate for more than three years in any term of six years; nor shall any person, being a delegate, be capable of holding any office under the united states, for which he, or another for his benefit receives any salary, fees or emolument of any kind.

Each state shall maintain its own delegates in a meeting of the states, and while they act as members of the committee of the states.

In determining questions in the united states in Congress assembled, each state shall have one vote.

Freedom of speech and debate in Congress shall not be impeached or questioned in any Court, or place out of Congress, and the members of congress shall be protected in their persons from arrests and imprisonments, during the time of their going to and from, and attendance on congress, except for treason, felony, or breach of the peace.

Article VI. No state, without the Consent of the united states in congress assembled, shall send any embassy to, or receive any embassy from, or enter into any conference, agreement, alliance or treaty with any King prince or state; nor shall any person holding any office of profit or trust under the united states, or any of them, accept of any present, emolument, office or title of any kind whatever from any king, prince or foreign state; nor shall the united states in congress assembled, or any of them, grant any title of nobility.

No two or more States shall enter into any treaty, confederation or alliance whatever between them, without the consent of the United States in Congress assembled, specifying accurately the purposes for which the same is to be entered into, and how long it shall continue.

No State shall lay any imposts or duties, which may interfere with any stipulations in treaties, entered into by the united States in Congress assembled, with any King, Prince or State, in pursuance of any treaties already proposed by Congress, to the courts of France and Spain.

No vessel of war shall be kept up in time of peace by any State, except such number only, as shall be deemed necessary by the united States in Congress assembled, for the defence of such State, or its trade; nor shall any body of forces be kept up by any State in time of peace, except such number only, as in the judgment of the united States in Congress assembled, shall be deemed requisite to garrison the forts necessary for the defence of such State; but every State shall always keep up a well regulated and disciplined militia, sufficiently armed and accoutred, and shall provide and constantly have ready for use, in public stores, a due number of field pieces and tents, and a proper quantity of arms, ammunition and camp equipage.

No State shall engage in any war without the consent of the united States in Congress assembled, unless such State be actually invaded by enemies, or shall have received certain advice of a resolution being formed by some nation of Indians to invade such State, and the danger is so imminent as not to admit of a delay, till the united States in Congress assembled can be consulted; nor shall any State grant commissions to any ships or vessels of war, nor letters of marque or reprisal, except it be after a declaration of war by the united States in Congress assembled, and then only against the kingdom or State and the subjects thereof, against which war has been so declared, and under such regulations as shall be established by the united States in Congress assembled, unless such State be infested by pirates, in which case vessels of war may be fitted out for that occasion, and kept so long as the danger shall continue, or until the united States in Congress assembled shall determine otherwise.

Article VII. When land-forces are raised by any State for the common defence [sic], all officers of or under the rank of colonel, shall be appointed by the legislature of each State respectively by whom such forces shall be raised, or in such manner as such State shall direct, and all vacancies shall be filled up by the State which first made the appointment.

Article VIII. All charges of war, and all other expenses that shall be incurred for the common defence or general welfare, and allowed by the united States in Congress assembled, shall be defrayed out of a common treasury, which shall be supplied by the several States in proportion to the value of all land within each State, granted to or surveyed for any person, as such land and the buildings and improvements thereon shall be estimated according to such mode as the united States in Congress assembled, shall from time to time direct and appoint.

The taxes for paying that proportion shall be laid and levied by the authority and direction of the legislatures of the several States within the time agreed upon by the united States in Congress assembled.

Article IX. The United States in Congress assembled, shall have the sole and exclusive right and power of determining on peace and war, except in the cases mentioned in the sixth article—of sending and receiving ambassadors—entering into treaties and alliances, provided that no treaty of commerce shall be made whereby the legislative power of the respective States shall be restrained from imposing such imposts and duties on foreigners, as their own people are subjected to, or from prohibiting the exportation or importation of any species of goods or commodities whatsoever—of establishing rules for deciding in all cases, what captures on land or water shall be legal, and in what manner prizes taken by land or naval forces in the service of the united States shall be divided or appropriated – of granting letters of marque and reprisal in times of peace—appointing courts for the trial of piracies and felonies committed on the high seas and establishing courts for receiving and determining finally appeals in all cases of captures, provided that no member of Congress shall be appointed a judge of any of the said courts.

The united States in Congress assembled shall also be the last resort on appeal in all disputes and differences now subsisting or that hereafter may arise between two or more States concerning boundary, jurisdiction or any other causes whatever; which authority shall always be exercised in the manner following. Whenever the legislative or executive authority or lawful agent of any State in controversy with another shall present a petition to Congress stating the matter in question and praying for a hearing, notice thereof shall be given by order of Congress to the legislative or executive authority of the other State in controversy, and a day assigned for the appearance of the parties by their lawful agents, who shall then be directed to appoint by joint consent, commissioners or judges to constitute a court for hearing and determining the matter in question: but if they cannot agree, Congress shall name three persons out of each of the united States, and from the list of such persons each party shall alternately strike out one, the petitioners beginning, until the number shall be reduced to thirteen; and from that number not less than seven, nor more than nine names as Congress shall direct, shall in the presence of Congress be drawn out by lot, and the persons whose names shall be so drawn or any five of them, shall be commissioners or judges, to hear and finally determine the controversy, so always as a major part of the judges who shall hear the cause shall agree in the determination: and if either party shall neglect to attend at the day appointed, without showing reasons, which Congress shall judge sufficient, or being present shall refuse to strike, the Congress shall proceed to nominate three persons out of each State, and the secretary of Congress shall strike in behalf of such party absent or refusing; and the judgment and sentence of the court to be appointed, in the manner before prescribed, shall be final and conclusive; and if any of the parties shall refuse to submit to the authority of such court, or to appear or defend their claim or cause, the court shall nevertheless proceed to pronounce sentence, or judgment, which shall in like manner be final and decisive, the judgment or sentence and other proceedings being in either case transmitted to Congress, and lodged among the acts of Congress for the security of the parties concerned: provided that every commissioner, before he sits in judgment, shall take an oath to be administered by one of the judges of the supreme or superior court of the State, where the cause shall be tried, "well and truly to hear and determine the matter in question, according to the best of his judgment, without favor, affection or hope of reward": provided also, that no State shall be deprived of territory for the benefit of the united States.

All controversies concerning the private right of soil claimed under different grants of two or more States, whose jurisdictions as they may respect such lands, and the States which passed such grants are adjusted, the said grants or either of them being at the same time claimed to have originated antecedent to such settlement of jurisdiction, shall on the petition of either party to the Congress of the united States, be finally determined as near as may be in the same manner as is before prescribed for deciding disputes respecting territorial jurisdiction between different States.

The united States in Congress assembled shall also have the sole and exclusive right and power of regulating the alloy and value of coin struck by their own authority, or by that of the respective States—fixing the standards of weights and measures throughout the united States—regulating the trade and managing all affairs with the Indians, not members of any of the States, provided that the legislative right of any State within its own limits be not infringed or violated—establishing or regulating post offices from one State to another, throughout all the united States, and exacting such postage on the papers passing through the same as may be requisite to defray the expences [sic] of the said office—appointing all officers of the land forces, in the service of the united States, excepting regimental officers—appointing all the officers of the naval forces, and commissioning all officers whatever in the service of the united States—making rules for the government and regulation of the said land and naval forces, and directing their operations.

The united States in Congress assembled shall have authority to appoint a committee, to sit in the recess of Congress, to be denominated 'A Committee of the States,' and to consist of one delegate from each State; and to appoint such other committees and civil officers as may be necessary for managing the general affairs of the united States under their direction—to appoint one of their members to preside, provided that no person be allowed to serve in the office of president more than one year in any term of three years; to ascertain the necessary sums of money to be raised for the service of the united States, and to appropriate and apply the same for defraying the public expences—to borrow money, or emit bills on the credit of the united States, transmitting every half year to the respective States an account of the sums of money so borrowed or emitted,—to build and equip a navy—to agree upon the number of land forces, and to make requisitions from each State for its quota, in proportion to the number of white inhabitants in such State; which requisition shall be binding, and thereupon the legislature of each State shall appoint the regimental officers, raise the men and cloth, arm and equip them in a soldier-like manner, at the expence of the united States; and the officers and men so cloathed, armed and equipped shall march to the place appointed, and within the time agreed on by the united States in Congress assembled. But if the united States in Congress assembled shall, on consideration of circumstances judge proper that any State should not raise men, or should raise a smaller number than its quota, and that any other state should raise a greater number of men than the quota thereof, such extra number shall be raised, officered, cloathed, armed and equipped in the same manner as the quota of each State, unless the legislature of such State shall judge that such extra number cannot be safely spread out of the same, in which case they shall raise, officer, cloath, arm and equip as many of such extra number as they judge can be safely spared. And the officers and men so cloathed, armed, and equipped, shall march to the place appointed, and within the time agreed on by the united States in Congress assembled.

The united States in Congress assembled shall never engage in a war, nor grant letters of marque or reprisal in time of peace, nor enter into any treaties or alliances, nor coin money, nor regulate the value thereof, nor ascertain the sums and expences necessary for the defence and welfare of the united States, or any of them, nor emit bills, nor borrow money on the credit of the united States, nor appropriate money, nor agree upon the number of vessels of war, to be built or purchased, or the number of land or sea forces to be raised, nor appoint a commander in chief of the army or navy, unless nine States assent to the same: nor shall a question on any other point, except for adjourning from day to day be determined, unless by the votes of tha majority of the united States in Congress assembled.

The Congress of the united States shall have power to adjourn to any time within the year, and to any place within the united States, so that no period of adjournment be for a longer duration than the space of six months, and shall publish the journal of their proceedings monthly, except such parts thereof relating to treaties, alliances or military operations, as in their judgment require secrecy; and the yeas and nays of the delegates of each State on any question shall be entered on the journal, when it is desired by any delegates; and the delegates of a State, or any of them, at his or their request shall be furnished with a transcript of the said journal, except such parts as are above excepted, to lay before the legislatures of the several States.

Article X. The Committee of the States, or any nine of them, shall be authorised to execute, in the recess of Congress, such of the powers of Congress as the united States in Congress assembled, by the consent of nine States, shall from time to time think expedient to vest them with; provided that no power be delegated to the said Committee, for the exercise of which, by the Articles of Confederation, the voice of nine States in the Congress of the united States assembled is requisite.

Article XI. Canada acceding to this confederation, and adjoining in the measures of the united States, shall be admitted into, and entitled to all the advantages of this Union; but no other colony shall be admitted into the same, unless such admission be agreed to by nine States.

Article XII. All bills of credit emitted, monies borrowed and debts contracted by, or under the authority of Congress, before the assembling of the united States, in pursuance of the present confederation, shall be deemed and considered as a charge against the united States, for payment and satisfaction whereof the said united States, and the public faith are hereby solemnly pledged.

Article XIII. Every State shall abide by the determination of the united States in Congress assembled, on all questions which by this confederation are submitted to them. And the Articles of this Confederation shall be inviolably observed by every State, and the Union shall be perpetual; nor shall any alteration at any time hereafter be made in any of them; unless such alteration be agreed to in a Congress of the united States, and be afterwards confirmed by the legislatures of every State.

And Whereas it hath pleased the Great Governor of the World to incline the hearts of the legislatures we respectively represent in Congress, to approve of, and to authorize us to ratify the said Articles of Confederation and perpetual Union. Know Ye that we the undersigned delegates, by virtue of the power and authority to us given for that purpose, do by these presents, in the name and in behalf of our respective constituents, fully and entirely ratify and confirm each and every of the said Articles of Confederation and perpetual Union, and all and singular the matters and things therein contained: And we do further solemnly plight and engage the faith of our respective constituents, that they shall abide by the determinations of the united States in Congress assembled, on all questions, which by the said Confederation are submitted to them. And that the Articles thereof shall be inviolably observed by the States we respectively represent, and that the Union shall be perpetual.

In Witness whereof we have hereunto set our hands in Congress. Done at Philadelphia in the State of Pennsylvania the ninth day of July in the Year of our Lord One Thousand Seven Hundred and Seventy-Eight, and in the Third Year of the independence of America.

[Editor's note: signers' names have been omitted]

Review Questions

1. What powers were reserved for the states?
2. What reasons were given for the establishment of a league of friendship among the states?
3. How did the Articles differentiate between an army (force) and the militia?
4. Who was allowed to declare war? What other rights did that body alone hold?
5. How many states had to agree in order for the body to make decisions and take action?

Thought Questions

1. What was the status of paupers, fugitives, and vagabonds under this system? Did they have any value in society? Compare this to the status of such people today.
2. Article V says no delegate can receive a salary. Do you think this was a better system?
3. The U.S. government has the ability to regulate the value of money, weights, and measures even today. How does this help to create uniformity in a society? How well would society function if the government didn't have this power?
4. These articles claimed that the "union shall be perpetual." Do any provisions in the articles invite disunity?
5. What are some potential problems with these articles?

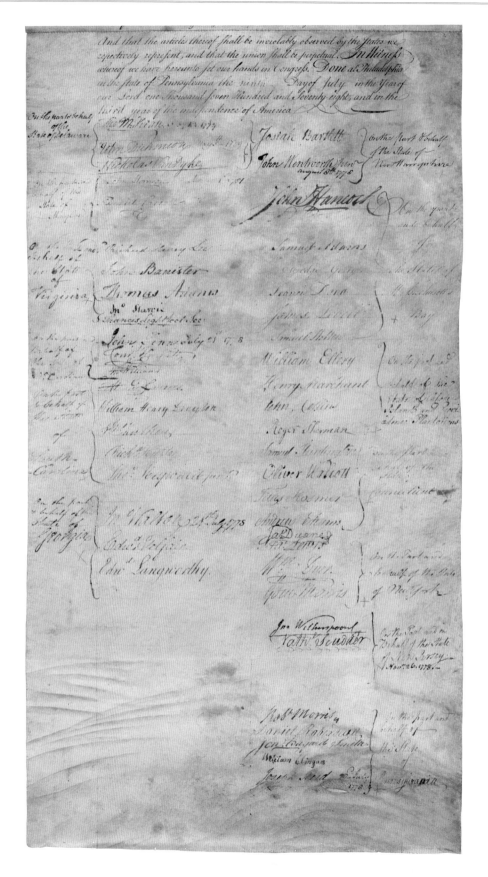

The U.S. Constitution

During the summer of 1787, the Constitutional Convention met in Philadelphia to draft a new document that would restructure the United States government on the grounds that the Articles of Confederation did not grant sufficient power to the federal government to enable it to collect taxes, regulate trade, and enforce laws. Twelve states' representatives were involved in the process (no delegates attended from Rhode Island), but James Madison was the most prominent contributor to the writing process. The U.S. Constitution was ratified on June 21, 1788, when it replaced the Articles as the standard for the federal and state governments' respective jurisdiction. The Constitution is the foundation of all legal decisions made in the most powerful court of the United States, the Supreme Court.

Preamble.

We the People of the United States, in Order to form a more perfect Union, establish Justice, insure domestic Tranquility, provide for the common defence, promote the general Welfare, and secure the Blessings of Liberty to ourselves and our Posterity, do ordain and establish this Constitution for the United States of America.

Article I.

Section 1. All legislative Powers herein granted shall be vested in a Congress of the United States, which shall consist of a Senate and House of Representatives.

Section 2. *Clause 1:* The House of Representatives shall be composed of Members chosen every second Year by the People of the several States, and the Electors in each State shall have the Qualifications requisite for Electors of the most numerous Branch of the State Legislature. *Clause 2:* No Person shall be a Representative who shall not have attained to the Age of twenty five Years, and been seven Years a Citizen of the United States, and who shall not, when elected, be an Inhabitant of that State in which he shall be chosen. *Clause 3:* Representatives and direct Taxes shall be apportioned among the several States which may be included within this Union, according to their respective Numbers, which shall be determined by adding to the whole Number of free Persons, including those bound to Service for a Term of Years, and excluding Indians not taxed, three fifths of all other

Persons. The actual Enumeration shall be made within three Years after the first Meeting of the Congress of the United States, and within every subsequent Term of ten Years, in such Manner as they shall by Law direct. The Number of Representatives shall not exceed one for every thirty Thousand, but each State shall have at Least one Representative; and until such enumeration shall be made, the State of New Hampshire shall be entitled to choose three, Massachusetts eight, Rhode-Island and Providence Plantations one, Connecticut five, New-York six, New Jersey four, Pennsylvania eight, Delaware one, Maryland six, Virginia ten, North Carolina five, South Carolina five, and Georgia three. *Clause 4*: When vacancies happen in the Representation from any State, the Executive Authority thereof shall issue Writs of Election to fill such Vacancies. *Clause 5*: The House of Representatives shall choose their Speaker and other Officers; and shall have the sole Power of Impeachment.

Section 3. *Clause 1*: The Senate of the United States shall be composed of two Senators from each State, chosen by the Legislature thereof, for six Years; and each Senator shall have one Vote. *Clause 2*: Immediately after they shall be assembled in Consequence of the first Election, they shall be divided as equally as may be into three Classes. The Seats of the Senators of the first Class shall be vacated at the Expiration of the second Year, of the second Class at the Expiration of the fourth Year, and of the third Class at the Expiration of the sixth Year, so that one third may be chosen every second Year; and if Vacancies happen by Resignation, or otherwise, during the Recess of the Legislature of any State, the Executive thereof may make temporary Appointments until the next Meeting of the Legislature, which shall then fill such Vacancies. *Clause 3*: No Person shall be a Senator who shall not have attained to the Age of thirty Years, and been nine Years a Citizen of the United States, and who shall not, when elected, be an Inhabitant of that State for which he shall be chosen. *Clause 4*: The Vice President of the United States shall be President of the Senate, but shall have no Vote, unless they be equally divided. *Clause 5*: The Senate shall choose their other Officers, and also a President pro tempore, in the Absence of the Vice President, or when he shall exercise the Office of President of the United States. *Clause 6*: The Senate shall have the sole Power to try all Impeachments. When sitting for that Purpose, they shall be on Oath or Affirmation. When the President of the United States is tried, the Chief Justice shall preside: And no Person shall be convicted without the Concurrence of two thirds of the Members present. *Clause 7*: Judgment in Cases of Impeachment shall not extend further than to removal from Office, and disqualification to hold and enjoy any Office of honor, Trust or Profit under the United States: but the Party convicted shall nevertheless be liable and subject to Indictment, Trial, Judgment and Punishment, according to Law.

Section 4. *Clause 1*: The Times, Places and Manner of holding Elections for Senators and Representatives, shall be prescribed in each State by the Legislature thereof; but the Congress may at any time by Law make or alter such Regulations, except as to the Places of choosing Senators. *Clause 2*: The Congress shall assemble at least once in every Year, and such Meeting shall be on the first Monday in December, unless they shall by Law appoint a different Day.

Section 5. *Clause 1*: Each House shall be the Judge of the Elections, Returns and Qualifications of its own Members, and a Majority of each shall constitute a Quorum to do Business; but a smaller Number may adjourn from day to day, and may be authorized to compel the Attendance of absent Members, in such Manner, and under such Penalties as each House may provide. *Clause 2*: Each House may determine the Rules of its Proceedings, punish its Members for disorderly Behaviour, and, with the Concurrence of two thirds, expel a Member. *Clause 5*: Each House shall keep a Journal of its Proceedings, and from time to time publish the same, excepting such Parts as may in their Judgment require Secrecy; and the Yeas and Nays of the Members of either House on any question shall, at the Desire of one fifth of those Present, be entered on the Journal. *Clause 4*: Neither House, during the Session of Congress, shall, without the Consent of the other, adjourn for more than three days, nor to any other Place than that in which the two Houses shall be sitting.

Section 6. *Clause 1*: The Senators and Representatives shall receive a Compensation for their Services, to be ascertained by Law, and paid out of the Treasury of the United States. They shall in all Cases, except Treason, Felony and Breach of the Peace, be privileged from Arrest during their Attendance at the Session of their respective Houses, and in going to and returning from the same; and for any Speech or Debate in either House, they shall not be questioned in any other Place. *Clause 2*: No Senator or Representative shall, during the Time for which he was elected, be appointed to any civil Office under the Authority of the United States, which shall have been created, or the Emoluments whereof shall have been encreased during such time; and no Person holding any Office under the United States, shall be a Member of either House during his Continuance in Office.

Section 7. *Clause 1*: All Bills for raising Revenue shall originate in the House of Representatives; but the Senate may propose or concur with Amendments as on other Bills. *Clause 2*: Every Bill which shall have passed the House of Representatives and the Senate, shall, before it become a Law, be presented to the President of the United States; If he approve he shall sign it, but if not he shall return it, with his Objections to that House in which it shall have originated, who shall enter the Objections at large on their Journal, and proceed to reconsider it. If after such Reconsideration two thirds of that House shall agree to pass the Bill, it shall be sent, together with the Objections, to the other House, by which it shall likewise be reconsidered, and if approved by two thirds of that House, it shall become a Law. But in all such Cases the Votes of both Houses shall be determined by yeas and Nays, and the Names of the Persons voting for and against the Bill shall be entered on the Journal of each House respectively. If any Bill shall not be returned by the President within ten Days (Sundays excepted) after it shall have been presented to him, the Same shall be a Law, in like Manner as if he had signed it, unless the Congress by their Adjournment prevent its Return, in which Case it shall not be a Law. *Clause 3*: Every Order, Resolution, or Vote to which the Concurrence of the Senate and House of Representatives may be necessary (except on a question of Adjournment) shall be presented to the President of the United States; and before the Same shall take Effect, shall be approved by him, or being disapproved by him, shall be repassed by two thirds of the Senate and House of Representatives, according to the Rules and Limitations prescribed in the Case of a Bill.

Section 8. *Clause 1*: The Congress shall have Power To lay and collect Taxes, Duties, Imposts and Excises, to pay the Debts and provide for the common Defence and general Welfare of the United States; but all Duties, Imposts and Excises shall be uniform throughout the United States; *Clause 2*: To borrow Money on the credit of the United States; *Clause 3*: To regulate Commerce with foreign Nations, and among the several States, and with the Indian Tribes; *Clause 4*: To establish an uniform Rule of Naturalization, and uniform Laws on the subject of Bankruptcies throughout the United States; Clause 5: To coin Money, regulate the Value thereof, and of foreign Coin, and fix the Standard of Weights and Measures; *Clause 6*: To provide for the Punishment of counterfeiting the Securities and current Coin of the United States; *Clause 7*: To establish Post Offices and post Roads; *Clause 8*: To promote the Progress of Science and useful Arts, by securing for limited Times to Authors and Inventors the exclusive Right to their respective Writings and Discoveries; *Clause 9*: To constitute Tribunals inferior to the Supreme Court; *Clause 10*: To define and punish Piracies and Felonies committed on the high Seas, and Offences against the Law of Nations; *Clause 11*: To declare War, grant Letters of Marque and Reprisal, and make Rules concerning Captures on Land and Water; *Clause 12*: To raise and support Armies, but no Appropriation of Money to that Use shall be for a longer Term than two Years; *Clause 13*: To provide and maintain a Navy; *Clause 14*: To make Rules for the Government and Regulation of the land and naval Forces; *Clause 15*: To provide for calling forth the Militia to execute the Laws of the Union, suppress Insurrections and repel Invasions; *Clause 16*: To provide for organizing, arming, and disciplining, the Militia, and for governing such Part of them as may be employed in the Service of the United States, reserving to the States respectively, the Appointment of the Officers, and the Authority of training the Militia according to the discipline prescribed by Congress; *Clause 17*: To exercise exclusive Legislation in all Cases whatsoever, over such District (not exceeding ten Miles square) as may, by Cession of particular States, and the Acceptance of Congress, become the Seat of the Government of the United States, and to exercise like Authority over all Places purchased by the Consent of the Legislature of the State in which the Same shall be, for the Erection of Forts, Magazines, Arsenals, dock-Yards, and other needful Buildings; —And *Clause 18*: To make all Laws which shall be necessary and proper for carrying into Execution the foregoing Powers, and all other Powers vested by this Constitution in the Government of the United States, or in any Department or Officer thereof.

Section 9. *Clause 1*: The Migration or Importation of such Persons as any of the States now existing shall think proper to admit, shall not be prohibited by the Congress prior to the Year one thousand eight hundred and eight, but a Tax or duty may be imposed on such Importation, not exceeding ten dollars for each Person. *Clause 2*: The Privilege of the Writ of Habeas Corpus shall not be suspended, unless when in Cases of Rebellion or Invasion the public Safety may require it. *Clause 3*: No Bill of Attainder or ex post facto Law shall be passed. *Clause 4*: No Capitation, or other direct, Tax shall be laid, unless in Proportion to the Census or Enumeration herein before directed to be taken. *Clause 5*: No Tax or Duty shall be laid on Articles exported from any State. *Clause 6*: No Preference shall be given by any Regulation of Commerce or Revenue to the Ports of one State over those of another: nor shall Vessels bound to, or from, one State, be obliged to enter, clear, or pay Duties in another. *Clause 7*: No Money shall be drawn from the Treasury, but in Consequence of Appropriations made by Law; and a regular Statement and Account of the Receipts and Expenditures of all public Money shall be published from time to time. *Clause 8*: No Title of Nobility shall be granted by the United States: And no Person holding any Office of Profit or Trust under them, shall, without the Consent of the Congress, accept of any present, Emolument, Office, or Title, of any kind whatever, from any King, Prince, or foreign State.

Section 10. *Clause 1*: No State shall enter into any Treaty, Alliance, or Confederation; grant Letters of Marque and Reprisal; coin Money; emit Bills of Credit; make any Thing but gold and silver Coin a Tender in Payment of Debts; pass any Bill of Attainder, ex post facto Law, or Law impairing the Obligation of Contracts, or grant any Title of Nobility. *Clause 2*: No State shall, without the Consent of the Congress, lay any Imposts or Duties on Imports or Exports, except what may be absolutely necessary for executing its inspection Laws: and the net Produce of all Duties and Imposts, laid by any State on Imports or Exports, shall be for the Use of the Treasury of the United States; and all such Laws shall be subject to the Revision and Control of the Congress. *Clause 3*: No State shall, without the Consent of Congress, lay any Duty of Tonnage, keep Troops, or Ships of War in time of Peace, enter into any Agreement or Compact with another State, or with a foreign Power, or engage in War, unless actually invaded, or in such imminent Danger as will not admit of delay.

Article II.

Section 1. *Clause 1*: The executive Power shall be vested in a President of the United States of America. He shall hold his Office during the Term of four Years, and, together with the Vice President, chosen for the same Term, be elected, as follows. *Clause 2*: Each State shall appoint, in such Manner as the Legislature thereof may direct, a Number of Electors, equal to the whole Number of Senators and Representatives to which the State may be entitled in the Congress: but no Senator or Representative, or Person holding an Office of Trust or Profit under the United States, shall be appointed an Elector. *Clause 3*: The Electors shall meet in their respective States, and vote by Ballot for two Persons, of whom one at least shall not be an Inhabitant of the same State with themselves. And they shall make a List of all the Persons voted for, and of the Number of Votes for each; which List they shall sign and certify, and transmit sealed to the Seat of the Government of the United States, directed to the President of the Senate. The President of the Senate shall, in the Presence of the Senate and House of Representatives, open all the Certificates, and the Votes shall then be counted. The Person having the greatest Number of Votes shall be the President, if such Number be a Majority of the whole Number of Electors appointed; and if there be more than one who have such Majority, and have an equal Number of Votes, then the House of Representatives shall immediately choose by Ballot one of them for President; and if no Person have a Majority, then from the five highest on the List the said House shall in like Manner choose the President. But in choosing the President, the Votes shall be taken by States, the Representation from each State having one Vote; A quorum for this Purpose shall consist of a Member or Members from two thirds of the States, and a Majority of all the States shall be necessary to a Choice. In every Case, after the Choice of the President, the Person having the greatest Number of Votes of the Electors shall be the Vice President. But if there should remain two or more who have equal Votes, the Senate shall choose from them by Ballot the Vice President. *Clause 4*: The Congress may determine the Time of choosing the Electors, and the Day on which they shall give their Votes; which Day shall be the same throughout the United States. *Clause 5*: No Person except a natural born Citizen, or a Citizen of the United States, at the time of the Adoption of this Constitution, shall be eligible to the Office of President; neither shall any Person be eligible to that Office who shall not have attained to the Age of thirty five Years, and been fourteen Years a Resident within the United States. *Clause 6*: In Case of the Removal of the President from Office, or of his Death, Resignation, or Inability to discharge the Powers and Duties of the said Office, the Same shall devolve on the Vice President, and the Congress may by Law provide for the Case of Removal, Death, Resignation or Inability, both of the President and Vice President, declaring what Officer shall then act as President, and such Officer shall act accordingly, until the Disability be removed, or a President shall be elected. *Clause 7*: The President shall, at stated Times, receive for his Services, a Compensation, which shall neither be increased nor diminished during the Period for which he shall have been elected, and he shall not receive within that Period any other Emolument from the United States, or any of them. *Clause 8:* Before he enter on the Execution of his Office, he shall take the following Oath or Affirmation:—"I do solemnly swear (or affirm) that I will faithfully execute the Office of President of the United States, and will to the best of my Ability, preserve, protect and defend the Constitution of the United States."

Section 2. *Clause 1:* The President shall be Commander in Chief of the Army and Navy of the United States, and of the Militia of the several States, when called into the actual Service of the United States; he may require the Opinion, in writing, of the principal Officer in each of the executive Departments, upon any Subject relating to the Duties of their respective Offices, and he shall have Power to grant Reprieves and Pardons for Offences against the United States, except in Cases of Impeachment. *Clause 2:* He shall have Power, by and with the Advice and Consent of the Senate, to make Treaties, provided two thirds of the Senators present concur; and he shall nominate, and by and with the Advice and Consent of the Senate, shall appoint Ambassadors, other public Ministers and Consuls, Judges of the supreme Court, and all other Officers of the United States, whose Appointments are not herein otherwise provided for, and which shall be established by Law: but the Congress may by Law vest the Appointment of such inferior Officers, as they think proper, in the President alone, in the Courts of Law, or in the Heads of Departments. *Clause 3:* The President shall have Power to fill up all Vacancies that may happen during the Recess of the Senate, by granting Commissions which shall expire at the End of their next Session.

Section 3. He shall from time to time give to the Congress Information of the State of the Union, and recommend to their Consideration such Measures as he shall judge necessary and expedient; he may, on extraordinary Occasions, convene both Houses, or either of them, and in Case of Disagreement between them, with Respect to the Time of Adjournment, he may adjourn them to such Time as he shall think proper; he shall receive Ambassadors and other public Ministers; he shall take Care that the Laws be faithfully executed, and shall Commission all the Officers of the United States.

Section 4. The President, Vice President and all civil Officers of the United States, shall be removed from Office on Impeachment for, and Conviction of, Treason, Bribery, or other high Crimes and Misdemeanors.

Article III.

Section 1. The judicial Power of the United States, shall be vested in one supreme Court, and in such inferior Courts as the Congress may from time to time ordain and establish. The Judges, both of the supreme and inferior Courts, shall hold their Offices during good Behaviour, and shall, at stated Times, receive for their Services, a Compensation, which shall not be diminished during their Continuance in Office.

Section 2. *Clause 1:* The judicial Power shall extend to all Cases, in Law and Equity, arising under this Constitution, the Laws of the United States, and Treaties made, or which shall be made, under their Authority;—to all Cases affecting Ambassadors, other public Ministers and Consuls;—to all Cases of admiralty and maritime Jurisdiction;—to Controversies to which the United States shall be a Party;—to Controversies between two or more States;—between a State and Citizens of another State;—between Citizens of different States,

—between Citizens of the same State claiming Lands under Grants of different States, and between a State, or the Citizens thereof, and foreign States, Citizens or Subjects. *Clause 2*: In all Cases affecting Ambassadors, other public Ministers and Consuls, and those in which a State shall be Party, the supreme Court shall have original Jurisdiction. In all the other Cases before mentioned, the supreme Court shall have appellate Jurisdiction, both as to Law and Fact, with such Exceptions, and under such Regulations as the Congress shall make. *Clause 3*: The Trial of all Crimes, except in Cases of Impeachment, shall be by Jury; and such Trial shall be held in the State where the said Crimes shall have been committed; but when not committed within any State, the Trial shall be at such Place or Places as the Congress may by Law have directed.

Section 3. *Clause 1*: Treason against the United States, shall consist only in levying War against them, or in adhering to their Enemies, giving them Aid and Comfort. No Person shall be convicted of Treason unless on the Testimony of two Witnesses to the same overt Act, or on Confession in open Court. *Clause 2*: The Congress shall have Power to declare the Punishment of Treason, but no Attainder of Treason shall work Corruption of Blood, or Forfeiture except during the Life of the Person attainted.

Article IV.

Section 1. Full Faith and Credit shall be given in each State to the public Acts, Records, and judicial Proceedings of every other State. And the Congress may by general Laws prescribe the Manner in which such Acts, Records and Proceedings shall be proved, and the Effect thereof.

Section 2. *Clause 1*: The Citizens of each State shall be entitled to all Privileges and Immunities of Citizens in the several States. *Clause 2*: A Person charged in any State with Treason, Felony, or other Crime, who shall flee from Justice, and be found in another State, shall on Demand of the executive Authority of the State from which he fled, be delivered up, to be removed to the State having Jurisdiction of the Crime. *Clause 3*: No Person held to Service or Labour in one State, under the Laws thereof, escaping into another, shall, in Consequence of any Law or Regulation therein, be discharged from such Service or Labour, but shall be delivered up on Claim of the Party to whom such Service or Labour may be due.

Section 3. *Clause 1*: New States may be admitted by the Congress into this Union; but no new State shall be formed or erected within the Jurisdiction of any other State; nor any State be formed by the Junction of two or more States, or Parts of States, without the Consent of the Legislatures of the States concerned as well as of the Congress. *Clause 2*: The Congress shall have Power to dispose of and make all needful Rules and Regulations respecting the Territory or other Property belonging to the United States; and nothing in this Constitution shall be so construed as to Prejudice any Claims of the United States, or of any particular State.

Section 4. The United States shall guarantee to every State in this Union a Republican Form of Government, and shall protect each of them against Invasion; and on Application of the Legislature, or of the Executive (when the Legislature cannot be convened) against domestic Violence.

Article V.

Felony - An offence, as murder or burglary or further offence

The Congress, whenever two thirds of both Houses shall deem it necessary, shall propose Amendments to this Constitution, or, on the Application of the Legislatures of two thirds of the several States, shall call a Convention for proposing Amendments, which, in either Case, shall be valid to all Intents and Purposes, as Part of this Constitution, when ratified by the Legislatures of three fourths of the several States, or by Conventions in three fourths thereof, as the one or the other Mode of Ratification may be proposed by the Congress; Provided that no Amendment which may be made prior to the Year One thousand eight hundred and eight shall in any Manner affect the first and fourth Clauses in the Ninth Section of the first Article; and that no State, without its Consent, shall be deprived of its equal Suffrage in the Senate.

Article VI.

Clause 1: All Debts contracted and Engagements entered into, before the Adoption of this Constitution, shall be as valid against the United States under this Constitution, as under the Confederation. *Clause 2*: This Constitution, and the Laws of the United States which shall be made in Pursuance thereof; and all Treaties made, or which shall be made, under the Authority of the United States, shall be the supreme Law of the Land; and the Judges in every State shall be bound thereby, any Thing in the Constitution or Laws of any State to the Contrary notwithstanding. *Clause 3*: The Senators and Representatives before mentioned, and the Members of the several State Legislatures, and all executive and judicial Officers, both of the United States and of the several States, shall be bound by Oath or Affirmation, to support this Constitution; but no religious Test shall ever be required as a Qualification to any Office or public Trust under the United States.

Article VII.

The Ratification of the Conventions of nine States, shall be sufficient for the Establishment of this Constitution between the States so ratifying the Same.

Done in Convention by the Unanimous Consent of the States present the Seventeenth Day of September in the Year of our Lord one thousand seven hundred and Eighty seven and of the Independence of the United States of America the Twelfth In witness whereof We have hereunto subscribed our Names,

[Editor's note: signers' names omitted. Italics and other formatting added for ease of reading.]

Ratification - the act of ratifying, confirmation, sanction.

Review Questions

1. What were the six purposes of the U.S. Constitution (found in the Preamble)?
2. What were the required qualifications of a senator? A representative?
3. Describe the process of the Electoral College (see Article II)
4. What was the one kind of trial not by jury? (see Article III)
5. What fraction of states' approval was needed to ratify amendments to the Constitution?

Thought Questions

1. Do you think the president should have veto power over legislation? Explain your answer.
2. What justifications does the Constitution list for impeaching the president? Do you agree? Should there be others?
3. Why do you think foreigners are barred from holding office as president, in the Senate, and in the House of Representatives? Is this fair? Why or why not?
4. What are the federal government's duties, as outlined in Article IV, Section 4? What additional duties does the federal government now claim? Are these additional responsibilities justified?
5. Article VI says, "No religious Test shall ever be required as a Qualification to any Office or public Trust under the United States." Yet most of the early American documents place a high value on religion. Why do you think this condition was added?

The Amendments to the U.S. Constitution

To grant a measure of flexibility to the U.S. Constitution, Article V permits a process for passing amendments to the Constitution. A resolution must be passed by both houses of Congress with a two-thirds vote, and then it must be ratified by three-quarters of the states. Amendments are not dependent on the approval of the president. Within a year of the ratification of the Constitution, the Bill of Rights, containing the first ten amendments to the Constitution, was introduced. Between 1798 and 1870, five more amendments were passed, and by 1992, the total had risen to twenty-seven amendments. The only amendment to be repealed has been the eighteenth (Prohibition), which was nullified by the twenty-first amendment.

Amendment 1. (Ratified in 1791.)

Congress shall make no law respecting an establishment of religion, or prohibiting the free exercise thereof; or abridging the freedom of speech, or of the press; or the right of the people peaceably to assemble, and to petition the Government for a redress of grievances.

Amendment 2. (Ratified in 1791.)

A well-regulated Militia, being necessary to the security of a free State, the right of the people to keep and bear Arms, shall not be infringed.

Amendment 3. (Ratified in 1791.)

No Soldier shall, in time of peace be quartered in any house, without the consent of the Owner, nor in time of war, but in a manner to be prescribed by law.

Amendment 4. (Ratified in 1791.)

The right of the people to be secure in their persons, houses, papers, and effects, against unreasonable searches and seizures, shall not be violated, and no Warrants shall issue, but upon probable cause, supported by Oath or affirmation, and particularly describing the place to be searched, and the persons or things to be seized.

Amendment 5. (Ratified in 1791.)

No person shall be held to answer for a capital, or otherwise infamous crime, unless on a presentment or indictment of a Grand Jury, except in cases arising in the land or naval forces, or in the Militia, when in actual service in time of War or public danger; nor shall any person be subject for the same offence to be twice put in jeopardy of life or limb; nor shall be compelled in any criminal case to be a witness against himself, nor be deprived of life, liberty, or property, without due process of law; nor shall private property be taken for public use, without just compensation.

Amendment 6. (Ratified in 1791.)

In all criminal prosecutions, the accused shall enjoy the right to a speedy and public trial, by an impartial jury of the State and district wherein the crime shall have been committed, which district shall have been previously ascertained by law, and to be informed of the nature and cause of the accusation; to be confronted with the witnesses against him; to have compulsory process for obtaining witnesses in his favor, and to have the Assistance of Counsel for his defence.

Amendment 7. (Ratified in 1791.)

In Suits at common law, where the value in controversy shall exceed twenty dollars, the right of trial by jury shall be preserved, and no fact tried by a jury, shall be otherwise re-examined in any Court of the United States, than according to the rules of the common law.

Amendment 8. (Ratified in 1791.)

Excessive bail shall not be required, nor excessive fines imposed, nor cruel and unusual punishments inflicted.

Amendment 9. (Ratified in 1791.)

The enumeration in the Constitution, of certain rights, shall not be construed to deny or disparage others retained by the people.

Amendment 10. (Ratified in 1795.)

The powers not delegated to the United States by the Constitution, nor prohibited by it to the States, are reserved to the States respectively, or to the people.

Amendment 11. (Ratified in 1795.)

The Judicial power of the United States shall not be construed to extend to any suit in law or equity, commenced or prosecuted against one of the United States by Citizens of another State, or by Citizens or Subjects of any Foreign State.

Amendment 12. (Ratified in 1804.)

The Electors shall meet in their respective states, and vote by ballot for President and Vice-President, one of whom, at least, shall not be an inhabitant of the same state with themselves; they shall name in their ballots the person voted for as President, and in distinct ballots the person voted for as Vice-President, and they shall make distinct lists of all persons voted for as President, and of all persons voted for as Vice-President, and of the number of votes for each, which lists they shall sign and certify, and transmit sealed to the seat of the government of the United States, directed to the President of the Senate;—The President of the Senate shall, in the presence of the Senate and House of Representatives, open all the certificates and the votes shall then be counted;—The person having the greatest number of votes for President, shall be the President, if such number be a majority of the whole number of Electors appointed; and if no person have such majority, then from the persons having the highest numbers not exceeding three on the list of those voted for as President, the House of Representatives shall choose immediately, by ballot, the President. But in choosing the President, the votes shall be taken by states, the representation from each state having one vote; a quorum for this purpose shall consist of a member or members from two-thirds of the states, and a majority of all the states shall be necessary to a choice. And if the House of Representatives shall not choose a President whenever the right of choice shall devolve upon them, before the fourth day of March next following, then the Vice-President shall act as President, as in the case of the death or other constitutional disability of the President.—The person having the greatest number of votes as Vice-President, shall be the Vice-President, if such number be a majority of the whole number of Electors appointed, and if no person have a majority, then from the two highest numbers on the list, the Senate shall choose the Vice-President; a quorum for the purpose shall consist of two-thirds of the whole number of Senators, and a majority of the whole number shall be necessary to a choice. But no person constitutionally ineligible to the office of President shall be eligible to that of Vice-President of the United States.

Amendment 13. (Ratified in 1865, except Mississippi. Ratified in Mississippi in 1995.)

Section 1. Neither slavery nor involuntary servitude, except as a punishment for crime whereof the party shall have been duly convicted, shall exist within the United States, or any place subject to their jurisdiction.

Section 2. Congress shall have power to enforce this article by appropriate legislation.

Amendment 14. (Ratified in 1868.)

Section 1. All persons born or naturalized in the United States, and subject to the jurisdiction thereof, are citizens of the United States and of the State wherein they reside. No State shall make or enforce any law which shall abridge the privileges or immunities of citizens of the United States; nor shall any State deprive any person of life, liberty, or property, without due process of law; nor deny to any person within its jurisdiction the equal protection of the laws.

Section 2. Representatives shall be apportioned among the several States according to their respective numbers, counting the whole number of persons in each State, excluding

Indians not taxed. But when the right to vote at any election for the choice of electors for President and Vice President of the United States, Representatives in Congress, the Executive and Judicial officers of a State, or the members of the Legislature thereof, is denied to any of the male inhabitants of such State, being twenty-one years of age, and citizens of the United States, or in any way abridged, except for participation in rebellion, or other crime, the basis of representation therein shall be reduced in the proportion which the number of such male citizens shall bear to the whole number of male citizens twenty-one years of age in such State.

Section 3. No person shall be a Senator or Representative in Congress, or elector of President and Vice President, or hold any office, civil or military, under the United States, or under any State, who, having previously taken an oath, as a member of Congress, or as an officer of the United States, or as a member of any State legislature, or as an executive or judicial officer of any State, to support the Constitution of the United States, shall have engaged in insurrection or rebellion against the same, or given aid or comfort to the enemies thereof. But Congress may by a vote of two-thirds of each House, remove such disability.

Section 4. The validity of the public debt of the United States, authorized by law, including debts incurred for payment of pensions and bounties for services in suppressing insurrection or rebellion, shall not be questioned. But neither the United States nor any State shall assume or pay any debt or obligation incurred in aid of insurrection or rebellion against the United States, or any claim for the loss or emancipation of any slave; but all such debts, obligations and claims shall be held illegal and void.

Section 5. The Congress shall have power to enforce, by appropriate legislation, the provisions of this article.

Amendment 15. (Ratified in 1870.)

Section 1. The right of citizens of the United States to vote shall not be denied or abridged by the United States or by any State on account of race, color, or previous condition of servitude.

Section 2. The Congress shall have power to enforce this article by appropriate legislation.

Amendment 16. (Ratified in 1913.)

The Congress shall have power to lay and collect taxes on incomes, from whatever source derived, without apportionment among the several States, and without regard to any census or enumeration.

Amendment 17. (Ratified in 1913.)

The Senate of the United States shall be composed of two Senators from each State, elected by the people thereof, for six years; and each Senator shall have one vote. The electors in each State shall have the qualifications requisite for electors of the most numerous branch of the State legislatures.

When vacancies happen in the representation of any State in the Senate, the executive authority of such State shall issue writs of election to fill such vacancies: Provided, That the legislature of any State may empower the executive thereof to make temporary appointments until the people fill the vacancies by election as the legislature may direct.

This amendment shall not be so construed as to affect the election or term of any Senator chosen before it becomes valid as part of the Constitution.

Amendment 18. (Ratified in 1919.)

Section 1. After one year from the ratification of this article the manufacture, sale, or transportation of intoxicating liquors within, the importation thereof into, or the exportation thereof from the United States and all territory subject to the jurisdiction thereof for beverage purposes is hereby prohibited.

Section 2. The Congress and the several States shall have concurrent power to enforce this article by appropriate legislation.

Section 3. This article shall be inoperative unless it shall have been ratified as an amendment to the Constitution by the legislatures of the several States, as provided in the Constitution, within seven years from the date of the submission hereof to the States by the Congress.

Amendment 19. (Ratified in 1920.)

The right of citizens of the United States to vote shall not be denied or abridged by the United States or by any State on account of sex. Congress shall have power to enforce this article by appropriate legislation.

Amendment 20. (Ratified in 1933.)

Section 1. The terms of the President and Vice President shall end at noon on the 20th day of January, and the terms of Senators and Representatives at noon on the 3d day of January, of the years in which such terms would have ended if this article had not been ratified; and the terms of their successors shall then begin.

Section 2. The Congress shall assemble at least once in every year, and such meeting shall begin at noon on the 3d day of January, unless they shall by law appoint a different day.

Section 3. If, at the time fixed for the beginning of the term of the President, the President elect shall have died, the Vice President elect shall become President. If a President shall not have been chosen before the time fixed for the beginning of his term, or if the President elect shall have failed to qualify, then the Vice President elect shall act as President until a President shall have qualified; and the Congress may by law provide for the case wherein neither a President elect nor a Vice President elect shall have qualified, declaring who shall then act as President, or the manner in which one who is to act shall be selected, and such person shall act accordingly until a President or Vice President shall have qualified.

Section 4. The Congress may by law provide for the case of the death of any of the persons from whom the House of Representatives may choose a President whenever the right of choice shall have devolved upon them, and for the case of the death of any of the persons from whom the Senate may choose a Vice President whenever the right of choice shall have devolved upon them.

Section 5. Sections 1 and 2 shall take effect on the 15th day of October following the ratification of this article.

Section 6. This article shall be inoperative unless it shall have been ratified as an amendment to the Constitution by the legislatures of three-fourths of the several States within seven years from the date of its submission.

Amendment 21. (Ratified in 1933.)

Section 1. The eighteenth article of amendment to the Constitution of the United States is hereby repealed.

Section 2. The transportation or importation into any State, Territory, or possession of the United States for delivery or use therein of intoxicating liquors, in violation of the laws thereof, is hereby prohibited.

Section 3. This article shall be inoperative unless it shall have been ratified as an amendment to the Constitution by conventions in the several States, as provided in the Constitution, within seven years from the date of the submission hereof to the States by the Congress.

Amendment 22. (Ratified in 1951.)

Section 1. No person shall be elected to the office of the President more than twice, and no person who has held the office of President, or acted as President, for more than two years of a term to which some other person was elected President shall be elected to the office of the President more than once. But this article shall not apply to any person holding the office of President when this article was proposed by the Congress, and shall not prevent any person who may be holding the office of President, or acting as President, during the term within which this article becomes operative from holding the office of President or acting as President during the remainder of such term.

Section 2. This article shall be inoperative unless it shall have been ratified as an amendment to the Constitution by the legislatures of three-fourths of the several states within seven years from the date of its submission to the states by the Congress.

Amendment 23. (Ratified in 1961.)

Section 1. The District constituting the seat of government of the United States shall appoint in such manner as the Congress may direct: A number of electors of President and Vice President equal to the whole number of Senators and Representatives in Congress to which the District would be entitled if it were a state, but in no event more than the least populous state; they shall be in addition to those appointed by the states, but they shall be considered, for the purposes of the election of President and Vice President, to be electors appointed by a state; and they shall meet in the District and perform such duties as provided by the twelfth article of amendment.

Section 2. The Congress shall have power to enforce this article by appropriate legislation.

Amendment 24. (Ratified in 1964.)

Section 1. The right of citizens of the United States to vote in any primary or other election for President or Vice President, for electors for President or Vice President, or for

Senator or Representative in Congress, shall not be denied or abridged by the United States or any state by reason of failure to pay any poll tax or other tax.

Section 2. The Congress shall have power to enforce this article by appropriate legislation.

Amendment 25. (Ratified in 1967.)

Section 1. In case of the removal of the President from office or of his death or resignation, the Vice President shall become President.

Section 2. Whenever there is a vacancy in the office of the Vice President, the President shall nominate a Vice President who shall take office upon confirmation by a majority vote of both Houses of Congress.

Section 3. Whenever the President transmits to the President pro tempore of the Senate and the Speaker of the House of Representatives his written declaration that he is unable to discharge the powers and duties of his office, and until he transmits to them a written declaration to the contrary, such powers and duties shall be discharged by the Vice President as Acting President.

Section 4. Whenever the Vice President and a majority of either the principal officers of the executive departments or of such other body as Congress may by law provide, transmit to the President pro tempore of the Senate and the Speaker of the House of Representatives their written declaration that the President is unable to discharge the powers and duties of his office, the Vice President shall immediately assume the powers and duties of the office as Acting President. Thereafter, when the President transmits to the President pro tempore of the Senate and the Speaker of the House of Representatives his written declaration that no inability exists, he shall resume the powers and duties of his office unless the Vice President and a majority of either the principal officers of the executive department or of such other body as Congress may by law provide, transmit within four days to the President pro tempore of the Senate and the Speaker of the House of Representatives their written declaration that the President is unable to discharge the powers and duties of his office. Thereupon Congress shall decide the issue, assembling within forty-eight hours for that purpose if not in session. If the Congress, within twenty-one days after receipt of the latter written declaration, or, if Congress is not in session, within twenty-one days after Congress is required to assemble, determines by two-thirds vote of both Houses that the President is unable to discharge the powers and duties of his office, the Vice President shall continue to discharge the same as Acting President; otherwise, the President shall resume the powers and duties of his office.

Amendment 26. (Ratified in 1971.)

Section 1. The right of citizens of the United States, who are eighteen years of age or older, to vote shall not be denied or abridged by the United States or any state on account of age.

Section 2. The Congress shall have the power to enforce this article by appropriate legislation.

Amendment 27. (Ratified in 1992.)

No law, varying the compensation for the services of the Senators and Representatives, shall take effect, until an election of Representatives shall have intervened.

[Editor's note: formatting added for ease of reading.]

Review Questions

1. What is a defendant saying if they "plead the fifth"?
2. Did the thirteenth amendment exempt prison labor systems? Explain.
3. With what kind of tax did the sixteenth amendment deal?
4. Which amendment repealed prohibition (repealed Amendment 18)?
5. What is the sequence of succession if the president dies or is impeached? (See the twenty-fifth amendment).

Thought Questions

1. How has the first amendment (article one in the Bill of Rights) raised controversy in the last few years? (There are several possible answers).
2. What do you think "cruel and unusual punishment" means? How is the term interpreted in debates about the death penalty?
3. Is it important to vote for president and vice president separately? Why or why not?
4. Why was the voting age moved to eighteen? (Hint: related to the military draft). Do you think other age limits should be similarly changed? Support your answer.
5. Why is it important that the Constitution be amendable? What do you think will be the next amendment?

The Northwest Ordinance

The Northwest Ordinance was adopted by the Second Continental Congress on July 13, 1787. The full name of the bill was "An Ordinance for the Government of the Territory of the United States North-West of the River Ohio." The bill was probably written by Nathan Dane, a delegate from Massachusetts, and Rufus King, a delegate from New Jersey. The purpose of the bill was to end competing claims for the territory northwest of the Ohio River. In the process of establishing a government for the Northwest Territory, it laid out precedent for exploring and settling what is now Ohio, Indiana, Illinois, Michigan, and Wisconsin; it articulated the means by which a new state could be added to the Union; and it established a bill of rights for those new states, including prohibition of slavery.

An Ordinance for the Government of the Territory of the United States, North-West of the River Ohio.

Be it ordained by the United States in Congress assembled, That the said territory, for the purposes of temporary government, be one district, subject, however, to be divided into two districts, as future circumstances may, in the opinion of Congress, make it expedient.

Be it ordained by the authority aforesaid, That the estates, both of resident and nonresident proprietors in the said territory, dying intestate, shall descent to, and be distributed among their children, and the descendants of a deceased child, in equal parts; the descendants of a deceased child or grandchild to take the share of their deceased parent in equal parts among them: And where there shall be no children or descendants, then in equal parts to the next of kin in equal degree; and among collaterals, the children of a deceased brother or sister of the intestate shall have, in equal parts among them, their deceased parents' share; and there shall in no case be a distinction between kindred of the whole and half blood; saving, in all cases, to the widow of the intestate her third part of the real estate for life, and one third part of the personal estate; and this law relative to descents and dower, shall remain in full force until altered by the legislature of the district. And until the governor and judges shall adopt laws as hereinafter mentioned, estates in the said territory may be devised or bequeathed by wills in writing, signed and sealed by him or her in whom the estate may be (being of full age), and attested by three witnesses; and real estates may be conveyed by lease and release, or bargain and sale, signed, sealed and delivered by the person being of full age, in whom the estate may be, and attested by two witnesses, provided such wills be duly proved, and such conveyances be acknowledged, or the execution thereof duly proved, and be recorded within one year after proper magistrates, courts, and registers shall be appointed for that purpose; and personal property may be transferred by delivery; saving, however to the French and Canadian inhabitants, and other settlers of the Kaskaskies, St. Vincents and the neighboring villages who have heretofore professed themselves citizens of Virginia, their laws and customs now in force among them, relative to the descent and conveyance, of property.

Be it ordained by the authority aforesaid, That there shall be appointed from time to time by Congress, a governor, whose commission shall continue in force for the term of three years, unless sooner revoked by Congress; he shall reside in the district, and have a freehold estate therein in 1,000 acres of land, while in the exercise of his office.

There shall be appointed from time to time by Congress, a secretary, whose commission shall continue in force for four years unless sooner revoked; he shall reside in the district, and have a freehold estate therein in 500 acres of land, while in the exercise of his office. It shall be his duty to keep and preserve the acts and laws passed by the legislature, and the public records of the district, and the proceedings of the governor in his executive department, and transmit authentic copies of such acts and proceedings, every six months, to the Secretary of Congress: There shall also be appointed a court to consist of three judges, any two of whom to form a court, who shall have a common law jurisdiction, and reside in the district, and have each therein a freehold estate in 500 acres of land while in the exercise of their offices; and their commissions shall continue in force during good behavior.

The governor and judges, or a majority of them, shall adopt and publish in the district such laws of the original States, criminal and civil, as may be necessary and best suited to the circumstances of the district, and report them to Congress from time to time: which laws shall be in force in the district until the organization of the General Assembly therein, unless disapproved of by Congress; but afterwards the Legislature shall have authority to alter them as they shall think fit.

The governor, for the time being, shall be commander in chief of the militia, appoint and commission all officers in the same below the rank of general officers; all general officers shall be appointed and commissioned by Congress.

Previous to the organization of the general assembly, the governor shall appoint such magistrates and other civil officers in each county or township, as he shall find necessary for the preservation of the peace and good order in the same: After the general assembly shall be organized, the powers and duties of the magistrates and other civil officers shall be regulated and defined by the said assembly; but all magistrates and other civil officers not herein otherwise directed, shall during the continuance of this temporary government, be appointed by the governor.

For the prevention of crimes and injuries, the laws to be adopted or made shall have force in all parts of the district, and for the execution of process, criminal and civil, the governor shall make proper divisions thereof; and he shall proceed from time to time as circumstances may require, to lay out the parts of the district in which the Indian titles shall have been extinguished, into counties and townships, subject, however, to such alterations as may thereafter be made by the legislature.

So soon as there shall be five thousand free male inhabitants of full age in the district, upon giving proof thereof to the governor, they shall receive authority, with time and place, to elect a representative from their counties or townships to represent them in the general assembly: Provided, That, for every five hundred free male inhabitants, there shall be one representative, and so on progressively with the number of free male inhabitants shall the right of representation increase, until the number of representatives shall amount to twenty five; after which, the number and proportion of representatives shall be regulated by the legislature: Provided, That no person be eligible or qualified to act as a representative unless he shall have been a citizen of one of the United States three years, and be a resident in the district, or unless he shall have resided in the district three years; and, in either case, shall likewise hold in his own right, in fee simple, two hundred acres of land within the same; Provided, also, That a freehold in fifty acres of land in the district, having been a citizen of one of the states, and being resident in the district, or the like freehold and two years residence in the district, shall be necessary to qualify a man as an elector of a representative.

The representatives thus elected, shall serve for the term of two years; and, in case of the death of a representative, or removal from office, the governor shall issue a writ to the county or township for which he was a member, to elect another in his stead, to serve for the residue of the term.

The general assembly or legislature shall consist of the governor, legislative council, and a house of representatives. The Legislative Council shall consist of five members, to continue in office five years, unless sooner removed by Congress; any three of whom to be a quorum: and the members of the Council shall be nominated and appointed in the following manner, to wit: As soon as representatives shall be elected, the Governor shall appoint a time and place for them to meet together; and, when met, they shall nominate ten persons, residents in the district, and each possessed of a freehold in five hundred acres of land, and return their names to Congress; five of whom Congress shall appoint and commission to serve as aforesaid; and, whenever a vacancy shall happen in the council, by death or removal from office, the house of representatives shall nominate two persons, qualified as aforesaid, for each vacancy, and return their names to Congress; one of whom congress shall appoint and commission for the residue of the term. And every five years, four months at least before the expiration of the time of service of the members of council, the said house shall nominate ten persons, qualified as aforesaid, and return their names to Congress; five of whom Congress shall appoint and commission to serve as members of the council five years, unless sooner removed. And the governor, legislative council, and House of Representatives, shall have authority to make laws in all cases, for the good government of the district, not repugnant to the principles and articles in this ordinance established and declared. And all bills, having passed by a majority in the house, and by a majority in the council, shall be referred to the governor for his assent; but no bill, or legislative act whatever, shall be of any force without his assent. The governor shall have power to convene, prorogue, and dissolve the general assembly, when, in his opinion, it shall be expedient.

The governor, judges, legislative council, secretary, and such other officers as Congress shall appoint in the district, shall take an oath or affirmation of fidelity and of office; the governor before the president of congress, and all other officers before the Governor. As soon as a legislature shall be formed in the district, the council and house assembled in one room, shall have authority, by joint ballot, to elect a delegate to Congress, who shall have a seat in Congress, with a right of debating but not voting during this temporary government.

And, for extending the fundamental principles of civil and religious liberty, which form the basis whereon these republics, their laws and constitutions are erected; to fix and establish those principles as the basis of all laws, constitutions, and governments, which forever hereafter shall be formed in the said territory: to provide also for the establishment of States, and permanent government therein, and for their admission to a share in the federal councils on an equal footing with the original States, at as early periods as may be consistent with the general interest:

It is hereby ordained and declared by the authority aforesaid, That the following articles shall be considered as articles of compact between the original States and the people and States in the said territory and forever remain unalterable, unless by common consent, to wit:

Article 1.

No person, demeaning himself in a peaceable and orderly manner, shall ever be molested on account of his mode of worship or religious sentiments, in the said territory.

Article 2.

The inhabitants of the said territory shall always be entitled to the benefits of the writ of habeas corpus, and of the trial by jury; of a proportionate representation of the people in the legislature; and of judicial proceedings according to the course of the common law. All persons shall be bailable, unless for capital offenses, where the proof shall be evident or the presumption great. All fines shall be moderate; and no cruel or unusual punishments shall be inflicted. No man shall be deprived of his liberty or property, but by the judgment of his peers or the law of the land; and, should the public exigencies make it necessary, for the common preservation, to take any person's property, or to demand his particular services, full compensation shall be made for the same. And, in the just preservation of rights and property, it is understood and declared, that no law ought ever to be made, or have force in the said territory, that shall, in any manner whatever, interfere with or affect private contracts or engagements, bona fide, and without fraud, previously formed.

Article 3.

Religion, morality, and knowledge, being necessary to good government and the happiness of mankind, schools and the means of education shall forever be encouraged. The utmost good faith shall always be observed towards the Indians; their lands and property shall never be taken from them without their consent; and, in their property, rights, and liberty, they shall never be invaded or disturbed, unless in just and lawful wars authorized by Congress; but laws founded in justice and humanity, shall from time to time be made for preventing wrongs being done to them, and for preserving peace and friendship with them.

Article 4.

The said territory, and the States which may be formed therein, shall forever remain a part of this Confederacy of the United States of America, subject to the Articles of Confederation, and to such alterations therein as shall be constitutionally made; and to all the acts and ordinances of the United States in Congress assembled, conformable thereto. The inhabitants and settlers in the said territory shall be subject to pay a part of the federal debts contracted or to be contracted, and a proportional part of the expenses of government, to be apportioned on them by Congress according to the same common rule and measure by which apportionments thereof shall be made on the other States; and the taxes for paying their proportion shall be laid and levied by the authority and direction of the legislatures of the district or districts, or new States, as in the original States, within the time agreed upon by the United States in Congress assembled. The legislatures of those districts or new States, shall never interfere with the primary disposal of the soil by the United States in Congress assembled, nor with any regulations Congress may find necessary for securing the title in such soil to the bona fide purchasers. No tax shall be imposed on lands the property of the United States; and, in no case, shall nonresident proprietors be taxed higher than residents. The navigable waters leading into the Mississippi and St. Lawrence, and the carrying places between the same, shall be common highways and forever free, as well to the inhabitants of the said territory as to the citizens of the United States, and those of any other States that may be admitted into the confederacy, without any tax, impost, or duty therefor.

Article 5.

There shall be formed in the said territory, not less than three nor more than five States; and the boundaries of the States, as soon as Virginia shall alter her act of cession, and consent to the same, shall become fixed and established as follows, to wit: The western State in the said territory, shall be bounded by the Mississippi, the Ohio, and Wabash Rivers; a direct line drawn from the Wabash and Post Vincents, due North, to the territorial line between the United States and Canada; and, by the said territorial line, to the Lake of the Woods and Mississippi. The middle State shall be bounded by the said direct line, the Wabash from Post Vincents to the Ohio, by the Ohio, by a direct line, drawn due north from the mouth of the Great Miami, to the said territorial line, and by the said territorial line. The eastern State shall be bounded by the last mentioned direct line, the Ohio, Pennsylvania, and the said territorial line: Provided, however, and it is further understood and declared, that the boundaries of these three States shall be subject so far to be altered, that, if Congress shall hereafter find it expedient, they shall have authority to form one or two States in that part of the said territory which lies north of an east and west line drawn through the southerly bend or extreme of Lake Michigan. And, whenever any of the said States shall have sixty thousand free inhabitants therein, such State shall be admitted, by its delegates, into the Congress of the United States, on an equal footing with the original States in all respects whatever, and shall be at liberty to form a permanent constitution and State government: Provided, the constitution and government so to be formed, shall be republican, and in conformity to the principles contained in these articles; and, so far as it can be consistent with the general interest of the confederacy, such admission shall be allowed at an earlier period, and when there may be a less number of free inhabitants in the State than sixty thousand.

Article 6.

There shall be neither slavery nor involuntary servitude in the said territory, otherwise than in the punishment of crimes whereof the party shall have been duly convicted: Provided, always, That any person escaping into the same, from whom labor or service is lawfully claimed in any one of the original States, such fugitive may be lawfully reclaimed and conveyed to the person claiming his or her labor or service as aforesaid.

Be it ordained by the authority aforesaid: That the resolutions of the 23rd of April, 1784, relative to the subject of this ordinance, be, and the same are hereby repealed and declared null and void.

[Editor's note: formatting added for ease of reading.]

Review Questions
1. Into how many districts was the territory in question to be divided?
2. What public officials did the ordinance establish in the northwest territories?
3. As practice in picking out the key ideas, summarize at least the first two articles.
4. On a map, draw out the potential boundaries of the new states (see article five). What modern states are contained in this area?
5. Were the new territories to be Free or Slave states?

Thought Questions
1. Only a significant population of "free males" was enough to merit representation for the territories. What does this tell you about the views on women and slaves?
2. What are the fundamental principles of civil and religious liberty? Is this emphasis ironic in light of the exclusion of women and slaves? Explain.
3. Compare the sentiments in article three with modern views on religion and education.
4. Why do you think waterways were exempt from ownership? What makes them different?
5. Why are countries and states referred to as feminine? Is this still in practice today?

The Missouri Compromise
Henry Clay

Henry Clay (1777–1852) was born in Virginia, but after finishing school, he moved to Kentucky to practice law. Before the age of thirty, Clay had been elected to the Senate to fill a temporary vacancy. He went on to serve terms in both the Senate and House. In 1818, when Missouri and Maine wished to enter the Union as new states, political debate arose as to whether they would be slave states or free states, and how that would impact the balance of states on each side of the slavery question. Clay devised the following compromise as a means of diverting the conflict. (John C. Calhoun's speech on the slavery question—also in this book—was written as a rebuttal to Clay's proposal.) Despite intense debate, the Missouri Compromise passed in 1820. Unfortunately, Clay's compromise only worked temporarily: it was repealed in 1854 by the Kansas-Nebraska Act, and three years later in *Dred Scott v. Sandford*, the Supreme Court ruled it unconstitutional.

An Act to authorize the people of the Missouri territory to form a constitution and state government, and for the admission of such state into the Union on an equal footing with the original states, and to prohibit slavery in certain territories.

Section 1. Be it enacted by the Senate and House of Representatives of the United States of America, in Congress assembled, That the inhabitants of that portion of the Missouri territory included within the boundaries herein after designated, be, and they are hereby, authorized to form for themselves a constitution and state government, and to assume such name as they shall deem proper; and the said state, when formed, shall be admitted into the Union, upon an equal footing with the original states, in all respects whatsoever.

Section 2. And be it further enacted, That the said state shall consist of all the territory included within the following boundaries, to wit: Beginning in the middle of the Mississippi river, on the parallel of thirty-six degrees of north latitude; thence west, along that parallel of latitude, to the St. Francois river; thence up, and following the course of that river, in the middle of the main channel thereof, to the parallel of latitude of thirty-six degrees and thirty minutes; thence west, along the same, to a point where the said parallel is intersected by a meridian line passing through the middle of the mouth of the Kansas river, where the same empties into the Missouri river, thence, from the point aforesaid north, along the said meridian line, to the intersection of the parallel of latitude which passes through the rapids of the river Des Moines, making the said line to correspond with the Indian boundary line; thence east, from the point of intersection last aforesaid, along the said parallel of latitude, to the middle of the channel of the main fork of the said river Des Moines; thence down arid along the middle of the main channel of the said river Des Moines, to the mouth of the same, where it empties into the Mississippi river; thence, due east, to the middle of the main channel of the Mississippi river; thence down, and following the course of the Mississippi river, in the middle of the main channel thereof, to the place of beginning: Provided, The said state shall ratify the boundaries aforesaid. And provided also, That the said state shall have concurrent jurisdiction on the river Mississippi, and every other river bordering on the said state so far as the said rivers shall form a common boundary to the said state; and any other state or states, now or hereafter to be formed and bounded by the same, such rivers to be common to both; and that the river Mississippi, and the navigable rivers and waters leading into the same, shall be common highways, and for ever free, as well to the inhabitants of the said state as to other citizens of the United States, without any tax, duty impost, or toll, therefore, imposed by the said state.

Section 3. And be it further enacted, That all free white male citizens of the United States, who shall have arrived at the age of twenty-one years, and have resided in said territory: three months previous to the day of election, and all other persons qualified to vote for representatives to the general assembly of the said territory, shall be qualified to be elected and they are hereby qualified and authorized to vote, and choose representatives to form a convention, who shall be apportioned amongst the several counties as follows:

From the county of Howard, five representatives. From the county of Cooper, three representatives. From the county of Montgomery, two representatives. From the county of Pike, one representative. From the county of Lincoln, one representative. From the county of St. Charles, three representatives. From the county of Franklin, one representative. From the county of St. Louis, eight representatives. From the county of Jefferson, one representative. From the county of Washington, three representatives. From the county of St. Genevieve, four representatives. From the county of Madison, one representative. From the county of Cape Girardeau, five representatives. From the county of New Madrid, two representatives. From the county of Wayne, and that portion of the county of Lawrence which falls within the boundaries herein designated, one representative.

And the election for the representatives aforesaid shall be holden on the first Monday, and two succeeding days of May next, throughout the several counties aforesaid in the said territory, and shall be, in every respect, held and conducted in the same manner, and under the same regulations as is prescribed by the laws of the said territory regulating elections therein for members of the general assembly, except that the returns of the election in that portion of Lawrence county included in the boundaries aforesaid, shall be made to the county of Wayne, as is provided in other cases under the laws of said territory.

Section 4. And be it further enacted, That the members of the convention thus duly elected, shall be, and they are hereby authorized to meet at the seat of government of said territory on the second Monday of the month of June next; and the said convention, when so assembled, shall have power and authority to adjourn to any other place in the said territory, which to them shall seem best for the convenient transaction of their business; and which convention, when so met, shall first determine by a majority of the whole number elected, whether it be, or be not, expedient at that time to form a constitution and state government for the people within the said territory, as included within the boundaries above designated; and if it be deemed expedient, the convention shall be, and hereby is, authorized to form a constitution and state government; or, if it be deemed more expedient, the said convention shall provide by ordinance for electing representatives to form a constitution or frame of government; which said representatives shall be chosen in such manner, and in such proportion as they shall designate; and shall meet at such time and place as shall be prescribed by the said ordinance; and shall then form for the people of said territory, within the boundaries aforesaid, a constitution and state government: Provided, That the same, whenever formed, shall be republican, and not repugnant to the constitution of the United States; and that the legislature of said state shall never interfere with the primary disposal of the soil by the United States, nor with any regulations Congress may find necessary for securing the title in such soil to the bona fide purchasers; and that no tax shall be imposed on lands the property of the United States; and in no case shall non-resident proprietors be taxed higher than residents.

Section 5. And be it further enacted, That until the next general census shall be taken, the said state shall be entitled to one representative in the House of Representatives of the United States.

Section 6. And be it further enacted, That the following propositions be, and the same are hereby, offered to the convention of the said territory of Missouri, when formed, for their free acceptance or rejection, which, if accepted by the convention, shall be obligatory upon the United States:

First. That section numbered sixteen in every township, and when such section has been sold, or otherwise disposed of, other lands equivalent thereto, and as contiguous as may be, shall be granted to the state for the use of the inhabitants of such township, for the use of schools.

Second. That all salt springs, not exceeding twelve in number, with six sections of land adjoining to each, shall be granted to the said state for the use of said state, the same to be selected by the legislature of the said state, on or before the first day of January, in the year one thousand eight hundred and twenty-five; and the same, when so selected, to be used under such terms, conditions, and regulations, as the legislature of said state shall direct: Provided, That no salt spring, the right whereof now is, or hereafter shall be, confirmed or adjudged to any individual or individuals, shall, by this section, be granted to the said state: And provided also, That the legislature shall never sell or lease the same, at anyone time, for a longer period than ten years, without the consent of Congress.

Third. That five per cent. of the net proceeds of the sale of lands lying within the said territory or state, and which shall be sold by Congress, from and after the first day of January next, after deducting all expenses incident to the same, shall be reserved for making public roads and canals, of which three fifths shall be applied to those objects within the state, under the direction of the legislature thereof; and the other two fifths in defraying, under the direction of Congress, the expenses to be incurred in making of a road or roads, canal or canals, leading to the said state.

Fourth. That four entire sections of land be, and the same are hereby, granted to the said state, for the purpose of fixing their seat of government thereon; which said sections shall, under the direction of the legislature of said state, be located, as near as may be, in one body, at any time, in such townships and ranges as the legislature aforesaid may select, on any of the public lands of the United States: Provided, That such locations shall be made prior to the public sale of the lands of the United States surrounding such location.

Fifth. That thirty-six sections, or one entire township, which shall be designated by the President of the United States, together with the other lands heretofore reserved for that purpose, shall be reserved for the use of a seminary of learning, and vested in the legislature of said state, to be appropriated solely to the use of such seminary by the said legislature: Provided, That the five foregoing propositions herein offered, are on the condition that the convention of the said state shall provide, by an ordinance, irrevocable without the consent or the United States, that every and each tract of land sold by the United States, from and after the first day of January next, shall remain exempt from any tax laid by order or under the authority of the state, whether for state, county, or township, or any other purpose whatever, for the term of five years from and after the day of sale; And further, That the bounty lands granted, or hereafter to be granted, for military services during the late war, shall, while they continue to be held by the patentees, or their heirs remain exempt as aforesaid from taxation for the term of three year; from and after the date of the patents respectively.

Section 7. And be it further enacted, That in case a constitution and state government shall be formed for the people of the said territory of Missouri, the said convention or representatives, as soon thereafter as may be, shall cause a true and attested copy of such constitution or frame of state government, as shall be formed or provided, to be transmitted to Congress.

Section 8. And be it further enacted. That in all that territory ceded by France to the United States, under the name of Louisiana, which lies north of thirty-six degrees and thirty minutes north latitude, not included within the limits of the state, contemplated by this act, slavery and involuntary servitude, otherwise than in the punishment of crimes, whereof the parties shall have been duly convicted, shall be, and is hereby, forever prohibited: Provided always, That any person escaping into the same, from whom labour or service is lawfully claimed, in any state or territory of the United States, such fugitive may be lawfully reclaimed and conveyed to the person claiming his or her labour or service as aforesaid.

[Editor's note: italics and other formatting added for ease of reading.]

Review Questions

1. What were to be the boundaries of the new state of Missouri?
2. Based on a geographical map, sketch out the rough shape of the state described in this act.
3. What was the territory ceded by France called?
4. To what did the addendum "Provided...As aforesaid" refer?
5. Where was slavery prohibited, according to this act?

Thought Questions

1. Under the Missouri Compromise, would you have lived in a slave-owning state?
2. What did the Missouri Compromise hope to accomplish? How successful was it?
3. How would you have felt if you were against slavery, but your state was a slave-holding state?
4. How do you think the lines drawn by the Missouri Compromise were chosen?
5. What were the ultimate consequences of dividing the country this way? Was it a good idea?

The Emancipation Proclamation
Abraham Lincoln

On January 1, 1863, in the third year of the Civil War, Abraham Lincoln presented a proclamation declaring all slaves in the United States to be free. The previous September, Lincoln had decreed an ultimatum to seceding states: return to the Union or all slaves in those states would be declared free. Although the Emancipation Proclamation is widely regarded as pronouncing the end of slavery, its overall effect was more of a symbolic gesture because states that had not seceded from the Union were not included, and the proclamation had no power to physically free slaves; however, the proclamation opened the door to freedoms later realized by the thirteenth, fourteenth, and fifteenth amendments to the Constitution. In this sense, it was an important beginning for the freedom movement. In addition, the Emancipation Proclamation permitted former slaves to serve in the army to fight for their own freedom.

Whereas on the twenty-second day of September, in the year of our Lord one thousand eight hundred and sixty-two, a proclamation was issued by the President of the United States, containing, among other things, the following, to wit:

"That on the first day of January, in the year of our Lord one thousand eight hundred and sixty-three, all persons held as slaves within any State or designated part of a State the people whereof shall then be in rebellion against the United States shall be then, thenceforward, and forever free; and the executive government of the United States, including the military and naval authority thereof, will recognize and maintain the freedom of such persons and will do no act or acts to repress such persons, or any of them, in any efforts they may make for their actual freedom.

"That the executive will on the first day of January aforesaid, by proclamation, designate the States and parts of States, if any, in which the people thereof, respectively, shall then be in rebellion against the United States; and the fact that any State or the people thereof shall on that day be in good faith represented in the Congress of the United States by members chosen thereto at elections wherein a majority of the qualified voters of such States shall have participated shall, in the absence of strong countervailing testimony, be deemed conclusive evidence that such State and the people thereof are not then in rebellion against the United States."

Now, therefore, I, Abraham Lincoln, President of the United States, by virtue of the power in me vested as Commander-In-Chief of the Army and Navy of the United States in time of actual armed rebellion against the authority and government of the United States, and as a fit and necessary war measure for suppressing said rebellion, do, on this first day of January, in the year of our Lord one thousand eight hundred and sixty-three, and in accordance with my purpose so to do, publicly proclaimed for the full period of one hundred days from the first day above mentioned, order and designate as the States and parts of States wherein the people thereof, respectively, are this day in rebellion against the United States the following, to wit:

Arkansas, Texas, Louisiana (except the parishes of St. Bernard, Palquemines, Jefferson, St. John, St. Charles, St. James, Ascension, Assumption, Terrebone, Lafourche, St. Mary, St. Martin, and Orleans, including the city of New Orleans), Mississippi, Alabama, Florida, Georgia, South Carolina, North Carolina, and Virginia (except the forty-eight counties designated as West Virginia, and also the counties of Berkeley, Accomac, Morthhampton, Elizabeth City, York, Princess Anne, and Norfolk, including the cities of Norfolk and Portsmouth), and which excepted parts are for the present left precisely as if this proclamation were not issued.

And by virtue of the power and for the purpose aforesaid, I do order and declare that all persons held as slaves within said designated States and parts of States are, and henceforward shall be, free; and that the Executive Government of the United States, including the military and naval authorities thereof, will recognize and maintain the freedom of said persons.

And I hereby enjoin upon the people so declared to be free to abstain from all violence, unless in necessary self-defence; and I recommend to them that, in all case when allowed, they labor faithfully for reasonable wages.

And I further declare and make known that such persons of suitable condition will be received into the armed service of the United States to garrison forts, positions, stations, and other places, and to man vessels of all sorts in said service.

And upon this act, sincerely believed to be an act of justice, warranted by the Constitution upon military necessity, I invoke the considerate judgment of mankind and the gracious favor of Almighty God.

Review Questions

1. When did the president issue his actual proclamation?
2. What evidence was used to determine which states were not in rebellion?
3. Which states were in rebellion at the time of this speech?
4. What recommendations did Lincoln give to the freed slaves?
5. Upon what grounds did Lincoln invoke the favor of God?

Thought Questions

1. Is there a difference between symbolic freedom and physical freedom? Which is more stable? Which is more valuable?
2. Which type of freedom did this document create? Support your answer.
3. Why weren't the rebellious states represented in Congress?
4. Would your home have been part of the rebellious states/counties or the non-rebellious ones?
5. Freed slaves were invited to join the military under this proclamation. What did this offer symbolize? Did it represent a change in the way white Americans viewed black people?

The Pledge of Allegiance
Francis Bellamy

Francis Bellamy (1855–1931) was born in New York, where as an adult he was ordained as a minister and then left the church to pursue a career as a journalist. Bellamy's career change coincided with a movement led by James Bailey Upham, a fellow journalist, to provide all public schools with a flag and educate students about the flag-raising ceremony. Through his friendship with Upham, Bellamy was chosen to write a pledge to be recited at the National Public Schools Celebration of Columbus Day. Bellamy's pledge was published anonymously in 1892. The authorship of the pledge was later contested by Upham, but in 1939, the United States Flag Association ruled in favor of Bellamy. The pledge was officially recognized by Congress on June 22, 1942, and in 1945 it was named "The Pledge of Allegiance." In recent years, the words "under God," which were added by President Eisenhower in 1954, have caused controversy between those who object to the addition of the words and those who consider them an integral part of the pledge.

I pledge allegiance to the Flag
Of the United States of America,
And to the Republic for which it stands:
One Nation under God, indivisible,
With Liberty and Justice for all.

Review Questions

1. What does a "pledge" mean?
2. What are you promising when you say this pledge?
3. What is a *republic*? Is the United States a republic? What characteristics of a republic does the United States have? What characteristics does it lack?
4. Would this pledge be as effective if it used the words "I pledge allegiance to the president"? How would such a pledge be different?
5. What did this pledge say about the foundations of our nation?

Thought Questions

1. When you pledge allegiance to the flag, are you promising loyalty to a piece of colored cloth? What does the flag represent?
2. Discuss the controversy over the words "under God." Do you think it's an important issue? Why or why not? Support your answer.
3. How would you define *liberty*? *Justice*? Is there a universal definition?
4. Does the United States provide liberty for all today? What about justice?
5. Is it ever possible to truly provide liberty and justice for all? Why or why not?

Dred Scott v. Sandford
Roger B. Taney

Roger Brooke Taney (1777–1864) was born in Maryland, where he practiced law until he was appointed attorney general and then secretary of the treasury during Andrew Jackson's presidency. In 1836, President Jackson appointed him fifth Chief Justice of the United States Supreme Court, and he served in that role until his death. Taney has become infamous for a case that came before the Supreme Court in 1857. A black slave, Dred Scott, had lived in the Illinois (a free state) and Wisconsin (a free territory) before returning to Missouri (a slave state). Scott sued to the courts on the grounds that living in a free state entitled him to freedom. The court ruled against him. The decision, written by Taney, declared that Scott could not be a citizen because he was black, and therefore he had no right to sue to the court. The court also declared the Missouri Compromise unconstitutional because it prohibited slavery in new states and territories. Taney's decision was highly controversial, and it brought the slavery question to new national prominence. (Note: Defendant John F. A. Sanford's name was misspelled as Sandford in the formal reports.)

There are two leading questions presented by the record: 1. Had the Circuit Court of the United States jurisdiction to hear and determine the case between these parties? And 2. If it had jurisdiction, is the judgment it has given erroneous or not?

The plaintiff in error, who was also the plaintiff in the court, was, with his wife and children, held slaves by the defendant, in the State of Missouri; and he brought this action in the Circuit Court of the United States for that district, to assert the title of himself and his family to freedom.

The declaration is in the form usually adopted in that State to try questions of this description, and contains the averment necessary to give the court jurisdiction; that he and the defendant are citizens of different States; that is, that he is a citizen of Missouri, and the defendant a citizen of New York.

The defendant pleaded in abatement to the jurisdiction of the court, that the plaintiff was not a citizen of the State of Missouri, as alleged in his declaration, being a Negro of African descent, whose ancestors were of pure African blood, and who were brought into this country and sold as slaves.

Before we speak of the pleas in bar, it will be proper to dispose of the questions which have arisen on the plea in abatement.

That plea denies the right of the plaintiff to sue in a court of the United States, for the reasons therein stated.

If the question raised by it is legally before us, and the court should be of opinion that the facts stated in it disqualify the plaintiff from becoming a citizen, in the sense in which that word is used in the Constitution of the United States, then the judgment of the Circuit Court is erroneous, and must be reversed.

The question is simply this: Can a Negro, whose ancestors were imported into this country, and sold as slaves, become a member of the political community formed and brought into existence by the Constitution of the United States, and as such become entitled to all the rights, and privileges, and immunities, guaranteed by that instrument to the citizen? One of which rights is the privilege of suing in a court of the United States in the cases specified in the Constitution.

It will be observed, that the plea applies to that class of persons only whose ancestors were Negroes of the African race, and imported into this country, and sold and held as slaves. The only matter in issue before the court, therefore, is, whether the descendants of such slaves, when they shall be emancipated, or who are born of parents who had become free before their birth, are citizens of a State, in the sense in which the word citizen is used in the Constitution of the United States.

The words 'people of the United States' and 'citizens' are synonymous terms, and mean the same thing. They both describe the political body who, according to our republican institutions, form the sovereignty, and who hold the power and conduct the Government through their representatives. They are what we familiarly call the 'sovereign people,' and every citizen is one of this people, and a constituent member of this sovereignty. The question before us is, whether the class of persons described in the plea in abatement compose a portion of this people, and are constituent members of this sovereignty? We think they are not, and that they are not included, and were not intended to be included, under the word 'citizens' in the Constitution, and can therefore claim none of the rights and privileges which that instrument provides for and secures to citizens of the United States. On the contrary, they were at that time considered as a subordinate and inferior class of beings, who had been subjugated by the dominant race, and, whether emancipated or not, yet remained subject to their authority, and had no rights or privileges but such as those who held the power and the Government might choose to grant them.

In discussing this question, we must not confound the rights of citizenship which a State may confer within its own limits, and the rights of citizenship as a member of the Union. It does not by any means follow, because he has all the rights and privileges of a citizen of a State, that he must be a citizen of the United States. He may have all of the rights and privileges of the citizen of a State, and yet not be entitled to the rights and privileges of a citizen in any other State. For, previous to the adoption of the Constitution of the United States, every State had the undoubted right to confer on whomsoever it pleased the character of citizen, and to endow him with all its rights. But this character of course was confined to the boundaries of the State, and gave him no rights or privileges in other States beyond those secured to him by the laws of nations and the comity of States. Nor have the several States surrendered the power of conferring these rights and privileges by adopting the Constitution of the United States. Each State may still confer them upon an alien, or any one it thinks proper, or upon any class or description of persons; yet he would not be a citizen in the sense in which that word is used in the Constitution of the United States, nor entitled to sue as such in one of its courts, nor to the privileges and immunities of a citizen in the other States. The rights which he would acquire would be restricted to the State which gave them.

It is very clear, therefore, that no State can, by any act or law of its own, passed since the adoption of the Constitution, introduce a new member into the political community created by the Constitution of the United States. It cannot make him a member of this community by making him a member of its own. And for the same reason it cannot introduce any person, or description of persons, who were not intended to be embraced in this new political family, which the Constitution brought into existence, but were intended to be excluded from it.

The question then arises, whether the provisions of the Constitution, in relation to the personal rights and privileges to which the citizen of a State should be entitled, embraced the Negro African race, at that time in this country, or who might afterwards be imported, who had then or should afterwards be made free in any State; and to put it in the power of a single State to make him a citizen of the United States, and endue him with the full rights of citizenship in every other State without their consent? Does the Constitution of the United States act upon him whenever he shall be made free under the laws of a State, and raised there to the rank of a citizen, and immediately clothe him with all the privileges of a citizen in any other State, and in its own courts?

The court think the affirmative of these propositions cannot be maintained. And if it cannot, the plaintiff in error could not be a citizen of the State of Missouri, within the meaning of the Constitution of the United States, and, consequently, was not entitled to sue in its courts.

It is true, every person, and every class and description of persons, who were at the time of the adoption of the Constitution recognized as citizens in the several States, became also citizens of this new political body; but none other; it was formed by them, and for them and their posterity, but for no one else. And the personal rights and privileges guarantied to citizens of this new sovereignty were intended to embrace those only who were then members of the several State communities, or who should afterwards by birthright or otherwise become members, according to the provisions of the Constitution and the principles on which it was founded.

It becomes necessary, therefore, to determine who were citizens of the several States when the Constitution was adopted. And in order to do this, we must recur to the Governments and institutions of the thirteen colonies, when they separated from Great Britain and formed new sovereignties, and took their places in the family of independent nations. We must inquire who, at that time, were recognized as the people or citizens of a State.

In the opinion of the court, the legislation and histories of the times, and the language used in the Declaration of Independence, show, that neither the class of persons who had been imported as slaves, nor their descendants, whether they had become free or not, were then acknowledged as a part of the people, nor intended to be included in the general words used in that memorable instrument.

It is difficult at this day to realize the state of public opinion in relation to that unfortunate race, which prevailed in the civilized and enlightened portions of the world at the time of the Declaration of Independence, and when the Constitution of the United States was framed and adopted.

They had for more than a century before been regarded as beings of an inferior order, and altogether unfit to associate with the white race, either in social or political relations; and so far inferior, that they had no rights which the white man was bound to respect; and that the Negro might justly and lawfully be reduced to slavery for his benefit. He was bought and sold, and treated as an ordinary article of merchandise and traffic, whenever a profit could be made by it. This opinion was at that time fixed and universal in the civilized portion of the white race. It was regarded as an axiom in morals as well as in politics, which no one thought of disputing, or supposed to be open to dispute; and men in every grade and position in society daily and habitually acted upon it in their private pursuits, as well as in matters of public concern, without doubting for a moment the correctness of this opinion.

A Negro of the African race was regarded by them as an article of property, and held, and bought and sold as such, in every one of the thirteen colonies which united in the Declaration of Independence, and afterwards formed the Constitution of the United States. The slaves were more or less numerous in the different colonies, as slave labor was found more or less profitable. But no one seems to have doubted the correctness of the prevailing opinion of the time.

The legislation of the different colonies furnishes positive and indisputable proof of this fact.

The language of the Declaration of Independence is equally conclusive:

It begins by declaring that, 'when in the course of human events it becomes necessary for one people to dissolve the political bands which have connected them with another, and to assume among the powers of the earth the separate and equal station to which the laws of nature and nature's God entitle them, a decent respect for the opinions of mankind requires that they should declare the causes which impel them to the separation.'

It then proceeds to say: 'We hold these truths to be self-evident: that all men are created equal; that they are endowed by their Creator with certain unalienable rights; that among them is life, liberty, and the pursuit of happiness; that to secure these rights, Governments are instituted, deriving their just powers from the consent of the governed.'

The general words above quoted would seem to embrace the whole human family, and if they were used in a similar instrument at this day would be so understood. But it is too clear for dispute, that the enslaved African race were not intended to be included, and formed no part of the people who framed and adopted this declaration; for if the language, as understood in that day, would embrace them, the conduct of the distinguished men who framed the Declaration of Independence would have been utterly and flagrantly inconsistent with the principles they asserted; and instead of the sympathy of mankind, to which they so confidently appealed, they would have deserved and received universal rebuke and reprobation.

Yet the men who framed this declaration were great men—high in literary acquirements—high in their sense of honor, and incapable of asserting principles inconsistent with those on which they were acting. They perfectly understood the meaning of the language they used, and how it would be understood by others; and they knew that it would not in any part of the civilized world be supposed to embrace the Negro race, which, by common consent, had been excluded from civilized Governments and the family of nations, and doomed to slavery. They spoke and acted according to the then established doctrines and principles, and in the ordinary language of the day, and no one misunderstood them. The unhappy black race were separated from the white by indelible marks, and laws long before established, and were never thought of or spoken of except as property, and when the claims of the owner or the profit of the trader were supposed to need protection.

This state of public opinion had undergone no change when the Constitution was adopted, as is equally evident from its provisions and language.

The brief preamble sets forth by whom it was formed, for what purposes, and for whose benefit and protection. It declares that it is formed by the people of the United States; that is to say, by those who were members of the different political communities in the several States; and its great object is declared to be to secure the blessings of liberty to themselves and their posterity. It speaks in general terms of the people of the United States, and of citizens of the several States, when it is providing for the exercise of the powers granted or the privileges secured to the citizen. It does not define what description of persons are intended to be included under these terms, or who shall be regarded as a citizen and one of the people. It uses them as terms so well understood, that no further description or definition was necessary.

But there are two clauses in the Constitution which point directly and specifically to the Negro race as a separate class of persons, and show clearly that they were not regarded as a portion of the people or citizens of the Government then formed.

One of these clauses reserves to each of the thirteen States the right to import slaves until the year 1808, if it thinks proper. And the importation which it thus sanctions was unquestionably of persons of the race of which we are speaking, as the traffic in slaves in the United States had always been confined to them. And by the other provision the States pledge themselves to each other to maintain the right of property of the master, by delivering up to him any slave who may have escaped from his service, and be found within their respective territories. By the first above-mentioned clause, therefore, the right to purchase and hold this property is directly sanctioned and authorized for twenty years by the people who framed the Constitution. And by the second, they pledge themselves to maintain and uphold the right of the master in the manner specified, as long as the Government they then formed should endure. And these two provisions show, conclusively, that neither the description of persons therein referred to, nor their descendants, were embraced in any of the other provisions of the Constitution; for certainly these two clauses were not intended to confer on them or their posterity the blessings of liberty, or any of the personal rights so carefully provided for the citizen.

Indeed, when we look to the condition of this race in the several States at the time, it is impossible to believe that these rights and privileges were intended to be extended to them.

The legislation of the States therefore shows, in a manner not to be mistaken, the inferior and subject condition of that race at the time the Constitution was adopted, and long afterwards, throughout the thirteen States by which that instrument was framed; and it is hardly consistent with the respect due to these Stakes, to suppose that they regarded at that time, as fellow-citizens and members of the sovereignty, a class of beings whom they had thus stigmatized; whom, as we are bound, out of respect to the State sovereignties, to assume they had deemed it just and necessary thus to stigmatize, and upon whom they had impressed such deep and enduring marks of inferiority and degradation; or, that when they met in convention to form the Constitution, they looked upon them as a portion of their constituents, or designed to include them in the provisions so carefully inserted for the security and protection of the liberties and rights of their citizens. It cannot be supposed that they intended to secure to them rights, and privileges, and rank, in the new political body throughout the Union, which every one of them denied within the limits of its own dominion. More especially, it cannot be believed that the large slaveholding States regarded them as included in the word citizens, or would have consented to a Constitution which might compel them to receive that character from another State. For if they were so received, and entitled to the privileges and immunities of citizens, it would exempt them from the operation of the special laws and from the police regulations which they considered to be necessary for their own safety. It would give to persons of the Negro race, who were recognized as citizens in any one State of the Union, the right to enter every other State whenever they pleased, singly or in companies, without pass or passport, and without obstruction, to sojourn there as long as they pleased, to go where they pleased at every hour of the day or night without molestation, unless they committed some violation of law for which a white man would be punished; and it would give them the full liberty of speech in public and in private upon all subjects upon which its own citizens might speak; to hold public meetings upon political affairs, and to keep and carry arms wherever they went. And all of this would be done in the face of the subject race of the same color, both free and slaves, and inevitably producing discontent and insubordination among them, and endangering the peace and safety of the State.

Upon a full and careful consideration of the subject, the court is of opinion, that, upon the facts stated in the plea in abatement, Dred Scott was not a citizen of Missouri within the meaning of the Constitution of the United States, and not entitled as such to sue in its courts; and, consequently, that the Circuit Court had no jurisdiction of the case, and that the judgment on the plea in abatement is erroneous.

We proceed, therefore, to inquire whether the facts relied on by the plaintiff entitled him to his freedom.

In considering this part of the controversy, two questions arise: Was he, together with his family, free in Missouri by reason of the stay in the territory of the United States hereinbefore mentioned? If they were not, is Scott himself free by reason of his removal to Rock Island, in the State of Illinois, as stated in the above admissions?

We proceed to examine the first question.

The act of Congress, upon which the plaintiff relies, declares that slavery and involuntary servitude, except as a punishment for crime, shall be forever prohibited in all that part of the territory ceded by France, under the name of Louisiana, which lies north of thirty-six degrees thirty minutes north latitude, and not included within the limits of Missouri. And the difficulty which meets us at the threshold of this part of the inquiry is, whether Congress was authorized to pass this law under any of the powers granted to it by the Constitution; for if the authority is not given by that instrument, it is the duty of this court to declare it void and inoperative, and incapable of conferring freedom upon any one who is held as a slave under the laws of any one of the States.

The counsel for the plaintiff has laid much stress upon that article in the Constitution which confers on Congress the power 'to dispose of and make all needful rules and regulations respecting the territory or other property belonging to the United States;' but, in the judgment of the court, that provision has no bearing on the present controversy, and the power there given, whatever it may be, is confined, and was intended to be confined, to the territory which at that time belonged to, or was claimed by, the United States, and was within their boundaries as settled by the treaty with Great Britain, and can have no influence upon a territory afterwards acquired from a foreign Government. It was a special provision for a known and particular territory, and to meet a present emergency, and nothing more.

If this clause is construed to extend to territory acquired by the present Government from a foreign nation, outside of the limits of any charter from the British Government to a colony, it would be difficult to say why it was deemed necessary to give the Government the power to sell any vacant lands belonging to the sovereignty which might be found within it; and if this was necessary, why the grant of this power should precede the power to legislate over it and establish a Government there; and still more difficult to say, why it was deemed necessary so specially and particularly to grant the power to make needful rules and regulations in relation to any personal or movable property it might acquire there. For the words, other property necessarily, by every known rule of interpretation, must mean property of a different description from territory or land. And the difficulty would perhaps be insurmountable in endeavoring to account for the last member of the sentence, which provides that 'nothing in this Constitution shall be so construed as to prejudice any claims of the United States or any particular State,' or to say how any particular State could have claims in or to a territory ceded by a foreign Government, or to account for associating this provision with the preceding provisions of the clause, with which it would appear to have no connection.

But the power of Congress over the person or property of a citizen can never be a mere discretionary power under our Constitution and form of Government. The powers of the Government and the rights and privileges of the citizen are regulated and plainly defined by the Constitution itself. And when the Territory becomes a part of the United States, the Federal Government enters into possession in the character impressed upon it by those who created it. It enters upon it with its powers over the citizen strictly defined, and limited by the Constitution, from which it derives its own existence, and by virtue of which alone it continues to exist and act as a Government and sovereignty. It has no power of any kind beyond it; and it cannot, when it enters a Territory of the United States, put off its character, and assume discretionary or despotic powers which the Constitution has denied to it. It cannot create for itself a new character separated from the citizens of the United States, and the duties it owes them under the provisions of the Constitution. The Territory being a part of the United States, the Government and the citizen both enter it under the authority of the Constitution, with their respective rights defined and marked out; and the Federal Government can exercise no power over his person or property, beyond what that instrument confers, nor lawfully deny any right which it has reserved.

The rights of private property have been guarded with equal care. Thus the rights of property are united with the rights of person, and placed on the same ground by the fifth amendment to the Constitution, which provides that no person shall be deprived of life, liberty, and property, without due process of law. And an act of Congress which deprives a citizen of the United States of his liberty or property, merely because he came himself or brought his property into a particular Territory of the United States, and who had committed no offence against the laws, could hardly be dignified with the name of due process of law.

And this prohibition is not confined to the States, but the words are general, and extend to the whole territory over which the Constitution gives it power to legislate, including those portions of it remaining under Territorial Government, as well as that covered by States. It is a total absence of power everywhere within the dominion of the United States, and places the citizens of a Territory, so far as these rights are concerned, on the same footing with citizens of the States, and guards them as firmly and plainly against any inroads which the General Government might attempt, under the plea of implied or incidental powers. And if Congress itself cannot do this—if it is beyond the powers conferred on the Federal Government—it will be admitted, we presume, that it could not authorize a Territorial Government to exercise them. It could confer no power on any local Government, established by its authority, to violate the provisions of the Constitution.

It seems, however, to be supposed that there is a difference between property in a slave and other property, and that different rules may be applied to it in expounding the Constitution of the United States.

But if the Constitution recognizes the right of property of the master in a slave, and makes no distinction between that description of property and other property owned by a citizen, no tribunal, acting under the authority of the United States, whether it be legislative, executive, or judicial, has a right to draw such a distinction, or deny to it the benefit of the provisions and guarantees which have been provided for the protection of private property against the encroachments of the Government.

Now the right of property in a slave is distinctly and expressly affirmed in the Constitution. The right to traffic in it, like an ordinary article of merchandise and property, was guaranteed to the citizens of the United States in every State that might desire it, for twenty years. And the Government in express terms is pledged to protect it in all future time, if the slave escapes from his owner. This is done in plain words—too plain to be misunderstood. And no word can be found in the Constitution which gives Congress a greater power over slave property, or which entitles property of that kind to less protection than property of any other description. The only power conferred is the power coupled with the duty of guarding and protecting the owner in his rights.

Upon these considerations, it is the opinion of the court that the act of Congress which prohibited a citizen from holding and owning property of this kind in the Territory of the United States north of the line therein mentioned, is not warranted by the Constitution, and is therefore void; and that neither Dred Scott himself, nor any of his family, were made free by being carried into this territory, even if they had been carried there by the owner, with the intention of becoming a permanent resident.

Upon the whole, therefore, it is the judgment of this court, that it appears by the record before us that the plaintiff in error is not a citizen of Missouri, in the sense in which that word is used in the Constitution; and that the Circuit Court of the United States, for that reason, had no jurisdiction in the case, and could give no judgment in it.

Its judgment for the defendant must, consequently, be reversed, and a mandate issued, directing the suit to be dismissed for want of jurisdiction.

Review Questions

1. What was the court's answer to the question: "Can a Negro [...] become a member of the political community"?
2. What was the relationship between the words "people of the United States" and "citizens" according to Taney? What did they mean?
3. What did Taney say about individual states giving out United States citizenship?
4. What was public opinion about black people at the time of the Declaration of Independence?
5. What parts of the Constitution approved of slavery and the "inferiority" of black people?

Thought Questions

1. How did Taney inherently make a distinction between the terms "persons," as in "class of persons" and "people," as in "people of the United States"? Does this seem contradictory to you?
2. How did Taney reconcile the "all men are created equal" of the Declaration of Independence with slavery? Does his logic (apart from the content of what he said) make sense?
3. Under which act of Congress did Dred Scott make his argument? (Hint: included in this book.) How did Taney undermine the authority of that act?
4. Why was it important, in terms of Taney's argument, that slaves were regarded as property?
5. This speech rightly caused anger among abolitionists. Can you pick out several phrases that might have been particularly offensive?

Brown v. Board of Education of Topeka
Earl Warren

Earl Warren (1891–1974) was born in California and worked there as a private lawyer and a district attorney before he was elected governor in 1942. After an unsuccessful bid for the vice presidency, in 1953, President Eisenhower appointed him the fourteenth Chief Justice of the Supreme Court. Warren held that role for sixteen years, retiring in 1969. One of Warren's most notable decisions came in 1954 in *Brown v. Board of Education of Topeka*, which was actually a collection of five related cases from Delaware, Kansas, South Carolina, Virginia, and Washington, D.C. Each case challenged the inferiority of schools segregated along racial lines. By deciding in favor of Brown, et. al., Warren rejected the doctrine of "separate but equal" that had governed race relations since the *Plessy v. Ferguson* decision in 1896. Warren's decision provided additional momentum for the burgeoning Civil Rights movement in the United States.

These cases come to us from the States of Kansas, South Carolina, Virginia, and Delaware. They are premised on different facts and different local conditions, but a common legal question justifies their consideration together in this consolidated opinion.

In each of the cases, minors of the Negro race, through their legal representatives, seek the aid of the courts in obtaining admission to the public schools of their community on a nonsegregated basis. In each instance, they had been denied admission to schools attended by white children under laws requiring or permitting segregation according to race. This segregation was alleged to deprive the plaintiffs of the equal protection of the laws under the Fourteenth Amendment. In each of the cases other than the Delaware case, a three-judge federal district court denied relief to the plaintiffs on the so-called "separate but equal" doctrine announced by this Court in *Plessy v. Ferguson*, 163 U.S. 537. Under that doctrine, equality of treatment is accorded when the races are provided substantially equal facilities, even though these facilities be separate. In the Delaware case, the Supreme Court of Delaware adhered to that doctrine, but ordered that the plaintiffs be admitted to the white schools because of their superiority to the Negro schools.

The plaintiffs contend that segregated public schools are not "equal" and cannot be made "equal," and that hence they are deprived of the equal protection of the laws. Because of the obvious importance of the question presented, the Court took jurisdiction. Argument was heard in the 1952 Term, and reargument was heard this Term on certain questions propounded by the Court.

Reargument was largely devoted to the circumstances surrounding the adoption of the Fourteenth Amendment in 1868. It covered exhaustively consideration of the Amendment in Congress, ratification by the states, then-existing practices in racial segregation, and the views of proponents and opponents of the Amendment. This discussion and our own investigation convince us that, although these sources cast some light, it is not enough to resolve the problem with which we are faced. At best, they are inconclusive. The most avid proponents of the post-War Amendments undoubtedly intended them to remove all legal distinctions among "all persons born or naturalized in the United States." Their opponents, just as certainly, were antagonistic to both the letter and the spirit of the Amendments and wished them to have the most limited effect. What others in Congress and the state legislatures had in mind cannot be determined with any degree of certainty.

An additional reason for the inconclusive nature of the Amendment's history with respect to segregated schools is the status of public education at that time. In the South, the movement toward free common schools, supported by general taxation, had not yet taken hold. Education of white children was largely in the hands of private groups. Education of Negroes was almost nonexistent, and practically all of the race were illiterate. In fact, any education of Negroes was forbidden by law in some states. Today, in contrast, many Negroes have achieved outstanding success in the arts and sciences, as well as in the business and professional world. It is true that public school education at the time of the Amendment had advanced further in the North, but the effect of the Amendment on Northern States was generally ignored in the congressional debates. Even in the North, the conditions of public education did not approximate those existing today. The curriculum was usually rudimentary; ungraded schools were common in rural areas; the school term was but three months a year in many states, and compulsory school attendance was virtually unknown. As a consequence, it is not surprising that there should be so little in the history of the Fourteenth Amendment relating to its intended effect on public education.

In the first cases in this Court construing the Fourteenth Amendment, decided shortly after its adoption, the Court interpreted it as proscribing all state-imposed discriminations against the Negro race. The doctrine of "separate but equal" did not make its appearance in this Court until 1896 in the case of *Plessy v. Ferguson*, supra, involving not education but transportation. American courts have since labored with the doctrine for over half a century. In this Court, there have been six cases involving the "separate but equal" doctrine in the field of public education. In *Cumming v. County Board of Education*, 175 U.S. 528, and *Gong Lum v. Rice*, 275 U.S. 78, the validity of the doctrine itself was not challenged. In more recent cases, all on the graduate school level, inequality was found in that specific benefits enjoyed by white students were denied to Negro students of the same educational qualifications. *Missouri ex rel. Gaines v. Canada*, 305 U.S. 337; *Sipuel v. Oklahoma*, 332 U.S. 631; *Sweatt v. Painter*, 339 U.S. 629; *McLaurin v. Oklahoma State Regents*, 339 U.S. 637. In none of these cases was it necessary to reexamine the doctrine to grant relief to the Negro plaintiff. And in *Sweatt v. Painter*, supra, the Court expressly reserved decision on the question whether *Plessy v. Ferguson* should be held inapplicable to public education.

In the instant cases, that question is directly presented. Here, unlike *Sweatt v. Painter*, there are findings below that the Negro and white schools involved have been equalized, or are being equalized, with respect to buildings, curricula, qualifications and salaries of teachers, and other "tangible" factors. Our decision, therefore, cannot turn on merely a comparison of these tangible factors in the Negro and white schools involved in each of the cases. We must look instead to the effect of segregation itself on public education.

In approaching this problem, we cannot turn the clock back to 1868, when the Amendment was adopted, or even to 1896, when *Plessy v. Ferguson* was written. We must consider public education in the light of its full development and its present place in American life throughout the Nation. Only in this way can it be determined if segregation in public schools deprives these plaintiffs of the equal protection of the laws.

Today, education is perhaps the most important function of state and local governments. Compulsory school attendance laws and the great expenditures for education both demonstrate our recognition of the importance of education to our democratic society. It is required in the performance of our most basic public responsibilities, even service in the armed forces. It is the very foundation of good citizenship. Today it is a principal instrument in awakening the child to cultural values, in preparing him for later professional training, and in helping him to adjust normally to his environment. In these days, it is doubtful that any child may reasonably be expected to succeed in life if he is denied the opportunity of an education. Such an opportunity, where the state has undertaken to provide it, is a right which must be made available to all on equal terms.

We come then to the question presented: Does segregation of children in public schools solely on the basis of race, even though the physical facilities and other "tangible" factors may be equal, deprive the children of the minority group of equal educational opportunities? We believe that it does.

In *Sweatt v. Painter*, supra, in finding that a segregated law school for Negroes could not provide them equal educational opportunities, this Court relied in large part on "those qualities which are incapable of objective measurement but which make for greatness in a law school." In *McLaurin v. Oklahoma State Regents*, supra, the Court, in requiring that a Negro admitted to a white graduate school be treated like all other students, again resorted to intangible considerations: "...his ability to study, to engage in discussions and exchange views with other students, and, in general, to learn his profession." Such considerations apply with added force to children in grade and high schools. To separate them from others of similar age and qualifications solely because of their race generates a feeling of inferiority as to their status in the community that may affect their hearts and minds in a way unlikely ever to be undone. The effect of this separation on their educational opportunities was well stated by a finding in the Kansas case by a court which nevertheless felt compelled to rule against the Negro plaintiffs:

> Segregation of white and colored children in public schools has a detrimental effect upon the colored children. The impact is greater when it has the sanction of the law, for the policy of separating the races is usually interpreted as denoting the inferiority of the Negro group. A sense of inferiority affects the motivation of a child to learn. Segregation with the sanction of law, therefore, has a tendency

to [retard] the educational and mental development of Negro children and to deprive them of some of the benefits they would receive in a racial[ly] integrated school system.

Whatever may have been the extent of psychological knowledge at the time of *Plessy v. Ferguson*, this finding is amply supported by modern authority. Any language in *Plessy v. Ferguson* contrary to this finding is rejected.

We conclude that, in the field of public education, the doctrine of "separate but equal" has no place. Separate educational facilities are inherently unequal. Therefore, we hold that the plaintiffs and others similarly situated for whom the actions have been brought are, by reason of the segregation complained of, deprived of the equal protection of the laws guaranteed by the Fourteenth Amendment. This disposition makes unnecessary any discussion whether such segregation also violates the Due Process Clause of the Fourteenth Amendment.

Because these are class actions, because of the wide applicability of this decision, and because of the great variety of local conditions, the formulation of decrees in these cases presents problems of considerable complexity. On reargument, the consideration of appropriate relief was necessarily subordinated to the primary question—the constitutionality of segregation in public education. We have now announced that such segregation is a denial of the equal protection of the laws. In order that we may have the full assistance of the parties in formulating decrees, the cases will be restored to the docket, and the parties are requested to present further argument on Questions 4 and 5 previously propounded by the Court for the reargument this Term. The Attorney General of the United States is again invited to participate. The Attorneys General of the states requiring or permitting segregation in public education will also be permitted to appear as *amici curiae* upon request to do so by September 15, 1954, and submission of briefs by October 1, 1954.

Review Questions

1. What was the common legal question of the cases Warren first mentioned?
2. In what Supreme Court case did the doctrine of "Separate but Equal" first appear?
3. Why was the history of the fourteenth amendment insufficient evidence in this case?
4. What was the "most important function of state and local governments," according to Warren?
5. What was Warren's conclusion about the "Separate but Equal" doctrine?

Thought Questions

1. Can things be different but equal? Why then was this particular doctrine so offensive?
2. Why did Warren think education was so important? Why do you think education is of value?
3. Warren said education was a right. Do you think education is a right or a privilege?
4. Have your school experiences been basically separated by race or basically integrated? How has this influenced your education?
5. Warren said that "a sense of inferiority affects the motivation of a child to learn." Explain why this might be so. Do you agree?

LEGAL DOCUMENTS

Writing Practice

While essays, articles, and speeches can explore options and present both sides of an issue, legal documents are designed to close loopholes and provide a clear set of standards for individuals and public officials to follow and enforce.

Look at the following paragraph from *The Federalist Papers*, Number 30:

> "What remedy can there be for this situation, but in a change of the system which has produced it in a change of the fallacious and delusive system of quotas and requisitions? What substitute can there be imagined for this *ignis fatuus* in finance, but that of permitting the national government to raise its own revenues by the ordinary methods of taxation authorized in every well-ordered constitution of civil government? Ingenious men may declaim with plausibility on any subject; but no human ingenuity can point out any other expedient to rescue us from the inconveniences and embarrassments naturally resulting from defective supplies of the public treasury."

As with other exercises, begin by rewriting the paragraph in your own words. Now, shifting your focus, rewrite the passage again, this time as if you were proposing a law or a resolution based on these ideas. You will need to define your terms, give clear parameters, aim for brevity and clarity, and (at your discretion) perhaps include a strategic bit of vagueness that will allow your proposal to be reinterpreted at a later date or applied to a different situation. For assistance, use what you have learned from reading the court decisions, declarations, contracts, and compromises in this book.

Looking Back, Looking Forward

Congratulations! You have now worked your way through forty-three classic documents from the history of American government. Along the way, you've assembled a variety of reading and thinking tools for future reading and writing experiences. So, you may be thinking, what now?

The Next Step

As you work to become a better, more informed individual, remember to look backward and forward. This collection is designed to show the profound impact documents and policies instituted in the past have had on life today. Very rarely are laws or issues in current events the result of a random event or choice. Instead, they reflect generations of past events and past decisions, all of which have contributed to the present situation. Events that happen today will have an effect in the future. Learning to read and think critically about these ideas is vital.

For students in ninth to twelfth grade, or for learners of any age who are ready to ask questions and think analytically about literature, a great resource is *How to Read the Federalist Papers*. This short book from the Heritage Foundation gives you tools to understand the importance of *The Federalist* in light of history and helps you connect its ideas to important contemporary issues.

Another resource to consider is the next book in the *Words Aptly Spoken* series, *Words Aptly Spoken: American Literature*. This book eases you into a study of American literature as it guides you through progressively more challenging books. It also leads you step-by-step through the process of writing an essay, giving you tools to improve not only your reading, but your writing as well.

Both of these books build on the skills you have begun to hone and will help you continue your journey through the world of literature.

Perspectives, Take Two

In today's society, mass media has an enormous impact on the way people view the world. Every day a million and one ideas compete for your attention. Most messages are designed to be absorbed passively and accepted without questioning. If nothing else, this book encourages you to practice reading—and, by default, listening and watching—with your brain fully engaged. If you can do this, you will be better prepared to distinguish between that which is merely enjoyable and that which is worthy of application to your own life.

In closing, as you continue this journey, it is worth repeating that participating in the great conversations of literature is an art that takes a lifetime to refine. However, it is an art that will yield a lifetime of fruit as you celebrate with family and friends the joy of laughing, crying, and simply bubbling over with excitement about the great stories which are now yours to share.

Best wishes on your journey!

Endnotes
Judy Palmer

In all these documents, we have tried to edit with the greatest accuracy of the original work rather than the commonly accepted version of the work. The greatest discrepancy, thus far, has been in the Gettysburg Address. Items with no changes or very minor have not been included. Use these notes as a reference for any discrepancies in document versions.

What's That You Say? Speeches

"Liberty or Death," by Patrick Henry
    Corrected mainly paragraphing to conform with: http://www.law.ou.edu/ushistory/henry.shtml http://www.history.org/Almanack/people/bios/pathenryspeech.html.

"First Inaugural Address," by George Washington
    Punctuation and capitalization needed to line up with the original document. See: http://www.historybuff.com/presidents/wash1.html.

"In Favor of the Federal Constitution" (excerpts), by James Madison
    Punctuation has been aligned with http://www.constitution.org/rc/rat_va_05.txt.

"The Monroe Doctrine," by James Monroe
    See: http://avalon.law.yale.edu/19th_century/monroe.asp.

"Seneca Falls Declaration of Sentiments," by Elizabeth Cady Stanton
    Edited per http://www.fordham.edu/halsall/mod/Senecafalls.html.

"On the Slavery Question," by John C. Calhoun
    For a manuscript copy, see: http://www.loc.gov/exhibits/treasures/trm043.html.
    For the text, see: http://www.nationalcenter.org/CalhounClayCompromise.html.

"A House Divided," by Abraham Lincoln
    Punctuation and some wording done per http://showcase.netins.net/web/creative/lincoln/speeches/house.htm.

"Inaugural Address," by Jefferson Davis
    Punctuation corrected per http://www.civilwarinteractive.com/DocsJeffDavisInaugural.htm.

"Gettysburg Address," by Abraham Lincoln
    Versions of the Gettysburg Address at different websites show extensive discrepancies.
    http://avalon.law.yale.edu/19th_century/gettyb.asp http://www.gettysburgaddress.com/HTMLS/ga.html
    We have used the text from the original writing at the National Archives.
    See: http://www.ourdocuments.gov/doc.php?doc=36.

"Atlanta Exposition Address," by Booker T. Washington
> See: http://www.fordham.edu/halsall/mod/1895washington-atlanta.html.

"The Man with the Muck-Rake," by Theodore Roosevelt
> Edited per
> http://www.greatamericandocuments.com/speeches/troosevelt-muck-rake.html.

"War Message," by Woodrow Wilson
> See: http://www.ourdocuments.gov/doc.php?doc=61&page=transcript.

"League of Nations Speech" (excerpt) by Henry Cabot Lodge
> The full speech is preserved in the *Congressional Record*, 66th Cong., 1st sess., 1919, 3779-84. See also: http://www.nhd.org/website/27023/sources/cabot.html.

"Pearl Harbor Address," by Franklin D. Roosevelt
> A copy of the first typed draft is available from the national archives at http://www.archives.gov/education/lessons/day-of-infamy.
>
> Audio recordings of the speech are available at http://www.archive.org/details/FranklinDelanoRooseveltDayOfInfamySpeech.
>
> For full text, see: http://avalon.law.yale.edu/wwii/dec03.asp#address.

"The Marshall Plan," by George C. Marshall
> See: http://www.usaid.gov/multimedia/video/marshall/marshallspeech.html.
> For the text of the Economic Cooperation Act (Public Law 472), which was based on Marshall's speech and passed April 3, 1948, see: http://www.archives.gov/exhibits/featured_documents/marshall_plan/.

"Inaugural Address," by John F. Kennedy
> See: http://avalon.law.yale.edu/20th_century/kennedy.asp.

"First Inaugural Address," by Ronald Reagan
> See: http://avalon.law.yale.edu/20th_century/reagan1.asp.

Is it Time to Rhyme? Poetry

"Pocahontas," William M. Thackeray
> This poem comes from Thackeray's 1855 collection *Ballads* (part II), published by Ticknor and Fields. The full book is available online from Google Books.

"Five Kernels of Corn," by Hezekiah Butterworth
> This poem comes from Butterworth's 1895 collection *In Old New England; The Romance of a Colonial Fireside*, published by D. Appleton and company. The full book is available online from Google Books.

"Nathan Hale," by Francis M. Finch
> This poem was presented at the centenary of the Linonian society at Yale in 1853. Like much of Finch's poetry, it was not published until after his death. In 1909, it was part of the collection *The Blue and the Gray, and other verses*, published by Henry Holt and Company and edited by Andrew D. White. The full book is available online from Google Books.

"Valley Forge" (excerpt), by Thomas B. Read
> This is an excerpt from section two, part six ("Headquarters") of Read's poem "The Wagoner of the Alleghanies," which was published in 1863 by J.B. Lippincott and Company. The full book is available online from Google Books.

"Defence of Fort McHenry," by Francis Scott Key
> This poem was first published in the *Baltimore American* on September 21, 1814, and subsequently in Analectic Magazine in November 1814.
> See: http://rpo.library.utoronto.ca/poem/1141.html.

"Defense of the Alamo," by Joaquin Miller
> This poem comes from Miller's 1898 collection *Poems of American Patriotism 1776-1898*, published by L.C. Page and Company. The full text is available online from Google Books.

"Liberty for All," by William L. Garrison
> This poem was first published in Garrison's Inaugural Editorial in The Liberator on January 1, 1831. For an online version, see: http://www.bartleby.com/248/171.html.

"The New Colossus," by Emma Lazarus
> This poem was published by Houghton, Mifflin, and Company in 1889 as part of the collection The Poems of Emma Lazarus, vol.1. The full text is available online from Google Books.

"The Men of the *Maine*," by Clinton Scollard
> This poem was published in 1903 by Fleming H. Revell Company as part of the collection *Ballads of Valor and Victory* by Scollard and Wallace Rice. The full text is available online from Google Books.

"Panama," by James Roche
> This poem was first published in January 1904 in *Scribner's Magazine* (volume 35, no. 1). An archive of the magazine is available from the HathiTrust Digital Library.
> See: http://hdl.handle.net/2027/mdp.39015030597077.

Can You Write That Down? Articles and Essays

"Apologia" (excerpt), by Christopher Columbus
> This is a selection from Columbus's reflections on his journeys, called *El Libro de las Profecías* (*Book of Prophecies*), which he probably composed between 1501 and 1502. This translation is by Kay Brigham (Barcelona: Libros CLIE, 1991).

"The Federalist: Number 30," by Alexander Hamilton
> See: http://avalon.law.yale.edu/18th_century/fed30.asp.

"The Federalist: Number 47," by James Madison
> See: http://avalon.law.yale.edu/18th_century/fed47.asp.

"Farewell Address," by George Washington

Punctuation and capitalization has been lined up with the original document; some spelling and capitalization in this document do not match rules we use today. See: http://earlyamerica.com/earlyamerica/milestones/farewell/text.html and *The Independent Chronicle*, September 26, 1796.

"The American Language" (excerpt), by H.L. Mencken
This selection comes from Mencken's 1919 book *The American Language: An Inquiry into the Development of English in the United States* (*1st edition, preface*), published by Alfred A. Knopf. The full text is available online from Google Books.

Where's the Evidence? Legal Documents

The Mayflower Compact
We currently use a modernized version. See http://www.constitution.org/bcp/mayfcomp.htm. If you want the original version, see http://www.americanhistory.com/history/mayflower.html.

The Declaration of Independence
In speaking of the *Declaration of Independence*, the "the" is not capitalized. See: http://www.archives.gov/exhibits/charters/declaration.html.

The Articles of the Confederation
See http://www.usconstitution.net/articles.html and http://www.ourdocuments.gov/doc.php?flash=true&doc=3.

The U.S. Constitution
See http://www.archives.gov/exhibits/charters/constitution.html.

Amendments to the *U. S. Constitution*
See http://www.usconstitution.net/const.html#Amends.

The Northwest Ordinance
Different editions of this document also show some discrepancies. See http://www.tngenweb.org/law/northwest1787.html and http://www.loc.gov/rr/program/bib/ourdocs/northwest.html.

The Missouri Compromise, by Henry Clay
See: http://www.ourdocuments.gov/doc.php?flash=true&doc=22&page=transcript.

The Emancipation Proclamation, by Abraham Lincoln
Edited per http://www.ourdocuments.gov/doc.php?flash=true&doc=34&page=transcript.

The Pledge of Allegiance, by Francis Bellamy
Pledge of Allegiance: See http://www.usflag.org/history/pledgeofallegiance.html. For the Red Skelton Pledge of Allegiance, see: http://www.usflag.org/skeltonspledge.html.

Dred Scott v. *Sandford* (excerpt), by Roger B. Taney
> This is an excerpt from the court's decision, delivered by Taney in December 1856. See: http://caselaw.lp.findlaw.com/scripts/getcase.pl?court=US&vol=60&invol=393.

Brown v. *Board of Education of Topeka*, by Earl Warren
> This decision was delivered by Warren on May 17, 1954. See: http://caselaw.lp.findlaw.com/cgi-bin/getcase.pl?court=US&vol=347&invol=483.

Photo Credits

The following images have been retrieved from the Library of Congress digital Prints and Photographs collection, unless otherwise noted. The reproduction number follows the photo description.

PAGE 13:
George Washington, LC-USZ62-12510
Thomas Jefferson LC-USZ62-53985
James Madison LC-USZ62-13004
George Clinton LC-USZ62-110647
Richard M. Johnson LC-USZ62-58484

PAGE 14:
George M. Dallas LC-USZ62-10549
William R. King LC-USZ62-109926
John C. Breckinridge LC-DIG-pga-03237
Abraham Lincoln LC-USZ62-5876
Hannibal Hamlin LC-DIG-cwpb-04944
Schuyler Colfax LC-USZ62-116494

PAGE 15:
Chester A. Arthur LC-USZ62-13021
Grover Cleveland LC-USZ62-48692
Thomas A. Hendricks LC-DIG-pga-02236
Levi P. Morton LC-DIG-cwpbh-04821
Adlai E. Stevenson LC-USZ62-108489
Garret A. Hobart LC-USZ62-40326
Theodore Roosevelt LC-USZ62-7233
Charles W. Fairbanks LC-DIG-hec-14934
James S. Sherman LC-USZ62-7891
Thomas R. Marshall LC-DIG-hec-17196

PAGE 16:
Calvin Coolidge LC-USZ62-110625
Charles G. Dawes LC-DIG-hec-20948
Charles Curtis LC-USZ62-41596
John N. Garner LC-DIG-hec-27054
Henry A. Wallace LC-USZ62-49956
Alben W. Barkley LC-DIG-hec-17396
Hubert H. Humphrey LC-USZ62-26628
Nelson A. Rockefeller LC-USZ62-69469

PAGE 17:
Walter Mondale LC-DIG-ppmsca-09739

PAGE 23:
Patrick Henry LC-USZ62-102566

PAGE 24:
Patrick Henry before the Virginia House of Burgesses May 30, 1765 (Peter Frederick Rothermel) LC-USZ62-3775

PAGE 27:
George Washington, first president of the United States (Gilbert Stuart) LC-USZ62-7265

PAGE 31:
James Madison, fourth President of the United States (Gilbert Stuart) LC-USZ62-13004

PAGE 33:
The Second Continental Congress voting independence. (Robert Pine and Edward Savage.) National Archives (http://www.archives.gov/research/american-revolution/pictures/images/revolutionary-war-021.jpg)148-CCD-35

PAGE 35:
James Monroe (based on a portrait by Gilbert Stuart) LC-USZ62-104958

PAGE 39:
Elizabeth Cady Stanton LC-USZ62-28195

PAGE 40:
Elizabeth Cady Stanton, seated, and Susan B. Anthony, standing, three-quarter length portrait LC-USZ61-791

PAGE 44:
Cotton picking in Alabama, Educational Technology Clearinghouse http://etc.usf.edu/clipart/54500/54521/54521_cotton-pick.htm

PAGE 51:
Abraham Lincoln LC-USZ62-5876

PAGE 57:
Jefferson Davis LC-USZ62-73642

PAGE 59:
Jefferson Davis house [i.e. Confederate Museum], Richmond, Va. LC-D4-18714

PAGE 61:
Abraham Lincoln with, from left: Col. Alexander S. Webb, Chief of Staff, 5th Corps.; Gen. George B. McClellan; Scout Adams; Dr. Jonathan Letterman, Army Medical Director; an unidentified person; and standing behind Lincoln, Gen. Henry J. Hunt. LC-USZ62-2276

PAGE 63:
Booker T. Washington LC-J694-255

PAGE 64:
Rural South Carolina near Manning LC-USF34-051911-D

PAGE 67:
Theodore Roosevelt LC-USZ62-49955

PAGE 69:
political cartoon: *Suppress them!* (Boardman Robinson) LC-USZ62-85459

PAGE 72:
political cartoon, cover of *Puck* magazine *His declaration of independence* (Udo J. Kepler) LC-DIG-ppmsca-25578

PAGE 77:
political cartoon *Well, what are you going to do about it?* (W. A. Rogers) LC 2a14497

PAGE 80:
political cartoon *No time to hesitate* (W. A. Rogers) LC 2a14515

PAGE 83:
Senator Henry Cabot Lodge, LC-DIG-hec-16581

PAGE 87:
The U.S.S. Neosho, navy oil tanker, cautiously backs away from her berth (right center) in a successful effort to escape the Japanese attack on Pearl Harbor, Dec. 7, 1941. At left the battleship U.S.S. California lists after aerial blows. Other crippled warships and part of the hull of the capsized U.S.S. Oklahoma may be seen in the background. The Neosho was later sunk in the Coral Sea. LC-USW33-038546-ZC

PAGE 88:
USS Arizona, at height of fire, following Japanese aerial attack on Pearl Harbor, Hawaii LC-DIG-fsa-8e09025

PAGE 91:
Gen. George Catlett Marshall LC-USZ62-61397

PAGE 107:
William Makepeace Thackeray (Frank Holl) LC-USZ62-92951

PAGE 108:
Wishham young woman (Edward S. Curtis), 1910 LC-USZ62-107917

PAGE 110:
The first Thanksgiving (Jean Leon Gerome Ferris) LC-USZ62-15195

PAGE 113:
Memories of the Union — execution of Nathan Hale on the site of east Broadway, corner of Market Street, New York, September 21, 1776 LC-USZ62-3754

PAGE 115:
Washington and Lafayette at Valley Forge (John Ward Dunsmore) LC-USZ62-104015

PAGE 116:
Soldiers standing in snow-covered military camp, possibly in Valley Forge, Pa., during American Revolution (George Peter) LC-DIG-det-4a25888

PAGE 119:
Francis Scott Key, LC-USZ62-53017

PAGE 120:
A view of the bombardment of Fort McHenry, near Baltimore, by the British fleet, LC-USZ62-61

PAGE 123:
Miller, Joaquin of Oregon, LOC LC-DIG-cwpbh-03677
The Alamo, San Antonio, Texas, LOC LC-USZ6-197

PAGE 124:
(top left) from *Journeys Through Bookland*, p. 48, Google Books.
(bottom right) from *Journeys Through Bookland*, p. 46, Google Books.

PAGE 130:
The wreck of the Maine, *American Leaders and Heroes*, page 241, Google Books

PAGE 134:
Panama Canal, LC-USZ62-117347

PAGE 139:
Christopher Columbus. Discoverer of America, LC-USZ62-105012

PAGE 141:
Alexander Hamilton (Daniel Huntington), LC-USZ62-96268

PAGE 145:
James Madison, LC-USZ62-13004

PAGE 151:
George Washington, LC-USZ62-7645

PAGE 161:
Washington at Mount Vernon 1797: agriculture is the most healthy, the most useful, and the most noble employment of man.--Washington (Currier & Ives), LC-USZ62-27

PAGE 163:
H. L. Mencken, LC-USZ62-42489

PAGE 171:
The Mayflower in Plymouth harbor (William Formby Halsall), LC-D416-677

PAGE 172:
The pilgrims signing the compact, on board the May Flower, Nov. 11th, 1620 (Tompkins Harrison Matteson), LC-DIG-ppmsca-07842

PAGE 173:
The Declaration committee (Currier & Ives), LC-USZC2-2243

PAGE 184:
Articles of Confederation, U.S. Archives, http://www.ourdocuments.gov/document_data/pdf/doc_003b.pdf

PAGE 194:
Bill of Rights, U.S. Archives, http://www.ourdocuments.gov/document_data/pdf/doc_013.pdf

PAGE 209:
Henry Clay, LC-USZ62-109953

PAGE 213:
Abraham Lincoln, LC-DIG-ppmsca-19204

PAGE 221:
Chief Justice Roger Taney,
   LC-USZ62-107588

PAGE 231:
Earl Warren, LC-USZ62-41653